The Red Riviera

Next Wave: New Directions in Women's Studies

A SERIES EDITED BY INDERPAL GREWAL,

CAREN KAPLAN, & ROBYN WIEGMAN

The Red Riviera

KRISTEN GHODSEE

Gender, Tourism, and
Postsocialism on the Black Sea

DUKE UNIVERSITY PRESS

DURHAM AND LONDON 2005

PRINTED IN THE UNITED STATES OF AMERICA ON ACID-FREE PAPER ∞

DESIGNED BY REBECCA GIMÉNEZ

TYPESET IN MINION BY KEYSTONE TYPESETTING

LIBRARY OF CONGRESS CATALOGING-IN-PUBLICATION DATA APPEAR

ON THE LAST PRINTED PAGE OF THIS BOOK.

Duke University Press gratefully acknowledges the support
of the Fletcher Family Research Fund at Bowdoin College, which
provided funds toward the production of this book.

to Josephine AND Mehdi

Contents

Acknowledgments

There are many people to whom I am deeply grateful for their encouragement, assistance, and support in the long process of writing this book. At Berkeley, I had the great fortune to be surrounded by magnificent professors and dedicated mentors. First and foremost, my thanks go out to my dissertation adviser and academic taskmaster, Pedro Noguera. Pedro was my steadfast ally from the day I set foot on campus, and his boundless enthusiasm for knowledge and social change have made their indelible marks on my career. More specifically, I want to thank him for following me out into the parking lot after a 1996 California-wide educational reform conference at the Berkeley Marina Hotel, and personally talking me out of leaving my Ph.D. program. Pedro's unquestioning confidence in me and his continuing friendship are responsible for much that I have achieved. It is no understatement to say that I could not have finished this book without him.

My deepest appreciation also goes out to Caren Kaplan for taking so much of her precious time to work together with me throughout graduate school. Caren was my tireless supporter, providing encouragement but also pushing me to expand my intellectual boundaries. Her feminist-theory class at Berkeley has the distinction of being the hardest class I took in all of my eleven years of higher education. The fascinating theoretical depths to which she brought me were the foundation of my own interest in Women's Studies, and the driving force behind my interest in gender and economic transition in Eastern Europe. But Caren's influence on my development goes beyond the example she set as an incredible scholar; she is also one of the most amazing women I have ever known. Despite the plethora of academic and personal commitments she had,

Caren was always there when her students needed her—fashionably dressed and in total control. My eternal gratitude is not enough to thank her for all the help she has given me over the years.

I would also like to recognize Irene Tinker for being my mentor and friend. When I would venture too far into the world of theory, Irene would always drag me back into the world of practice. Irene and her work have been a huge inspiration to me, and I can never thank her enough for her insightful thoughts and comments on my research. I am deeply indebted to Carol Stack and Jean Lave for teaching me the craft of ethnography. In particular, I want to thank Carol for writing books that demonstrate just how beautiful academic writing can be. At Berkeley, I also want to express my appreciation to Barbara Voytek, Harley Shaiken, Manuel Castells, David Stern, Percy Hintzen, Gil Eyal, Alexei Yurchak, Althea Graham-Cummings, Gi Gi Lang, and Johan. In North America more generally, I want to thank Anton Allahar, Susan Gal, Gail Kligman, Lynn Bolles, Inderpal Grewal, Betty Olson, and Josephine Gussa for reading or commenting on various drafts of the manuscript.

There were many phases of this project, and I am appreciative of the variety of organizations and institutions that provided funding in support of my research: The University of California, Berkeley, the Bulgarian-American Fulbright Commission, International Board on Research and Exchanges (IREX), the National Council for Eurasian and East European Research, Bowdoin College, and the East European Studies Program at the Woodrow Wilson International Center for Scholars. Also, I would like to acknowledge *Signs: Journal of Women in Culture and Society* for previously publishing an article which included portions of my conclusion.

In Bulgaria, I would like to say *blagodaria* to Julia Stefanova, Katya, Iolanta, Anatassia, and all the staff at the Bulgarian-American Fulbright Commission in Sofia. I would also like to recognize former Ambassador Richard Miles and his wife, Sharon Miles, for their assistance with my research in the field. *Merci* as well to former Deputy Minister for Tourism Marianna Assenova, Professor Maria Vodenska at Sofia University, Julia Watkins at the American University in Blagoevgrad, Juliet Peeva at the Ministry of Economy, Todor Radev at Albena, Nedyalka Sandalska at Balkan Holidays, former Deputy Minister of Transportation Velitchko

Velitchkov, Andrei Filipov at A.V.L., Mira Yanova at MBMD Research, Anelia Atanassova at LGI, and former Central Committee sociologist Vassilka Velitchkova. I especially appreciate the support of the American University's Sofia Office and the staff there: Marianna, Evelina, Galya, Galina, and Stanimir.

In Washington, D.C., I am grateful to Marty Sletzinger and Sabina Crisen in the East European Studies Program at the Woodrow Wilson International Center for Scholars for their generosity in supporting the preparation of the manuscript. Meredith Knepp deserves special mention for allowing me to bring my seven-month-old daughter to the Wilson Center as I made my first revisions. My two interns, Irena Crncevic and Laura Freschi, get special thanks for reading and proofing multiple drafts.

At Bowdoin College, I want to thank my marvelous colleagues, especially Jennifer Scanlon, Rachel Connelly, Jane Knox-Voina, Pamela Ballinger, Page Herrlinger, Karin Clough, and Anne Clifford for putting up with my many bouts of insanity and my annoying tendency to talk too much about my work. Special thanks to Jen and Rachel for being so supportive of my research and for making Gender and Women's Studies such a fabulous place to work. Their friendship and encouragement have been invaluable to me. And thanks to Anne for continuing to remind me about those "blue books" during each semester's course registration period, and for all her help with my bibliography. This book could not have been written without the writing assistance I was lucky enough to get from Genevieve Creedon, who understands the passion of writing and has a brilliant career as an editor in front of her if she wants it.

My deepest appreciation goes to Duke University Press and their brilliant staff, especially Christine Dahlin, Courtney Berger, and Justin Faerber. Most importantly, I want to acknowledge the guidance and support of Ken Wissoker, who helped me find my narrative voice and encouraged me to tell the stories of the ordinary tourism employees. Without his thoughtful guidance, this book would have been a useless jumble of jargon and academese. If the pantheon of Muses were reopened to new members, I would gladly break convention and nominate Ken as its first male demigod of creative inspiration.

Additionally, I want to express my deepest appreciation to the two men that I suddenly lost in September 2001. To Atsushi Shiratori, my best friend and an unapologetic capitalist, whose spectacular life was cut short on September 11th, and to my father, Mehdi Ghodsee, who unexpectedly passed away two weeks later. So much of what I have done in my life, including this book, was driven by my desire to live up to their expectations of me. I'm crossing my fingers that they get book reviews in the afterlife.

There are not enough synonyms for "thanks" in the English language to express how grateful I am to my hexagalactic partner in all things, Cosmonaut Filipov. Thanks for crashing my martini party and giving me a good reason to spend *a lot* of time in Bulgaria. Hugs and kisses to Tosca for keeping me company and sharing your healing nose with me when I needed it, and to Porthos for just being happy and dumb. Finally, thank you, thank you, thank you to Kristiana for being the most magical, joyful, and precious thing in my life. Mommy will have lots of time for your fairy dinner parties now.

Introduction

The sea breeze is salty and cooling. The operatic calls of the young men selling corn on the cob accompany the gruff hums of jet skis and the percussive gushing and smashing of the Black Sea. Topless Western European girls lounge beside portly Russian grandmothers. Wild gangs of preteen boys overrun the shoreline, dribbling soccer balls through the sand castles built by naked squealing toddlers. There are more than five thousand people enjoying the glorious day on the narrow band of beach in the resort of Albena.

The fine sands on the shore are similar to the soft, pale grains in Koh Samui or Antigua. But compared to the lush, tropical ambience of Thailand or the Caribbean, Bulgaria feels distinctly European. There are no palm trees, no thatched huts, and the local peddlers threading their way through the sun-worshipping tourists are paler-skinned and carefully covered with thick, white smears of waterproof sunscreen. Looking out toward the sea, you see the usual array of water-sport equipment found at any major beach resort—paragliders, water skis, and paddle boats. This could be Greece, Italy, or France, but a glance inland at the towering, cement hotels—monolithic pillars of totalitarian architecture—betrays the landscape's communist past.

Few people outside of Europe think of Bulgaria as a tourist destination, but German, British, French, and Scandinavian visitors have been descending on the country en masse since the mid-1960s. In addition to its pristine beaches, Bulgaria is blessed with four mountain ranges, including the Balkan Mountains after which the entire peninsula is named. The other three ranges are home to international ski resorts that attract winter holidaymakers from across the continent. Bulgaria is also well known among spa enthusiasts—the plentitude and variety of its mineral waters draw international visitors for both medicinal and recreational tourism. But it is the resorts on the country's eastern coastline that are the biggest lure, comparable to but cheaper than Spain or Turkey for the cognoscenti among European tourists on a budget. Of the five major resorts at the seaside, Albena is one of the most breathtaking. Its tree-covered hillsides and purplish cliffs slope sharply down to the blue-green waters of the Black Sea.

On the top floor of the tallest hotel in the center of Albena, Desislava is just finishing the lunch shift.[1] She wipes her hands on her apron before she taps a cigarette out of the pack and sits down by a window to smoke. Her dyed orange-reddish hair falls in curls to her shoulders. A stripe of chocolate-brown roots runs from her forehead toward the crown of her head. Her ever-so-slightly angled eyes are rimmed with fine wrinkles that fold up when she inhales. She holds the cigarette lightly between her index and middle fingers. Her fingernails are carefully manicured. From the Panorama Restaurant she can see the entire resort through the floor-to-ceiling windows. "So much has changed since 1989," she starts. "And so much has stayed the same."

Desislava, or Desi for short, is remarkably qualified to be a waitress. She has the equivalent of a master's degree in English philology, and she speaks four languages in addition to her native Bulgarian. She has been working in Albena for over twenty years. When she first graduated from the university before the collapse of communism, there was nothing in the world she wanted more than to work in one of the international tourist resorts on the seaside. Her fortunate assignment to Albena made her the envy of her friends and classmates. For all her loyalty and per-severance over the years, she expected nothing less than to be one of the lucky few assigned to the Panorama Restaurant. She tells me that she has earned her position. Even today, more than ten years after the onset of so-called "free markets," Desi is proud to work in tourism. There is no other job that she would rather do.

In the nearby city of Varna, a young woman named Svetla is the top student in her class at the German language secondary school. She has decided, against the advice of her parents, to sit for the university entrance exam in tourism. The exam requires the mastery of a minimum of two foreign languages, and Svetla's mother is afraid that the program is too competitive. Her father wants her to sit for an easier exam like law or medicine. But Svetla is committed to tourism. She knows that the best way to get a job in the Golden Sands resort is to graduate with a tourism degree, and she is willing to study an extra four or five hours a day to perfect her French before the exam. Her dream is to be a receptionist and to someday become the manager of her own hotel.

The high demand for and prestige of tourism employment in Bulgaria may seem at odds with common perceptions about the undesirability of work in the sector in advanced industrialized economies. But Desi, Svetla, and many other Bulgarians like them are responding to the particular history of Bulgarian tourism, which sets it apart from tourism sectors across the globe. This small Southeastern European country was one of the only places in the world to develop tourism under the direction of central planners during a communist era. Totalitarian tourism in Bulgaria was organized with reference to capitalist models, but independent of the dictates of supply and demand and liberated from the profit constraints of free-market competition. The peculiarities of its socialist development made employment in the sector exceptionally prestigious, and the internal dynamics of communist gender politics meant that it was Bulgarian women who worked the lion's share of these exclusive jobs.

Bulgaria's sudden insertion into global capitalism after 1989 drastically reshaped the Bulgarian economy. As the country's once vibrant industrial sector began to collapse, tourism emerged as one of the key powerhouses of the postsocialist economy. Representing at least 10 percent of Bulgaria's gross domestic product, tourism became the nation's largest generator of foreign exchange. Most importantly, tourism was one of the few sectors that continued to expand despite the onset of privatization and marketization. Tourism was labor-intensive—at a time when jobs in the formal economy were disappearing, employment in the sector grew. Yet despite high unemployment rates for men, fierce competition for jobs, and a general erosion in women's formal employment prospects after the onset of capitalism, Bulgarian women continued to dominate the sector even at the highest levels of management.

This is the story of the development and transformation of the Bulgarian tourism sector during both the communist and postcommunist

eras, and how this unique trajectory impacted the lives of the many women who worked in the sector as they struggled through the chaos of economic and political transition. This is a tale that starts with a revolutionary idea, an idea that promised social and economic justice for all workers and total equality for women. The story ends with the reality of economic collapse, government corruption, organized crime, widespread poverty, and reemerging social inequalities not only between men and women, but also between the ascending handful of the super-rich and the slowly sinking majority. Through it all, the women employed in Bulgaria's tourism sector negotiated their way through the rapidly changing institutional imperatives of emergent free markets by using the education and experience gained under the old system.

The success of these women was in many ways an unexpected outcome. Many scholars, international aid institutions, and nongovernmental organizations have suggested that all women in Bulgaria were negatively affected by the economic transition.[2] But there were some populations of women in Bulgaria that did relatively well after 1989. In general, the women who were better off after the collapse of communism had higher levels of general education, work experience with Westerners, and foreign-language training. My case study focuses on tourism because it was the sector of the communist economy that employed the highest concentration of women who had almost daily access to Western tourists. This access gave women employed in tourism a chance to practice and perfect their foreign-language skills, to interact with and understand capitalist culture, and to receive tips in hard currency. The long off-season also allowed women extended opportunities to pursue continuing education and training throughout their careers. Thus, women working in tourism under communism had a high concentration of the education and skills necessary to benefit from the economic transition. By 2002, about 20 percent of currently employed women and approximately 18 percent of the total female labor force were directly or indirectly employed in tourism.[3] Many of these women were able to use their education and experience to succeed in the postsocialist context. This is a significant enough number of women to challenge common perceptions that Bulgarian women in general were more negatively affected by the economic transition than men.

These higher levels of the right type of education and experience that were attained under communism have translated into new class privileges under capitalism. This has created significant economic disparities between different groups of women within Bulgarian society. While a small group of women experiences an increase in their standard of living, the majority of Bulgarian women slide into poverty. This is a process that mirrors the emerging economic inequalities in Bulgarian society as a whole, but few have yet to study these emerging class differences between women.

Since generalizations about women as a distinct and separate group miss these emerging social inequalities, it is necessary to dig beneath the gender-disaggregated national statistics. My arguments emerge not from distant observation or quantitative analysis, but from the experiences of Bulgarian women working in the tourism sector and how the process of economic transformation in 1989 irreversibly altered their trajectories.[4] Only the personal accounts of real women who survived the collapse of communism can provide the detail and insight necessary to understand how larger historical shifts in political and economic systems shape individual lives. Narrowing in on personal stories also allows me to examine the particular processes through which some women were able to adjust to capitalism using interpersonal, educational, and material resources designed for survival under communism—a radically different social, political, and economic system.

Throughout this book, I weave my arguments around the small histories of Bulgarians employed in the tourism sector, gathered during the fourteen months that I lived in Bulgaria in 1999 and 2000. In the chapters that follow, I momentarily slip into the shoes of women like Desi, the waitress in Albena. Her story provides the details that anchor much of my theoretical framework into the real lives of Bulgarian women. The story of Dora, a forty-two-year-old head chef in the seaside resort of Golden Sands, helps me to explore what life was like for Bulgarian women working in tourism under communism. While sharing meals and telling jokes with her and her family, I see the tale of Bulgaria's transition to capitalism through their eyes, and examine the effect of the collapse of communism on men and women across the nation.

Then there is Gergana, a young chambermaid working in the winter resort of Borovetz. By following her through a typical day of changing sheets and scrubbing toilets, I look at the particular economic context of tourism employment in Bulgaria after 1989 and how, despite high rates of postsocialist unemployment for men, the tourism sector has remained dominated by women. In this endeavor, I am also helped by Hristo, the bartender; Katina, the travel agent; Pencho, the ski instructor; and Petar, an unemployed miner. Their experiences allow me to explore the relatively high wages and high levels of job satisfaction found in the tourism sector.

I also travel back in time with Sonia, a receptionist who has been working in Bulgarian tourism for almost four decades. Sonia's memories and observations of the historical development of tourism in Bulgaria provide the foundation for my look at the unique political economy of the sector under communism and the peculiarities of command economics and secret police surveillance on the beaches of the Black Sea coast. Through her I also demonstrate how the isolation and control of the Bulgarian people and their inability to travel outside of the Eastern Bloc made work in tourism so exceptional. The daily contact with Western tourists and the constant access to otherwise unobtainable foreign currencies gave women like Sonia invaluable social and economic assets under communism. These would later prove invaluable to her ability to survive the economic transition.

Prolet was a reservations manager in Golden Sands before 1989, but took advantage of the new opportunities provided by the liberalization of the Bulgarian economy to start her own small business as a tour operator. The details of her personal trajectory provide the backdrop for my investigation of the privatization and marketization of tourism after 1989 and how these changes strengthened the position of Bulgarian women in the sector. I also look at the new, postsocialist forces that shaped the character of tourism employment after 1989—the emergence of a new democratic state, the small but increasing interest of foreign investors and transnational corporations, the suddenly ubiquitous presence of the Bulgarian Mafia, and the proliferation of nongovernmental organizations representing Bulgaria's new "civil society."

Finally, I take a step back from the tourism sector and consider the broader implications of my case study through the eyes of the director of one of Bulgaria's prominent women's NGOs. I discuss what women's NGOs in Bulgaria are doing to improve the lives of women and how their efforts ignore the successes of people like Desi, Dora, Gergana, Sonia, and Prolet. In fact, the work of women's NGOs may be contributing to the creation of ideologies that will make it more difficult for future generations of women to thrive in a free-market economy.

In addition to the more in-depth stories of these women, there are glimpses of many other Bulgarian men and women whose experiences give names and faces to the larger social, political, and economic processes that shaped and reshaped the development of Bulgaria's tourism sector over the last fifty years. It was through these extended conversations with maids, waitresses, cooks, receptionists, and the many others who work in Bulgarian tourism that my own observations and analysis came to life. In the details of their day-to-day routines were the experiences and outcomes that eventually fleshed out the bare bones of the abstract theories of economic transition. It was only through my understanding of the history of someone like Desi that I could begin to untangle the theoretical complexities of how some individual Bulgarians overcame the economic chaos that followed the collapse of communism while others did not.

Desi is thirty-eight years old. She was born in a village outside of the city of Varna to parents who were both farmers and committed communists. At eighteen, Desi passed the exams to study English at Varna University and became the first person in her family to receive a university education. Desi had a talent for foreign languages; she also studied German and excelled at the required Russian language courses. Upon graduation, she officially joined the Communist Party. This helped to place her in a three-year position as a waitress in a restaurant in Albena serving primarily English tourists.

Each day, Desi worked in a paradise of luxury compared to her small village. In an era when travel outside of the Eastern bloc was severely curtailed and contact between Westerners and ordinary Bulgarians was strictly forbidden, Desislava met and talked with British, German, and Scandinavian tourists on a daily basis. At a time when access to Western currencies was denied to all but the most privileged members of the communist elite, Desislava regularly took home pockets full of pounds, marks, and krone, which she could then exchange for Bulgarian leva on the black market for several times the official rate. She also had access to the special dollar stores where her hard currency could buy her Western cigarettes, alcohol, and denim jeans.

In Albena, the Western tourist season lasted only through July and August. For another four months, there were tourists and youth groups from the brother socialist countries. During the six months of the off-season, Desi was sent to different universities around the country to further her language training. In the five years that she worked in Albena during the communist era, she took language courses in German, Dutch, Danish, Swedish, and French.

In 1986, Desi married a man from her village who worked as a technician in the Golden Sands resort. He was also a member of the Communist Party. In 1988, she gave birth to a son, Kiril. Through their connections with the party, she and her husband were able to get their own apartment in a block in Varna. She moved out of her parents' house in the village and into the big city. She continued to work in Albena, but now used the off-season to do home studies and to spend time with her infant son. During the tourist season, Desi sent Kiril to her parents' village where her mother looked after him.

Everything suddenly changed in November 1989 when Todor Zhivkov, Bulgaria's communist leader for over three decades, unexpectedly resigned. Desi first felt the effects of the changes when the severe shortages of basic goods left the store shelves bare. But the economic disorder would be eclipsed in Desi's life by the death of her mother in 1991. As an only child, Desislava allowed her father to move into her apartment in Varna. At the same time, the number of tourists to Bulgaria increased, and Desi was working more days and longer hours.

Desi had considered leaving her job in Albena in the early 1990s to stay home for a few years and spend more time with her father and her son. She decided to keep working because the increase in tourists after the changes meant that there were many new people coming to Bulgaria for the first time, and she was curious to meet them. The departure of some of her colleagues also allowed for her promotion to a nicer restaurant in the center of the resort and a pay increase. Like Desi, her colleagues were used to leaving and returning to the labor force at will due to the possibility of extended maternity leaves under communism. The ones who left Albena in the early nineties never thought that they would have trouble coming back to their jobs at a later point.

As the nineties progressed, the economic situation worsened. Desi's father's pension was reduced. Her husband lost his job in the resort. Since he spoke no foreign languages and had only a technical engineering background, there was little he could do once the resorts were restructured and the Mafia began moving in. Desi's father sold the house in the village. Now, only Desi's tips and wages from the restaurant keep her family from going without good food, medicine, or heating in the winter when so many Bulgarians are forced to choose one over the others.

Each day Desi rides the employee microbus from Varna to Albena for about thirty minutes. She does not mind the commute; the narrow road winds its way up the picturesque coast. Through the trees and the breaks in the cliffs, Desi catches spectacular glimpses of the sea going in both directions. The smell of the fresh, salty air greets her in the morning, and the sight of the tourists and their children strolling through the resort—relaxed and content—calms her anxieties about the future of her own family. Every week new busloads of foreigners are dropped off in the resort, and every day a handful of them find their way up to the Panorama Restaurant. Each morning as the microbus sways its way to Albena, Desi muses about whom she might meet. A Dutch architect? A German bus driver? A Russian poet? Or perhaps even a young American woman studying Bulgarian tourism . . .

CULTURAL CAPITAL AND CAPITALISM

Desi's story provides valuable detail for understanding how and why the education and experience women gained while working in the tourism sector under communism was the key to their postsocialist success. By using Desi's experiences, we can begin to explore the mechanisms that allowed women like her to survive the economic transition relatively better off than many of her compatriots. To do this, however, I must use several theories that explain the complex relationship between education and social mobility in different economic contexts.

In their book, *Making Capitalism without Capitalists*, Gil Eyal, Ivan Szelenyi, and Ellen Townsley investigate the ways in which individual men and women in Central Europe successfully made the transition from life under communism to life under capitalism, and argue that those with higher levels of education have done better than those with money or political connections.[5] At the center of their analysis is trajectory adjustment theory, a compelling model that demonstrates why some portions of the population were thriving under the new capitalist system while others were not. Before the explanatory clarity of trajectory adjustment theory, however, there were two competing theories of how capitalism would be built after the collapse of communism: the theory of "capitalism-by-design" and the theory of "path dependence."[6]

The idea of capitalism-by-design was very simple. Proponents of this theory believed that 1989 was a complete break with the past, and that all of the former socialist countries were blank slates on which a new capitalist economy and democratic polity could be built by imported technologies, expertise, and institutions from the advanced capitalist countries.[7] The idea of capitalism-by-design informed all of the "shock therapy" policies whereby markets were liberalized almost overnight.

Western institutions such as stock markets and entire legal codes were imported and implemented in hopes that the right conditions would create capitalism, literally, by design.

The new institutional arrangements in society, like the advent of private ownership of industry, the possibility of starting small, private businesses, and the creation of national labor markets (by no longer guaranteeing full employment) were also supposed to reshape individual behavior. Those individuals whose entrepreneurial instincts had long been suppressed would suddenly spring forth and become the drivers of the new economy. Rising unemployment would lead to greater competition for jobs. This would lead to higher levels of productivity and lower wages, and Bulgarian entrepreneurs would be more competitive in international markets. The newly legal possibility for individuals to accumulate disproportionate amounts of wealth and to dispose of that wealth as they saw fit would create incentives for others in society to work hard and be creative in building the new capitalist reality. Capitalism and communism were seen as mutually exclusive systems, and individuals who had thrived under communism (bureaucrats and apparatchiks) would not be able to survive under a new system that rewarded ability and initiative.[8]

To use the example of Desi's experience under the paradigm of capitalism-by-design, 1989 represented a distinct break with the past as the communist government fell apart. Because full-time employment was no longer an obligation, many women in Albena decided to leave their jobs, while Desi used the opportunity to get promoted to a better position within the resort. From the institutional design point of view, this was a desirable outcome related to the emergence of new institutions (labor markets) in society. The women who left Albena probably did so because they viewed working as an obligation and therefore had little motivation and presumably low productivity. These are exactly the people that Albena as a private resort with a profit motive would want to get rid of. On the other hand, Desi enjoyed her work very much and was delighted with the new possibilities of more responsibility and higher pay in a better establishment—Desi is exactly the type of employee that Albena would want to keep. Thus, simply by changing the institutional arrangements and incentives, individual human behavior can be shaped so that those who are the most able will succeed in the new economic system. In other words, individual people make rational decisions in response to new economic conditions that ultimately benefit society as a whole.

The problem with the capitalism-by-design paradigm is that it does not take into account that the women working in Albena had entire lives' worth of experience under the old communist system that did not merely disappear because there was now unemployment. Even if Desi absolutely loved her job and was an excellent waitress, she might have still left Albena because it was the first time in her life that she had the choice as to whether or not she wanted to work. Furthermore, many of the women left the workforce assuming that their jobs would be there when they wanted them back. They were operating under the assumptions of the old institutions, rather than being directly influenced by the advent of the new ones.

Path dependence—the second theory of understanding the creation of capitalism in the former socialist countries—reintroduced the idea that there are structural constraints that limit an individual's ability to make rational decisions in response to the new system of incentives.[9] The idea behind path dependence was simply that capitalism would be different for each country depending on the status and type of communist state that existed before 1989. The sociologist David Stark recognized that different states had different approaches to privatization depending on how heavily indebted they were to the multinational lending institutions immediately before the collapse.[10] The process of privatization was very important in shaping the new institutions of private property and entre-preneurship, and in each country that process was path dependent on the previous economic situation. Stark rejects the capitalism-by-design thesis as far too simplistic in assuming that decades of understanding and expertise under one economic system could simply be washed away by the advent of another. Once again, to use Desi as an example, her life did not suddenly start all over again in 1989. Things began changing around her, but her ability to deal with those changes was determined by aspects of her life that developed under communism, the things that limited her range of choices: her job in the resort, her education, her husband, her son, etc.

Trajectory adjustment theory tries to combine both the capitalism-by-design and path dependence ideas into one mechanism for explaining how individuals made the transition from communism to capitalism. While capitalism-by-design placed too much of an emphasis on the new institutions that emerged after 1989 and the rationality of individuals if and when they chose to respond to them, path dependence implied that people could never fully escape their communist pasts when in fact there were many examples of individuals reinventing themselves under the new economic system. Trajectory adjustment theory mitigates these contradictions and relies heavily on Pierre Bourdieu's notions of the *habitus* and *champ* and on his ideas about social and cultural capital.[11]

Eyal, Szelenyi, and Townsley argue that individuals are able to adjust their personal and professional "trajectories" in response to exogenously imposed alterations in the economic system by changing their habitus to respond to new "rules of the game." Each individual has a "portfolio" of stocks in economic capital, cultural capital, and social/political capital that determines their habitus and thus, their place in the *champ*. Economic capital is material goods or money that can be used for productive purposes. Social or political capital is an individual's knowledge of and ability to utilize social networks and spheres of influence. Cultural capital is also sometimes called "human capital," which is an individual's education, skills, and experience. Cultural capital also includes the acquisition of "good taste"—a culturally appropriate knowledge of what constitutes good food, good art, good music, good manners, and so forth—which marks an individual as belonging or deserving to belong to a higher social position. This kind of cultural capital is also referred to as symbolic capital, because an individual's public "performance" of these discerning tastes symbolizes personal "success" to others in her social milieu. Much of Bourdieu's work focuses on how differential access to formal educational institutions and the learning of proper behaviors and tastes legitimate the unequal distributions of resources in advanced capitalist societies.[12]

To use Desi as an illustration, she had all three types of capital at her disposal in 1989 when the transition began. She had economic capital in the form of hard currency, the British pounds and German marks that she saved from her tips. She also had social/political capital in her membership in the Communist Party and her network of friends and colleagues at Albena. Finally, Desi had impressive amounts of cultural capital; she had a degree from a prestigious university, extensive training in several different languages, and many years of work experience with foreigners. According to the trajectory adjustment theory, these different forms of capital made up Desi's portfolio of stocks.

As the transition began, Desi rationally responded to the changing institutions in society by trading in or dumping less useful forms of capital in favor of those that had become more valuable under the new system. Under communism her old connections within the Communist Party were a very useful form of social capital that helped her get a job and apartment and move up within the established hierarchy. After the changes in 1989, however, this social capital was devalued considerably, and her cultural capital in the form of education, training, and language expertise became much more valuable. Furthermore, her economic capital in the form of hard currency, which was merely a bonus under communism, became important in the postsocialist period, when the Bulgarian currency was drastically devalued due to hyperinflation and the general economic instability that accompanied the transition. Having money in hard currency preserved the value of her savings, and allowed her to buy most of the things she needed even as prices rose. Desi slowly came to rely more on her economic and cultural capital as the transition proceeded, with her social capital becoming less and less significant.

As in the theory of capitalism-by-design, the relative value of Desi's different forms of capital was transformed due to external changes in the political and economic institutions in Bulgaria, and she rationally chose to rely on different forms of capital in response to those changes. But Desi's capital in 1989 was path dependent. The education and social networks she had in her portfolio were legacies of her social position during communism. Not everyone in Bulgaria, and certainly not every woman in Bulgaria, entered the postsocialist period with the same portfolio. Desi's husband, for instance, had excess stocks of social capital (his membership in the local Communist Party) that eventually proved useless in finding him a job after the changes. In the case of Central Europe, Eyal, Szelenyi, and Townsley demonstrate that the people who emerged as leaders after communism were the ones who had cultural capital, rather than those who had social or economic capital. This was also true in Bulgaria, particularly in the tourism sector, where those like

Desi who had excess stocks of cultural capital were able to survive and thrive after 1989.

For a wide variety of reasons, the most valuable forms of cultural capital after the collapse of communism were those of general education, work experience with foreigners (preferably Westerners), and fluency in foreign languages (again preferably Western ones). In chapters 1 and 2, I examine the particular historical circumstances surrounding the development of tourism in Bulgaria under communism that allowed women working in that sector to acquire disproportionate amounts of these forms of cultural capital—the state policies aimed at achieving full employment for all Bulgarian men and women and the unofficial gender regime that funneled women into the "service" sector. Women in tourism before 1989 were uniquely poised to do very well as the communist institutions were swept away and replaced by free-market competition in one of the most dynamic sectors of the Bulgarian economy. Desi the waitress, Dora the chef, Sonia the receptionist, and Prolet the reservations manager had all gained their cultural capital under the old system, but it became valuable only after the liberalization of the Bulgarian economy. In chapter 3, I examine this phenomenon in detail and propose that cultural capital is valuable only under capitalist regimes of accumulation where education and training are commodified in society and thereby made scarce. In other words, education becomes valuable only when it is difficult for people to get.

The dilemma of Svetla, the young secondary school student in Varna who aspires to study tourism, exemplifies the changes that the onset of capitalism in Bulgaria has brought to both young men and women. Under communism, higher education for all young Bulgarians was paid for by the state. Of course, there was fierce competition for places at the best universities and colleges in the country, but anyone who wanted to continue his or her education was virtually guaranteed a space in at least one institution to study something. Before 1989, pursuing a general or technical education was not a function of one's economic position, but, at least theoretically, purely a function of one's own desire and ability. Furthermore, higher education was not necessary to secure employment—that was guaranteed for life by the communist state. Therefore, women like Desi, Dora, Sonia, and Prolet who studied tourism at the university level did so because they were both capable and motivated. Unfortunately for Svetla, capability and motivation will no longer be enough.

The collapse of communism brought with it dramatic changes to everything, including Bulgaria's educational system. At precisely the historical moment that employment was no longer guaranteed by the state and knowledge and skills became more important than being a member of the Communist Party, higher education began to slip out of the reach of Bulgaria's recently impoverished majority. Whereas once access to higher education was a question of passing the right exams, since 1989 young people like Svetla have increasingly had to worry about how to pay the costs.

By 2004, most public universities offered full scholarships to only the top percentage of candidates who passed the entrance exam; those with lower scores were expected to pay if they wanted to attend. Additionally, Bulgaria has seen a steady increase in the presence of private universities, many of which will accept any student who can afford to pay. But the tuition demanded by these private schools far exceeds the annual earnings of the average Bulgarian family, and the quality of the education received at these new institutions is dubious. And even if a student is lucky enough to earn a full scholarship to a prestigious public university, rumors abound that good marks can be earned only through gifts and bribes to poorly paid and overworked faculty members.

For Svetla to attend university, she must earn a score that puts her in the top 20 percent of all students who pass the tourism exam. Without a full scholarship, Svetla's parents cannot afford to pay for her to study, and she will have to start looking for a job instead. The competition is stiff for the tourism exam, which is why her father is pressuring her to sit for the law and medicine exams as well. Furthermore, even though Svetla is very bright and works very hard, many of the young people that she is competing against have been studying with private tutors. Her parents cannot afford the tutors, so Svetla studies alone with secondhand language textbooks from the 1980s. The most fortunate of her classmates have been sent away for a month to England, France, or Germany to practice their language skills; Svetla practices on a computer in an Internet cafe near her secondary school. She still has a fair shot at scoring in the top 20 percent, but since 1989, higher education has increasingly become a luxury for wealthier Bulgarians. Despite these disadvantages, Svetla is dedicated to pursuing her dream. She has one more month to study.

Svetla does have one advantage: that there are women like Desi in charge of making hiring decisions in the tourism sector. Desi is suspicious of the degrees granted by the new private universities, and knows that many talented young people are having to forego higher education due to increasing costs and the pressure that many feel to work so they can help support their parents. Desi is well aware of how fortunate she was to grow up under communism, even though she was happy to see the system collapse. Desi likes to joke that she traded her freedom for an education. Svetla tells me that she would gladly give up her ability to travel abroad for a top place at Varna Economics University and the promise of a career in tourism.

Svetla and Desi are just two of the over three million Bulgarian women who have lived through the transition from communism to capitalism. Although their experiences cannot be overgeneralized, the different paths and opportunities available to them are in some ways representative of the emerging disparities between women in Bulgaria. A minority of women are poised to do well in a competitive labor market. This group includes an older generation of women (like Desi) with valuable cultural capital in the form of skills and experience inherited from communism and a younger generation of women (like Svetla's wealthy classmates) with enough economic capital to purchase the requisite cultural capital under the new free-market system. In both cases, it is the possession of cultural capital that increases economic privilege relative to the other group of women. Education and experience (rather than political affiliation) are now the keys to finding a job. The majority of Bulgarian women, like Svetla, have neither valuable skills acquired in the communist era nor the economic capital to invest in their own or their children's education. They are the ones who are the most likely to have been harmed by the economic transition.

To those studying the situation of women in Bulgaria, however, it is too easy to lump these two groups of women together and ignore the very important class divisions that are polarizing them. Of course, these new socioeconomic fissures between women mirror the class stratification of the entire Bulgarian society since 1989: a small minority ascends to middle- and upper-middle-class status while the majority slips into increasing poverty (not including the lucky few Bulgarian athletes, celebrities, businesspeople, politicians, and organized criminals who join the ranks of the international super-rich). Thus, while it is true that the majority of Bulgarian women are worse off after 1989, it is equally true that the majority of Bulgarian men have been negatively affected by the economic changes. Homogenizing Bulgarian women into one category fails to take account of the cultural capital that some of them (such as those employed in tourism) do have, and how this has helped them increase their economic position relative both to other women and to men.

In an interesting irony, the vast array of nongovernmental organizations for Bulgarian women make exactly this mistake. Since the end of communism, hundreds of millions of dollars in international aid have poured into the country to create "civil society," and women's organizations are ubiquitous. While the main concern of most Bulgarian women is access to education and/or employment opportunities, these organizations are busy advocating for women's rights by focusing on noneconomic gender issues such as sexual harassment or domestic violence. In the conclusion of this book, I broaden the implications of my case study of tourism and examine the politics of professionally advocating for women's rights in the postsocialist context.

Thus, although my primary subject is tourism and the many Bulgarian women who work in the sector, tourism cannot be studied in a vacuum no matter how separated the resorts are from the rest of the country. It is the social, political, and economic context of Bulgarian tourism, particularly its communist origins and the changes that capitalism has wrought since 1989, that have created the fascinating circumstances that allowed some Bulgarian women to succeed despite the many challenges. On the other hand, tourism in 2004 accounted for over 12 percent of Bulgaria's gross domestic product, and all of the indicators point to higher future growth in the sector. Because it makes up such a large part of the Bulgarian economy, what goes on in the tourism sector also influences the rest of the country. In many ways, Bulgaria's entire macroeconomic stability relies on tourism, and the women who, for the most part, run the sector have the future of Bulgaria in their hands. The individual stories of these few relatively successful women may help us understand the spirit and tenacity of those Bulgarians who were not crushed by the maelstrom of transition, and how their example can help us to find strategies for the resuscitation of the many Bulgarians who were.

Back in Albena, Desi pulls her hair back into a ponytail and secures it with a thin black elastic. There are a few stray strands of hair that frame her face; she slides them behind her ears. Her high cheekbones are now more prominent, and she applies a fresh coat of red lipstick. We are both still sitting in the Panorama Restaurant where we have been talking for almost two hours. She gazes out of the large window.

Through the glass, I can see almost the entire beach swarming with thousands of tiny, nearly naked human bodies in the late afternoon sun. There are heads bobbing up and down in the water near the shore; a little further in, a motorboat pulls seven or eight people astride a long, bright, yellow, plastic banana. As the motorboat accelerates, the banana swoops up into the air and then splashes back down, cutting a wide arc out to the two-kilometer buoy that bobs near the horizon. The brightly colored sun umbrellas on the beach are lined up with military precision. Standing tall, they lead from the thin boardwalk down to the shoreline. I imagine that if somebody gave the right command, the umbrellas could march off and invade the sea.

Desi looks at her watch. She will need to get ready for the dinner shift soon.

I turn my attention back to my notebook. She watches me for a few minutes as I write. I have taken almost twenty pages of notes from our interview, and she seems impressed at the volume as I flip back through the notes to check if I have any last-minute questions.

"I didn't think my life was so interesting," she says.

I stop flipping and look up at her. "Think of everything that has happened in your country over the last decade. Don't you think it's amazing how things have changed in your life since 1989?"

She extends her hand and inspects a small chip in her nail polish. "Not really," she says.

I laugh. "Well, it is interesting to me."

She shrugs. I thank her for her time, and we agree to meet again in a few days.

As she walks toward the kitchen, I look back at my notebook. It amazes me still how the details of the life of one waitress can seem inconsequential, and yet provide a window into an entire world of women living, working, and surviving on the other side of the globe. It is the stories of these women that can make sense of the often-senseless process of political and economic change, and that will help tell the captivating tale of women, tourism, and transition in this small but intriguing nation on the most southeasterly edge of Europe.

Shattered Windows, Broken Lives

It is impossible to understand the lives of Bulgarian women in tourism without understanding a little about the country they call their home, and almost every journey to Bulgaria begins in the capital city of Sofia. The Thracians called this city Sardonopolis; the Romans called it Serdica. To the Byzantines it was Triaditsa, while the early Bulgarians called it Sredetz. Some Bulgarian scholars claim that the area now surrounded by modern Sofia probably developed as a city at the same time as Troy and Mycenae, and point to selected writings of Thucydides, Herodotus, and Aristotle, who claim that it is the oldest city in Europe.[1] Archeological evidence points to human habitation in the area since 7000 B.C.E., and something like the nation of Bulgaria has existed for over a thousand years. It is this rich history that at least partially makes the country so attractive to tourists.

Historically, Bulgaria was a convenient crossroads between Europe and Asia, and its capital is a natural geographic middle point between the Black and Adriatic Seas. Bulgaria's romantic allure and geopolitical significance faded during the Cold War when it was just another communist country behind the Iron Curtain. After 1989, the nation peacefully emerged from communism as the "island of stability" in the Balkans—sandwiched between the violent revolution in Romania and the chaotic breakup of the former Yugoslavia. In 2003, Sofia was a bustling capital that was home to 1.2 million Bulgarians or more than 15 percent of the country's population.

Like Vesuvius towering over the city of Naples, Sofia has its own guardian mountain, Mount Vitosha, which watches over the chaos of Eastern European urbanity. The main boulevard and shopping district in

Sofia is named after the mountain, and is diminutively referred to as Vitoshka, or little Vitosha. On this street meander many well-dressed and fashionable young people, heads cocked slightly to the side as they chat on their state-of-the-art GSM phones, no larger than a box of Tic-Tacs. Interspersed among the high-street shops purveying the latest styles of Max Mara and Krizia are roped-off sidewalk cafes brimming with animated locals sipping black Bulgarian espressos and chain-smoking American and French "designer" cigarettes from deliberately displayed packs. Several stores, called "Pretty Shops," sell the haute couture equivalent of cosmetics: Estee Lauder, Clarins, Lancôme, and Shiseido.

At the top of Vitosha is a classical Orthodox church, Sveta Nedelya, just thirty steps away from the entrance of the luxurious Sofia Sheraton, which shares a building with the Offices of the Bulgarian Presidency. Postcard vendors, old women selling bundles of wildflowers, and young men surreptitiously selling pirated compact discs fill the wide plaza around the church. At the other end, toward the street's namesake mountain, is the National Palace of Culture. It stands within a large public park that is also full of outdoor cafes and cocktail bars amidst overgrown trees and artfully landscaped concrete. On the side streets leading off Vitosha are a diverse collection of fashionable, up-scale restaurants serving international cuisines, Internet cafes with high-speed web connections, and cinemas showing the latest American blockbusters. There is, of course, a flagship McDonalds and a more humble but no less crowded Dunkin' Donuts. Down the center of the street runs a well-used, but distinctively European, yellowish-orange electric tram that sporadically sucks up and spits out pedestrian traffic onto the tree-lined sidewalks. The private car traffic that zips up and down the street consists of hundreds of bright yellow taxis and a disturbing number of black, armored Mercedes and BMWS.

From the very top of Vitosha Street just past the Sveta Nedelya cathedral, the other main corridor in the center of the city begins. This boulevard, now called King Liberator (Tsar Osvoboditel), is paved with dark, yellowish-gold clay bricks that were a gift to Bulgaria from the Austrio-Hungarian Empire. Scattered among embassies, cafes, cocktail bars, and office buildings are the King's Palace (now an ethnographic museum), the parliament building and the Alexander Nevski Cathedral. The boule-

1. KING LIBERATOR STREET. PHOTO BY AUTHOR.

vard ends at the doors of Sofia University, the most prestigious institution of higher education in the country. If Vitosha is the center of the new Bulgaria, King Liberator is the center of the old Bulgaria. The communists celebrated all of the major national holidays with parades down this street. Private car traffic was forbidden, and security was extremely tight. This was the part of Sofia used to impress the foreign dignitaries. Even today, many of the buildings here have been repainted, and the eighty kilograms of gold that decorate the domes of the Nevski Cathedral have been carefully restored. It is one of the few streets in Sofia that still has functioning streetlights.

Private cars and taxis drive freely over the cracking yellow bricks; the street is now one of the main thoroughfares through the city. Directly across from the parliament building and the Orthodox cathedral is the Taboo Club, the most "luxurious" strip club in the city. Slightly further down the street toward the King's Palace is one of the more fashionable cafe/cocktail bars in Sofia: Lipstick. In the summer, the tables are tucked between shady, chestnut trees that sparkle at night with white Christmas-tree lights wrapped around their branches and trunks. The patio area is edged with a dainty, wrought-iron fence. Private security guards pat all male patrons down at the door, and Bulgarians pay their bills and leave immediately when the G-class Mercedes sport utility vehicles pull up in front of the cafe. With their multiple girlfriends and bodyguards in tow, the Bulgarian mobsters take over the bar after midnight. Lipstick, with its open-air seating area facing onto the street, is perfect for drive-by assassinations. Bulgarians do not want to be caught in the crossfire. To the casual Western observer, however, the flock of German luxury sedans outside may be nothing unusual. For many visitors, Lipstick is a pleasant place to spend the evening, people-watching the Bulgarian elite and ordering exotic cocktails from the waitresses who all speak perfect English.

Vitosha is a Potemkin village that fools foreigners into believing that over a decade of capitalism has been good for Bulgaria. Foreigners often have a difficult time reconciling the economic data they have on Bulgaria with the fantasy of wealth and prosperity that a stroll down Vitosha Street or a night at Lipstick engenders in all but the most observant visitors. To the casual tourist, the fleeting business traveler, or the World Bank financial consultant on a ten-day mission to "understand" Bulgaria, Vitoshka, King Liberator, and their immediate environs create the impression of a slightly anachronistic European country impressively catching up with new imperatives of global capitalism.

On the lower corners of Vitosha Street that border the park of the National Palace of Culture, there is usually an old woman or an old man on each side with large brown-paper sacks full of *gevretzi*, a kind of Bulgarian bread that is a cross between a bagel and a pretzel. These pretzel-bagels are a good way to fill your stomach in the morning and cost only thirty *stotinki* (about eighteen u.s. cents).[2] If you sit in a cafe across from these corners for an hour in the morning and watch the wide cross-section of Bulgarians buying these hot gevretzi, you begin to glimpse beneath the gilded veneer of Vitosha Street. On these two corners and others like them around the city, the *gevrek* venders feed the city's students, workers, and pensioners. They support an economy where the average monthly wage of the country's citizens is not enough to meet an individual's basic human needs for food, water, shelter, and the cost of basic utilities. And some cannot even afford the gevretzi.

Early in the morning, well before the shops open, and even before the dwindling handful of Roma children and amputees take up their begging posts—when the street is quiet and empty in anticipation of the orgy of real and imagined consumption that the day will bring—the curtain of

2. A STREET LEADING OFF LOWER VITOSHA. PHOTO BY AUTHOR.

dawn rises on the tragedy of Vitosha Street. Among the paper and plastic recyclers and the Roma "treasure" hunters, there are always a few pensioners, communism's forgotten mothers and fathers, sifting through the large metallic dumpsters for food. And not only on Vitosha, but in affluent and even semi-affluent neighborhoods around Sofia city, the "dumpster divers" have become a permanent fixture of the urban landscape. It is disconcerting to watch them, with their spotless, unwrinkled clothes, their polished shoes, and clean-shaven chins—these are not social misfits or homeless people. These are men and women who worked honestly for all of their lives under one economic system only to lose their rewards by the advent of another.

Sofia itself is like an old woman who was once remarkably beautiful. She does her best to bear with dignity her rapidly fading glory, but everywhere the signs of her steady degeneration are evident. Photographs of Sofia from as late as the 1980s show a clean, well-manicured city with long tree-lined boulevards and immaculately groomed cobblestone streets. The nineteenth-century buildings and monuments in the center of the city seemed always freshly painted or polished. I have been told that the streets and sidewalks in the downtown areas were once washed nightly with soap.

A stroll away from the main tourist pathways reveals the dilapidated underbelly of the city even in broad daylight. The unique hexagonal cement tiles that pave the wide sidewalks are now uneven and cracked from all the private cars parked on them. People in Bulgaria are forced to walk on the streets because the sidewalks are overrun with parked automobiles. The streets themselves are full of deep gaps in the pavement. The cash-starved municipality seldom repairs them. Only recently have the rubbish bins begun to appear around the city to mitigate the epidemic of littering that plagued Sofia in the 1990s. Some residents still dump trash out of their third- and fourth-floor windows. The trees along the streets are now wild and overgrown. No one cares for the grass in the numerous neighborhood parks and playgrounds where thousands of stray dogs roam in search of food. In addition to the fecal messes they leave, which render the parks unusable, the strays often form themselves into dangerous packs that attack unwary pedestrians. The beautiful, grand buildings of Sofia's past are falling to pieces; their paint has faded or flaked away. There is random graffiti on even the most treasured national monuments.

In what used to be one of the most fashionable neighborhoods in Sofia, there are shattered windows covered over with multiple layers of plastic clingwrap. Since the early 1990s, many of Bulgaria's top organized criminals have built or hired apartments in the neighborhood, slowly settling in among the resident pensioners and children of the former communist *nomenklatura*. The increasing tensions between different factions of Bulgaria's new mobster elite mean that small bombs are routinely detonated in parked cars. Various assassination attempts have wreaked destruction on millions of leva of private property for which there is no compensation. If they survive, the targets can easily afford to do the repairs necessary to their own property. For the elderly inhabitants of this neighborhood, whose monthly heating bills alone already exceed their meager pensions, one nearby explosion can mean the difference between barely surviving and falling into poverty. They cannot afford to replace the windows shattered by the explosions. Even if they could find a way, one woman I spoke to said that she would not spend the money to replace them for fear that there would be yet another explosion. For now, the plastic wrap is the best that most people can do. At least it still lets the light in.

Even people working for the government are not immune to the general erosion in living standards in the country. I once met with a senior expert from the Ministry of Economy in an open-air cafe, where I ordered two draught beers and a bag of imported Ruffles potato chips. The waiter opened the bag and shook the chips out onto a white napkin on a porcelain plate. At the end of the interview, there were maybe five or six chips left on the plate. As I paid the bill, I watched the senior expert carefully fold the white napkin over the remaining chips, and put them into her bag. When she saw that I was watching her, she said simply, "For my son." The chips had cost one lev (seventy u.s. cents) in the restaurant, and would cost about seventy-five stotinki (fifty cents) in the supermarket. But from the way she gingerly put them away, careful not to crush one, I knew that they would be a special treat.

The hardships that characterize life in Sofia, however, are amplified when they radiate out from the capital, touching the lives of almost all Bulgarians, even the middle classes. In the carefully landscaped garden of a summerhouse about twenty-five kilometers outside of Sofia, I watched a gaggle of meticulously dressed housewives of the Bulgarian upper-middle class chatting together at a child's birthday party. As the mother of the birthday boy brought out the meat that she had prepared for the grill, another housewife cooed and said, "Steak tips? How nice that you prepared steak tips. They have become so expensive. We cannot afford to eat them anymore at our house."

The other housewives nodded in agreement. The mother shrugged, looking down at what had once been a staple of the Bulgarian diet. "These are his favorite," she said.

Almost everyday while I was living in Bulgaria, I saw painful evidence of the rapidly declining living standard at all levels of society. I often felt as if everyone and everything around me were still trying to shake off the sudden evaporation of communism in the Eastern bloc. In all of my casual conversations with Bulgarians, I found that they most frequently attributed their sorrows to what they simply called "the changes," a Himalayan understatement for the total collapse of an entire political and economic system. In order to understand how women's lives have been affected, how expectations and opportunities for women in tourism have been transformed since 1989, I first need to step back and survey the larger ramifications of the collapse of Bulgarian communism, the system that had given them their now-valuable cultural capital.

One of the greatest failures of both Eastern and Western social science was that no one really saw the collapse of the Soviet Empire coming. So-called "experts" were just as shocked as the ordinary people when the Berlin Wall suddenly came down. After almost half a century of a Cold War that had brought the world to the brink of total nuclear annihilation, the enemy just disappeared. As the sociologist Manuel Castells explained: "The Soviet experiment marked decisively a twentieth century that, by and large, revolved around its development and consequences for the whole world. It cast a giant shadow not only over the geopolitics of states, but also over the imaginary constructions of social transformation . . . That all this effort, all this human suffering and passion, all these ideas, all these dreams, could have vanished in such a short period of time, revealing the emptiness of the debate, is a stunning expression of our collective capacity to build political fantasies so powerful that they end up changing history."[3]

In the beginning of my fieldwork, the massive scale of the collapse was almost impossible for me to imagine no matter how much I had heard or read about it. I tried to make comparisons with the United States. I would ask: What would have to change in my own country to replicate the sheer magnitude of "the changes"? At first, I thought about these things on a large scale. I imagined the president and some senators absconding with the entire federal budget and emigrating to North Korea or Cuba. I imagined a stock-market crash from which the United States could never recover, a second Great Depression spiraling out of control. I imagined the possibility of marshal law in New York City. I imagined President Bush the Second dissolving the legislative and judicial branches of the government and declaring himself supreme leader for life. I imagined all of my private property seized by the police: my car, my computer, my bank account. I tried to picture all of these things happening at the same time.

My first reaction to all this speculation was a smug confidence that these things could never happen—not in the United States of America, not in the proverbial land of the free. I found that my self-assurance was disconcerting. How many people, I asked myself, had believed the same thing about communism in 1988? How many Bulgarians had joined the Communist Party on November 1, 1989? Could our own apocalypse be just around the corner? How could I ever be prepared for something as huge as the end of the United States? This was truly beyond the scope of even my active imagination. Therefore, I felt that I could understand the experiences of my Bulgarian friends, family, and colleagues only in the abstract, as a theoretical possibility, and never as an actual material reality. As time passed, I realized that my inability to fully understand the implications of the collapse stemmed from my own lack of knowledge about what Bulgarian communism had meant for the people—men and women who had grown up under the "old system" and grown accustomed to its logic.

DORA

Dora, a forty-two-year-old head chef in the resort Golden Sands, had a life under communism that was typical for many Bulgarians. In her earliest years, she was taken care of by her mother, who had two years of paid maternity leave. Dora was then moved to the kindergarten at the canning factory where her mother worked. After that, she went to primary school and studied hard for the exams that would allow her, like Desi, to get a place in a prestigious language secondary school. Dora scored very well on her entrance exams and studied in the first German gymnasium (high school), where she decided that she wanted to work in tourism. After secondary school, Dora (like most girls) went straight on to higher education, while the boys fulfilled their two years of compulsory military service. Since the international culinary institute was one of the most competitive college programs, she worked very hard to pass the entrance exams. Once she graduated, Dora was required to work for three years in a job of the state's choosing. This placement was a way of repaying the state back for her education.

Dora, like most Bulgarians, seldom had to look for employment—it was the state's responsibility to utilize her skills. Most often, postgraduation placements at all educational levels turned into permanent positions. If an enterprise closed, or someone was no longer able to do her assigned job, the state was responsible for finding new workplaces for the employees: every able man and woman in Bulgaria was guaranteed employment. Individual Bulgarians worked in the same professions until they reached the age of retirement (fifty-five for women and sixty for men), and then they settled into old age with a comfortable state pension until the day they died. Dora was randomly assigned to work in the Golden Sands resort after college and would have had a relatively comfortable life had the system not collapsed in 1989.

Soon after she began working, Dora got married. Like all Bulgarians, Dora and her husband, Boyan, received a "newlywed" loan from the state. Comfortable living with Boyan's parents, Dora and her husband used the loan to buy a private car. When Dora became pregnant and they decided to buy their own apartment, Dora and Boyan had to sell the car in order to qualify for the 1 percent mortgage. If they owned a private car, the state required that the size of the down payment they needed to get the loan be exactly the value of a private car. Communist banking was the absolute inverse of its capitalist counterpart: the less collateral you had the more likely you were to get a loan.

As in many socialist societies, the personal accumulation of wealth was universally frowned upon in Bulgaria; membership in the Communist Party served to differentiate the social classes. To this end, the state wasted little of its precious hard currency to import consumer goods, and little "luxuries" were very hard to find. Most consumer goods such as clothes, music, shoes, and household appliances had to be smuggled into the country, bought on the black market, brought back by a well-connected relative, or bought in the overpriced, state-run Korecom stores for hard currency. While Bulgarians had all of their basic needs met by the state, many of them longed for the forbidden fruits of capitalism.[4] In university, Dora once spent an entire month's stipend to buy a smuggled, limited edition Queen LP and a poster of Freddie Mercury from a classmate whose sister-in-law was a stewardess for Balkan Air.

Although Dora misses the job security and the benefits of communism, she is happy that the system is gone. Under communism, she could not travel abroad. She did not even have a passport. Now, she can drive to Greece with her husband and their two sons anytime she wants. Although she cannot afford to do it, she tells me that it is the possibility of being able to go that makes her happy. "My country is no longer my prison," she says.

On an individual level, the socialist experiment in Bulgaria reshaped every detail of people's lives. The state was responsible for meeting basic needs from birth to death; a socialist citizen was delivered in a state-run hospital and buried by a state-run mortuary in a state-owned cemetery. Under communism, houses and apartments were privately owned, and unlike other socialist countries, Bulgaria did not suffer from severe housing shortages. In the cities, the communists erected thousands of *zhilishtni blokove* (housing blocks)—tall, utilitarian apartment buildings with standardized floor plans in neighborhoods called "Youth," "Friendship," and "Red Star." The allocation of apartments was determined by the place of employment—your position in society would essentially determine where the state allowed you to buy a house. The communist elite lived in the fashionable neighborhoods in the center of the city, while the workers were relegated to the extensive suburbs. For all Bulgarians, however, there were very strict rules about the size of privately owned dwellings; the number of rooms allowed was determined by a formula based on the number of family members that occupied the home. The only exception to this was that "professionals" were allowed an extra bedroom to use as an office. Once an appropriately sized apartment or house was found in an appropriate neighborhood, the state gave mortgages at a standard interest rate of 1 percent.

Like an overbearing father, the Bulgarian state was responsible for meeting the needs of its "children," and in return, it demanded absolute obedience. The children had no say in choosing their father. Like restless teenagers, they lived an existence starved for freedom and independence.[5] Dora says she could not think freely under communism. She lived in constant fear that someone would discover that her father listened to the BBC World Service on his shortwave radio, and that she would lose her job. She also hated that the government determined every aspect of her life, from what kind of food she ate to what color socks she wore. She had no control over the government. Unlike Desi, Dora never joined the Communist Party, and that was the only political choice she ever made. Even now she tells me that she has not voted in the last two elections.

"I am happy with the idea that I could vote if I wanted to," she says and shrugs. "But I'm not so sure that it would matter now either. Still, things are better."

Although she is happy that the communists are no longer in power, Dora fully recognizes that it was those very communists who set her country on the path to modernization and industrialization. She considers communism a necessary stage that Bulgaria had to pass through in order to "join the Western countries." Before Bulgaria's ideological and political alliance with the Soviet Union, the small nation was significantly less developed than the rest of Europe. Ottoman influence meant that social relations in Bulgaria were more feudal than in Hungary or Poland, and the country had little capitalist development prior to World War II.[6] The few industries that had begun to emerge revolved around food processing and textile production. Bulgaria became a communist country after 1944 with the strong support of the agricultural workers. Dora's own grandfather had been a farmer who joined the partisans in the mountains. Communism and centralized planning allowed for the rapid industrialization of the Bulgarian economy and the proletarianization of its overwhelmingly peasant population.[7]

Bulgaria was one of the founding members of the Council for Mutual Economic Assistance (CMEA or COMECON). This trade organization promoted socialist economic integration with the other communist Eastern European nations and eventually Mongolia, Vietnam, and Cuba. Bulgaria's transformation from a predominantly agricultural economy to an industrialized one was realized largely through its participation in the COMECON. In 1970, the COMECON nations were already the destination for 77 percent of Bulgaria's exports.[8] By 1989, the COMECON was absorbing a full 84 percent. These numbers were much lower for other European COMECON members. Czechoslovakia came second with 55 percent of its exports going to COMECON countries, with the German Democratic Republic coming in third at 43 percent, almost half the amount for Bulgaria.[9] These export "markets" allowed the Bulgarian industry to diversify and grow. Between 1939 and 1983, Bulgaria experienced a relatively rapid decrease in the importance of textile production and food processing and a concomitant growth of machinery, chemicals, and metallurgy. Indeed, between 1981 and 1983, 53.8 percent of Bulgaria's exports were in machinery.[10]

The Soviet Union was Bulgaria's largest export market. In 1970, the USSR alone was "purchasing" 54 percent of Bulgarian exports. By 1989, this number had risen to 65 percent. Bulgaria was more than twice as economically dependent on the USSR than any other European COMECON country.[11] Bulgaria was additionally dependent on the COMECON for 74 percent of its imports in 1989. It received 53 percent of its imports from the Soviet Union alone. Many of these imports were exchanged in a barter-like fashion, often for well below the market price which Bulgaria would have had to pay had it purchased these goods elsewhere. In fact, these low "prices," especially for oil, were an important part of Soviet aid and a significant producer of foreign exchange for Bulgaria, which would often resell these goods to its non-COMECON neighbors for a profit. As the "little brother" of the Soviet Union, Bulgaria saw a rapid increase in the standard of living for its citizens.[12] Between 1965 and 1983, the number of Bulgarians who owned televisions, refrigerators, electric washing machines, and private cars dramatically increased.[13]

In terms of human development, communism facilitated a great expansion in education and social services.[14] Generous social programs and nationalized health care led to declining infant mortality and increasing life expectancy. Infant mortality declined by more than half between 1960 and 1980.[15] During that same period, Bulgarian life expectancy increased by five years.[16] The communist state also strived to incorporate women and ethnic minorities into the educational system and labor force, endowing women in particular with the cultural capital that would be so valuable to them in the post-1989 period. The state also subsidized cultural activities and sports, producing world-renowned Bulgarian artists, entertainers, and athletes. Communism drastically transformed the Bulgarian society and economy in a relatively short period.

Precommunist gender relations were also radically transformed between 1944 and 1989 as the state attempted to abolish all legal, social, cultural, and moral prescriptions for the "proper" behavior of men and women. Furthermore, the communist state attempted to socialize domestic work as much as possible. In order to support women in their new roles as workers, communists supported policies that created public canteens and childcare facilities in addition to granting women generous maternity leaves, child allowances, and early retirement. Since the state guaranteed economic security and all basic human needs, the socialist man and woman theoretically had few purely economic incentives to marry. In fact, single mothers had considerably more benefits from the state than married women with children, creating disincentives to marriage and giving women relative independence from men.

Socialism never completely defeated local patriarchies, but in the process of creating their own more egalitarian gender regimes the countries of the Eastern bloc were able to boast some of the highest female labor participation rates in the world. In 1989, on the eve of the collapse, 84.7 percent of Bulgarian women were employed as waged workers outside of the home.[17] As paid workers, women like Dora had rights to all of the benefits of formal employment: their own wages and pensions, access to personal credit through workplace cooperative savings schemes, paid holidays, access to enterprise-owned hotels and camps, and so forth. Some women also managed to infiltrate traditionally male professions such as steel processing and engineering, and were thus able to earn some of the highest wages available in the economy.

While the state actively tried to eradicate the gender differences between men and women, it made social allowances for women's continued social and biological role as mothers. Under communism, Dora had been guaranteed maternity leave, which began forty-five days before her expected delivery date with the possibility of continuing until her child reached the age of three. For her first three children, the state paid for this leave until each child was two. After two years, the leave was unpaid with the provision that Dora's job would be held through the whole duration of her absence. If she chose to return to work before her child's second birthday, she was entitled to receive 50 percent of the national minimum wage for the portion of the leave she did not use. This was in addition to her wages. Alternatively, Dora could have granted permission to Boyan or to one of his or her parents to take the unused portion of her maternity leave. Golden Sands could not refuse to grant this leave if it was requested, and her three years of leave were recognized as labor service toward her pension.

Socialism had other benefits for women like Dora. Childcare facilities were guaranteed to working women by the state.[18] In addition to paid maternity and childcare leave, Boyan and Dora would have received a monthly child allowance until a child was sixteen (or eighteen if the child was still in school), the amount of which was determined by the size of the family.[19] There were also laws that restricted Dora from working at night and in certain professions that would endanger her reproductive abilities (such as work in nuclear power plants or in certain petrochemical factories). Although these laws reinforced labor segregation and helped to concentrate women in lower-paying jobs, they were meant to protect women from certain kinds of exploitation and could be challenged on an individual level if desired.

On a more personal level, the communist state consistently protected the rights of women in marriage and in the case of divorce. Under communism, Dora and Boyan were considered equal partners in their marriage, and all loans made to the couple and sales of family property required the signatures of both husband and wife. If Dora and Boyan had divorced, all property would have been divided equally, with Dora most likely being awarded custody of their children. Most importantly, the state would have automatically deducted child-support payments from Boyan's wages and transferred them to Dora every month. Divorced women with children could rely on this steady income that would always be collected no matter where in Bulgaria the father moved. Widows could rely on the state for their own pensions and additional social supports once their husbands had passed away. Young girls had access to education and many career opportunities.

The communist state did go a long way in attempting to create the conditions for women's full emancipation. Communism displaced patriarchy from the household to the state level, and committed resources to the support of women's dual roles as mothers and workers.[20] Social expectations for young women, firmly grounded in communist doctrine, always revolved around their fulfilling the roles of both worker and mother, never one at the exclusion of the other. Although Bulgarian women's lives were still very much determined by paternalistic control (for example, the state could still legislate how many children a married woman should have), the socialist system considered the emancipation of women one of its fundamental goals, and gender relations between men and women were relatively equal. When I press her on the issue, even Dora admits that things were easier for women under the "old system."

One day in the off-season, I am invited home for dinner with Dora's family. Dora's mother tells me a joke about a Bulgarian woman who sits bolt upright in the middle of the night in a panic. The woman jumps out of bed and rushes to the bathroom to look in the medicine cabinet. Then she runs into the kitchen and opens the refrigerator. Finally, she dashes to the window and looks out onto the street. Relieved, she returns to the bedroom. Her husband asks her, "What's wrong with you?"

"I had a terrible nightmare," she says. "I dreamt that we could still afford to buy medicine, that the refrigerator was absolutely full, and that the streets were safe and clean."

"How is that a nightmare?" the husband asks.

The woman shakes her head, "I thought the communists were back in power."

Dora sneers at her mother for "talking politics" at dinner, but I laugh.

The joke highlighted a popular nostalgia for the "good" parts of communism that was just starting to reemerge in the early years of the twenty-first century. In the summer of 2003, in the seaside resorts of Bulgaria, I had seen beach vendors selling Union of Soviet Socialist Republics (cccp) and German Democratic Republic (ddr) t-shirts to the tourists. At the same time, cd pirates in Sofia were running out of the compact disc "Golden Songs of Russia," with a red and yellow cover and the hymn of the ussr as the first track. In front of the Alexander Nevski Cathedral, Bulgarian antique dealers were selling all manner of socialist pins, buttons, and medals, old postcards of the now-destroyed mausoleum, and busts of Marx, Lenin, and Georgi Dimitrov.[21] It used to be only the tourists who picked up the communist trinkets, but in 2003 the antique dealers said that their most loyal customers were Bulgarians hoping to preserve a bit of their past for future generations. On the streets of Plovdiv or Varna and the cafes and bars of Sofia, it was not uncommon to hear a cell phone with its ring tone set to the chorus of "The Internationale."

On the one hand, these artifacts of the past probably had the appeal of kitsch for Bulgarians who had some time to distance themselves from the oppressive nature of the old system. On the other hand, the increasingly visible manifestations of communist nostalgia were also a product of the frustration that many Bulgarians like Dora's mother felt about their dramatically decreased standard of living since Bulgaria began its transition to free markets and liberal democracy. Between 1989 and 1998, the Bulgarian Gross Domestic Product (GDP) lost more than a third of its value.[22] In the period immediately following the transition, GDP per capita fell from $2,513 in 1989 to $946 in 1991, a massive decline in just two years.[23] By 2003, per capita GDP had still not recovered up to 1989 levels, and income polarization had increased.[24] Prices rose steadily throughout the 1990s, purchasing power decreased, and unemployment increased.[25]

For all but a handful of Bulgarians at the very top of society—a few businessmen, celebrities, athletes, politicians, and organized criminals—everyday survival had become increasingly difficult. Dora's family clearly recalled the severe shortages of the early 1990s. Staples of the Bulgarian diet—meat, cheese, and milk—were suddenly nowhere to be found. At dinner that night, Boyan explained to me how the politicians had gotten rich by exporting Bulgaria's agricultural produce for hard currency while their own people rationed the paltry remains. Organized criminals had terrorized the population, racketeering every small business out of profitability. Boyan had tried to start a small restaurant only to have to pay all of his profits in the form of "insurance" to the new Bulgarian Mafia. He now works at a petrol station. As Dora tries to hush him, Boyan (encouraged by Dora's mother) complains to me that they had sacrificed personal and economic security for the still-abstract American concepts of liberty and democracy. As an American, I almost feel like he is blaming me, and I quietly listen for over an hour as Boyan catalogues the various ills of postcommunist Bulgaria. There is no doubt that the promise of freedom rings very hollow in the ears of the bitter men and women who lived the majority of their lives under the old system. For those who still cling to the communist form of habitus that allowed them to live better before 1989, "the changes" have been harsh.

Dora and Boyan also fear for their teenage son. There is a growing drug problem among Bulgarian youth who have little to do with their time. In 2003, a dose of heroin on the street cost as little as $3. The number of young people drawn into heroin addiction continues to increase. They, too, are disenfranchised from Bulgarian society. In 2001, 35.3 percent of youth between the ages of fifteen and twenty-four were unemployed.[26] Their only hopes are pinned on finding a way to leave the country—a way to go to the West. In the late 1990s, there were always long queues for visas in front of the various consulates of the Western countries. One Bulgarian I interviewed actually met and courted his future wife in the long days he spent in lines trying to obtain entry to the West.

This uncertainty about the future has manifested itself as a deep-seated cynicism. Like Boyan, many Bulgarians are skeptical of the widely touted benefits of capitalism and globalization. In June 2000, 85.5 percent of Bulgarians surveyed believed that the situation in their country would continue to deteriorate, and 86 percent felt that it was either difficult to live or that their situation had become unbearable.[27] Another survey found that 57 percent of Bulgarians believed that "one can only get rich if he steals," as opposed to only 43 percent who believed one could obtain riches through honesty and hard work. Twenty-three point six percent felt that it was preferable that their children be corrupt rather than poor, while 34.5 percent of respondents felt that "in this world it [was] better for [their] children sometimes to lie."[28] In this same year, more than a quarter of all Bulgarians compared the situation in their country with the situation of countries in the developing world.

Most interesting of all was a question that asked a nationally representative sample of Bulgarians what they would be willing to stand in front of the parliament building in Sofia and protest.[29] Almost two-thirds of both men and women agreed that a drastic deterioration of the economic situation would warrant protest. In fact, the responses of men and women differed very little on most of the survey questions. Men, however, were more inclined to stand up for their recently gained civil rights; they were more willing to challenge corrupt politicians, manipulated elections, and protect the rights of minorities and the freedom of speech. Women, on the other hand, were more concerned with drastic increases in the costs for health and education. Interestingly, less than a third of either Bulgarian men or women would protest the introduction of new forms of dictatorship (a common synonym in Bulgaria for Soviet-style communism). This indicator also showed the biggest percentage difference between the sexes, with 31 percent of men saying they would protest this versus only 22 percent of women.

This difference in the willingness to protest highlights the emergence of new gender politics in the postsocialist period, and the erosion of the old equalities that the state forced on men and women before 1989. But a survey result such as this should be interpreted very carefully. One should not conclude from the survey finding, for instance, that differences between men's and women's responses are based either on biological or irreversible psychological differences between them. A popular discourse in Bulgaria now proposes that women prefer security and men prefer freedom due to some evolutionary differentiation of the sexes over the millennia. Indeed, in the postsocialist period both nationalists and free-market liberals have reimagined communism as a system that benefited only women and suppressed men and their "natural" entrepreneurial talents.[30]

Katherine Verdery has convincingly argued, however, that state socialism led to the inevitable infantilization of both men and women, who became equally dependent on a paternalistic state that met all of their basic needs. Both men and women were coddled by the omnipotent state—men with secure employment and freedom from the responsibilities of providing for their families, and women also with secure employment and extensive social supports for meeting the basic needs of their children.

While the gender roles of men and women did change significantly in Bulgaria during the forty-five–year experiment with communism, patriarchal traditions have made a comeback since the early 1990s. In Bulgaria, gender roles and the beliefs of men and women are being reconstructed in response to rapidly changing material realities. The transition from communism affected all individuals in different ways. The gendered response to the survey question is not because of inherent difference between men and women, but because men and women were responsible for different aspects of everyday life during the communist and postcommunist periods. Men's and women's experiences of the transition were dependent on which aspects of "the changes" they tended to have more contact with during that particular historical moment, and how those changes affected their beliefs and expectations. This is a very important point because there are many Bulgarians who now believe that women are "naturally" less suited to competition and capitalism when in fact there are many women who are doing relatively better than men.

Unemployment affected all Bulgarians, but the experience of unemployment was different for men and women. Men like Boyan were primarily employed in the industrial sector, and Bulgarian factories were among the first state-owned enterprises to be closed down. Boyan had been trained as a chemical engineer, and he had few skills that would help in finding another job. Furthermore, once Boyan was laid off, he had little in the way of traditional responsibilities to occupy his now copious amounts of free time. Many men like Boyan, therefore, experienced the effects of the transition almost immediately, and soon busied themselves with trying to find work or starting small businesses in the emerging private sector.

Women, alternatively, tended to work in the offices of the state's vast bureaucracy. They did not start losing their jobs until further into the transition years. In 1995, more than half of the Bulgarian economy remained within the public sector.[31] Many of these jobs were in feminized professions. The bloated public sector shrank rather slowly relative to the state-owned factories. This allowed women to be sheltered from the early effects of transition by a still-powerful state. Furthermore, some women were able to use their more general education and work experience (cultural capital) to find jobs in the private sector. Even after women did begin to lose their administrative jobs en masse, they still had many other responsibilities in the home to occupy their time, and continued to be dependent on the state for access to health care and education for their children. It was only after a total economic collapse in 1997 that the state was forced to dismantle the social safety net of kindergartens, schools, and hospitals that had allowed women to combine their productive and reproductive roles. In many ways, men personally felt the negative effects of the transition from socialism much earlier than women did, but they were more likely to find new, higher-paying jobs in the private sector because employers preferred workers who could not take maternity leave.

Therefore, it should not be surprising that women in the postsocialist period in Bulgaria have more of an affinity for the centralized state, since it was this very state that was still looking after their needs well into the transition period. The difference in men's and women's perception of the state was a product of unique historical circumstances that were lived in different ways by men and women. As the transition continued throughout the 1990s and living standards continued to deteriorate, women may have been more inclined to hope for a stronger state that would step in and stop the decline. This was not the product of a biological feminine tendency toward economic dependence, as the conservatives would have it, but a result of women's experience of the transition. Bulgarian women's personal and political commitment to a stronger state should not be viewed as a failure of women to adjust to the realities of the free-market system. Indeed, some scholars have recognized that most Bulgarians want the state to have a larger role in guaranteeing minimum social welfare.[32] This desire can be seen as a form of resistance to the free-market system. Under the current macroeconomic circumstances, Bulgaria cannot "afford" to have a larger state, and what Bulgaria can "afford" is largely determined by the International Monetary Fund and the World Bank.

And women are not doomed to fail under capitalism because they are women. The relative "success" or "failure" of women or men is determined by external criteria defined by international organizations—labor activity rates, unemployment rates, per capita income, and so forth. It is true that on many of these indicators (though certainly not on all) there are groups of women who have suffered disproportionately, but this does not immediately translate into a generalization about women as a whole. The important point is that acknowledging that men and women have been affected differently by the transition process does not necessarily mean that one group has to be worse off than the other. Some aspects of "the changes" were very bad for women, and other aspects were very bad for men. Similarly, some of the consequences of the transition might have benefited women while others favored men.

Although there were socialized gender expectations for men and women under communism, these differences did not translate into material inequalities between the sexes in terms of unequal access to resources. Bulgarian men and women fulfilled different social roles, worked different kinds of jobs, and accumulated different types of cultural capital, but they were equally dependent on the socialist state for almost every aspect of their lives. It was only after 1989 that difference in gender roles, and in particular gender differences in the allocation of cultural capital, began to translate into differences in the material standard of living. While in many cases, men were the beneficiaries of postsocialist changes in the gender regime, tourism is one sector where women entered the transition period with an advantage.

Under communism, Boyan had earned more than Dora as a chemical engineer. In fact, he once earned some of the highest wages available to a nonparty member. Today, Dora's salary as head chef is almost four times what Boyan earns at the petrol station. In their family, Boyan is the one more likely to long for socialism because he does not have the right portfolio of stocks of capital to succeed in the free-market economy. It is Dora's revalued cultural capital that largely supports them, not because Boyan is somehow less able, less motivated, or less suited to capitalism, but because of the different types of education and career they had under communism. Dora, and other women in tourism like her, just happened to possess the right package of skills for a competitive labor market, and it is women like Dora who are lost in the generalizations and national surveys that claim that Bulgarian women are worse off than men.

THREE WEEKS BEFORE SVETLA'S
UNIVERSITY ENTRANCE EXAM

Not far from Dora's and Boyan's apartment, Svetla is drinking her third bottle of Coca-Cola in an Internet cafe. She is reading French newspapers online and writing down new vocabulary words from the travel sections. With her tattered French-Bulgarian dictionary, she methodically looks up each new word and records the various meanings. Svetla has been in the cafe for almost five hours; her back is aching from sitting in the low plastic chair. She leans back for a moment to stretch. The young man who works with the computers walks over to her with a small bag of pretzels, and Svetla realizes that she has not eaten since she started. She thanks him with a smile, and clicks on to another Web site.

2

Making Mitko Tall

Some thirty kilometers south of Sofia is the city of Samokov, once an economic powerhouse both before and during the communist period. Samokov sits in a wide valley and is bisected by the Iskar River and surrounded by the pine-covered Rila Mountains. Driving into Samokov on the local highway, automobiles often have to swerve around horse-drawn wooden carts. Cars and petrol have become so expensive that many people still use the carts as a primary form of transportation. Samokov is full of ten- to twelve-story apartment blocks with rusting metal balconies and cement-gray facades. The long rows of these identi-cally unimaginative buildings are the highest structures in the valley—eyesores on an otherwise naturally beautiful horizon. The streets in many of the neighborhoods are so full of potholes that they are nothing more than uneven dirt roads punctuated with floating slabs of graying tar-mac. There are empty stores, empty warehouses, and empty factories, all boarded up and deserted. If you look at the layout of the city and the remnants of the streetlights and sidewalks, it is difficult to imagine that Samokov was once a modern European city. Today, even the locals admit that it is hardly better off than cities in the developing world that have never been invigorated by the prosperity of rural industrialization.

In a neighborhood on the other side of the Iskar River from the city's center, there is a block of apartments with seven identical buildings. In the fourth building, on the seventh floor, in a small two-bedroom apart-ment, lives a woman called Gergana. She shares this small apartment with her husband, her husband's mother and father, and her eight-year-old son, Mitko. Her mother- and father-in-law once had their own apart-ment nearby, but they could not survive on their small pensions. Their

3. DOWNTOWN SAMOKOV. PHOTO BY AUTHOR.

apartment is rented out to another young couple with two children. At first, it was very difficult for Gergana to have to live with her husband's parents, but her mother-in-law helps everyday with Mitko, and they are able to afford more things by living together. The utility offices are open only while Gergana is working, so she counts on her father-in-law to pay all of the bills that must be paid in person. Gergana's husband is unemployed and has been for the last four years. He finds occasional work as a construction worker in Sofia. The jobs are infrequent, and his unemployment compensation expired more than two years ago. Mostly, he spends his time looking for a new job in Samokov or watching imported Columbian soap operas dubbed into Bulgarian.

Gergana is almost twenty-seven years old. She got married when she was eighteen, directly after finishing secondary school. She had her son soon afterwards. She was only fourteen when communism ended in Bulgaria. She remembers the Samokov of her childhood as a beautiful little city on the river. Her dream had always been to work in Borovetz, the winter ski resort just minutes from Samokov in the shadow of Mount Moussala, the highest peak on the Balkan peninsula. The events of 1989 altered the course of Gergana's young life.

The first few years of "the changes" were terrible for Gergana and her family. "For almost two years there was nothing to buy in the stores. If you walked into a grocery store, there might be one or two tins of tomato sauce—even those would be snatched up and stored away. It was as if the entire country was in a twenty-four-month state of emergency," she says. In 1990 most sources of protein were rationed. Gergana and her family had to make do with just ten eggs and one kilogram of cheese each month. Gergana blames her small stature on the fact that she had nothing good to eat during her teenage years. She tells me, "One needs milk and meat to grow tall."

The only families that had food were those that grew their own produce, or those who had relatives who worked in Borovetz. After 1989, the newly elected Bulgarian Socialist Party exported everything that Bulgaria produced and kept only enough to supply the international tourist resorts that were still generating hard currency for the country. Despite the aggressive exporting, Bulgaria's foreign debt more than tripled during the same time that people were using ration coupons. Gergana, like many Bulgarians, believes that the politicians made off with all the money, and eventually used it to form the Bulgarian Mafia. At the same time, state assets were "spontaneously privatized" by many of the country's former elite, draining more money out of the government's budget. The desperation and lawlessness of the initial transition period manifested itself in soaring crime rates. Property was privatized through theft, robbery, racketeering, extortion, and murder. The young, the qualified, and the connected packed up their bags and fled the country—a mass exodus of muscle and brain.

If Gergana had had the opportunity, she would have left the country, too. Her husband, Petar, often talked of paying some truck drivers to smuggle them into Germany. Gergana was too afraid for Mitko to think of taking the risk of leaving the country illegally, but she lived with the constant fear that someday her husband would just go. In the early 1990s, Gergana says, she kept hoping that things would get better. Instead, their living standards continued to plummet. Although she says she never cared about politics, she believes that she would have taken to the streets in 1996 if she had been in Sofia. The whole economy finally imploded that year, as young Bulgarian protesters helped oust the ruling socialists. Things had been too bad for too long.

Gergana's hope for a better government was never realized. In January 1997, a coalition party strongly supported by the West, the Union of Democratic Forces (UDF, or CDC in Bulgarian), took power under the leadership of the prime minister, Ivan Kostov. The new government signed a three-year standby agreement with the International Monetary Fund (IMF), and committed to a Currency Board Arrangement (CBA) that linked the Bulgarian lev to the German mark. The painful process of privatization and marketization of the already tattered Bulgarian economy began, and conditions worsened for Gergana and her family when Petar lost his job in the mines.

Working closely with the IMF and the World Bank, Kostov implemented austerity measures to bolster macroeconomic stability. Deep cuts were made into what was left of the social safety net, depriving Gergana of many services on which she had come to rely. She now had to pay to take Mitko to see a doctor even when he was very ill. Bulgaria also began the "harmonization" in hopes of becoming a member of the European Union. This entailed changing laws, freeing more markets, and making environmental concessions to the EU, such as decommissioning Bulgaria's nuclear power plant. The cost of living continued to rise while fewer and fewer Bulgarians could find jobs and those with jobs never saw their salaries increase in line with inflation. Eventually, the UDF was voted out of office, only to be replaced by a new government led by Bulgaria's former king. Despite the change in government, the economic situation for most Bulgarians continued to worsen.

As a young woman, Gergana understood that securing employment in the winter resort was the best thing she could do for her family. Through a friend of a friend of a friend, she was hired on as a temporary employee during the high season one year. Although she had only a secondary-school education, she spoke Russian very well and could communicate in basic German. Eventually, she managed to stay on permanently. Gergana has worked for eight years as a chambermaid.

Her family has no car, but it is not far to walk to the central bus station. In the winter, the public buses still run frequently. Her days usually start at 6:30. She must be at the bus station to wait for the free employee bus at 7:40. If she misses the employee bus, she must pay for her own transportation and pay a ten-leva fine for being late. She works from 8 A.M. to 5 P.M. five days a week, with a two-day "weekend" which only

4. SAMOKOV BUS STATION IN THE SUMMER. PHOTO BY AUTHOR.

occasionally falls on Saturday and Sunday. Once at the hotel she changes into her uniform, a patterned smock over blue stretchy polyester pants and indoor slippers that are already torn from too much wear. She is one of the five lucky maids who work in the hotel all year round; there are five more who are hired only for the winter. During the season, Gergana is responsible for fifteen rooms. This is slightly more than the other maids in the resort, who are usually responsible for twelve or thirteen rooms. In the off-season, she is responsible for thirty rooms, but they are rarely all full. The receptionists at the front desk are very good at spreading the hotel guests evenly through the hotel in order to equalize the distribution of rooms that need to be cleaned.

Gergana loves Bulgarian music, but she is not allowed to bring a radio to work. She usually hums the latest folk-pop melodies as she cleans. On the day that I accompany her, she chats with me nonstop. "The maids are the most important people in the hotel," she says. "Beds and toilets are where people do the most personal things in our lives. No one likes to think of sharing a bed or a toilet with complete strangers. During the season, there are maybe a hundred different people who use the same bed and the same toilet. If they do not believe that these are perfectly clean, they will be very unhappy. I have to make sure that everything is absolutely sterile between the arrivals of different guests. If I do a bad job, no one will ever want to come to this hotel again. No one wants to pay money to sleep in a dirty bed or to use a dirty toilet."

Being a chambermaid is hard work, and the guests seldom leave tips. "First there are the bathrooms," she explains. "The toilets, showers, and sinks must all be scrubbed clean, and the floor must be mopped. Towels, toilet paper rolls, and complimentary toiletries need to be replaced. The carpets must be vacuumed. The beds must be made. The windows and mirrors must be cleaned. The balcony should be clear of all snow in the winter, and mopped in the summer. Then, there is the tidying up of the guests' belongings. This is always the hardest part because some of the guests are much more messy than others."

Gergana has to put everything she picks up off the floor or the bed into clear view and still make the room look neat. She is not allowed to hang up any clothes or fold anything away in the drawers. If the guests cannot find something, they are quick to accuse the maid of stealing. This is the most humiliating part of the job. Every year there are at least a dozen scandals where the foreign tourists blame the chambermaids for the theft of something they themselves have misplaced. The incidents are usually followed by profuse apologies when the object is found, but it makes little difference. A maid can be fired immediately if it is found that she has stolen anything, and Gergana lives in perpetual fear of being accused.

There are also cultural differences. When Gergana first started working in the hotel she was not accustomed to the British tourists who filled the hotel from December to March. In the beginning, she was surprised that the British would leave their dirty shoes on the dressers. As she tidied up the rooms, she would always put their shoes down on the floor only to discover that they were back up on the dresser again the next morning. In Bulgaria, it is unacceptable to leave shoes anywhere but on the floor. Now, she leaves the shoes where she finds them, although she still finds the practice rather unsanitary.

Different tourists also have different levels of tidiness. Although all of the nationalities are different, it is clear to Gergana when there is a woman staying in the room versus a pair of men. Women are neater, unless they have children. In that case, the tidiness of the woman in the room is overwhelmed by the sheer chaos that young children can wreak in a hotel—toilet paper strewn around the room or candy melted onto the light bulbs.

Once every ten days in the winter and once every five days in the off-season, one maid is responsible for doing the all-night shift. On each floor of the hotel there is a small "office" for the maids with a single bed and a small kitchen. The night shifts are hard for Gergana especially because there is a lot of vomit to be cleaned up in the winter season.[1] On regular days, however, the employee bus carries Gergana back to Sama-kov at 5 P.M. She has enough time to prepare supper for her family, clean her own house, and watch a little television before she collapses in bed around 11 P.M.

For all her efforts, Gergana earned 200 leva ($117) a month in 2003. This is a very good salary for a maid because she works in a state-owned hotel. In the other private hotels in Borovetz, the maids usually make about 150 leva ($88) a month. Gergana is also lucky that she is paid once a month, on time. Other maids will work for the entire season before their employers pay them their salary. For 15 leva a month she can eat subsi-dized meals at the hotel, and sometimes she is able to save some meat for Mitko. The hotel also pays her taxes for health insurance and pensions. Although she has a labor contract, it is always for a short term. She has been working for almost eight years on two- and three-month contracts. This way the hotel can get rid of her at anytime, and she is always afraid of losing her job.

Gergana's husband's parents, who were both civil servants, have pen-sions that do not add up to more than 220 leva a month. The rent from their apartment is only 150 leva a month, and they live in perpetual fear that their tenant will lose his job in the resort as a waiter, and be unable to pay. Gergana's husband's income is sporadic and can never be counted on. In total, the entire secure income of the five people living in Gergana's apartment is 570 leva ($335) a month. This amounts to about $67 a month per person. In the winter months, the heating bill alone can cost as much as 170 leva a month. This brings their collective income down to 400 leva ($235)—just $47 a person, close to the international poverty line of people living on less than $1 a day. If Gergana lost her job, her whole family would have to live on just 200 leva in the winter and 370 leva the rest of the year. It would be impossible for them to survive since none of their relatives has access to private plots of land on which to grow crops. They cannot keep chickens or pigs in the apartment.

Even so, Gergana's family are among the fortunate ones. The national average wage for the country in 2003 was 289 leva ($171), and unemployment in Samokov was more than 25 percent.[2] The majority of Bulgarians barely manage to survive each month in a country where most people felt relatively "well-off" before 1989. Economic differentiation in Bulgaria used to be based only on access to cars, summerhouses, and consumer goods—stereos, washing machines, blenders, Western clothes, and brand-name perfumes and cigarettes. The people who had these things had special connections and hard currency; their material wealth was an outward sign of their higher social status. But these goods were difficult for everyone else to find, and though they may have longed to possess them, their physical absence from ordinary stores kept them from most people's minds. No one went without food. Today, most Bulgarians like Gergana spend the majority of their incomes on food, and food has become the arbiter of social differentiation. The stores are always full of foodstuffs, but the decline in personal incomes has meant that many Bulgarians cannot afford to buy staple items of the national diet, let alone even the simplest of Western treats.

Only the superrich have been able to insulate themselves from the steady decline in real incomes and rising prices that has eroded the living standards of ordinary Bulgarians. According to one study, Bulgarians who considered themselves financially "normal" (not rich and not poor) spent 60.5 percent of their household budgets on food in December 2000.[3] This percentage would be much higher if not for the fact that more than a third of Bulgarian households grow and produce more than 50 percent of the food they consume. Even Bulgarians who considered their financial status as "very good" spent 38 percent of their household budgets on food. The UNDP also found that more than 80 percent of Bulgarians polled in December 2000 said their income was less than their normal expenditures. Forty percent of Bulgarians said that they coped with income shortfalls by "refraining from things that we are used to." Finally, the report found that in the winter months, household expenditures on food declined as Bulgarians "starved out" the colder months, sacrificing food for heat.[4]

While the statistics sketch the outline of the overall trends, the picture isn't complete until one stands in line at a supermarket deli counter with an ordinary Bulgarian woman feeling the weight of her increasing poverty. She might buy cheaper cuts of meat or forgo little luxuries altogether, while enduring one of the harshest ironies of the postsocialist period—that the stores are now full of imported foods from the West. Before 1989, Gergana dreamed of having exotic fruits or eating strawberries out of season. An era of constant shortage gave way to an era of plenty, but neither Gergana nor most other Bulgarians could afford to enjoy it. At the end of 2000, the real value of incomes had decreased drastically since the early 1990s; the real value of the minimum wage had fallen by 75 percent and the value of social pensions had fallen by 82 percent.[5] The main culprit in this precipitous decline in incomes has been a scourge of unemployment. It is impossible to understand the importance of tourism employment in Bulgaria without having a sense of the general conditions in the labor market. Precisely because jobs are so scarce, people like Gergana who are lucky enough to find work in the resorts are the envy of many Bulgarians.

EMPLOYMENT AND UNEMPLOYMENT IN BULGARIA

Gergana's husband, Petar, does not believe in God. Before 1989, he was a leader of the Komsomol, the communist youth organization in his region.[6] He was once a miner, one of the most respected professions under the old system. He misses the hard physical labor of picking at the stubborn, but always yielding, earth. Petar is a devout atheist. He believes with Marx that religion is merely the opiate of the masses. He sneers at the old women as they supplicate themselves before the church, bringing flowers and money to honor what Petar considers the false idols of Bulgaria's feudal past. He compares those who believe in Jesus with those weak-minded Bulgarians who call the newly established pay-by-the-minute psychic hotlines and live their lives by the imported German horoscopes translated into Bulgarian by the local newspapers. "God is just a distraction," he says, smoking a cigarette near the Samokov bus station.

Petar is a very big man. He is quite tall by Bulgarian standards, and his shoulders are broad. Looking at him, I think that he looks like the ideal proletarian—the honest-but-exploited worker in whose name the communist state once ruled. He is thirty-three years old. He has been without any steady employment since he was twenty-nine. I think the only reason he has agreed to talk with me is because he believes that I may be able to get him a job. I tell him that I do know some people in Borovetz, but that I cannot promise anything because I am a foreigner. He looks disappointed.

Petar wakes up every morning at 5:30 to be at the bus station at 6:00. On some days between April and November, contractors from Sofia will send vans to Samokov to pick up day laborers for construction sites in the city. On other days, a group of other unemployed men from Samokov will squeeze themselves into a small Russian Lada and make the hour journey to the capital to see if they can find work on their own. There are always too many men and not enough jobs. Three out of every five days, Petar will not find work. He will walk around the city and smoke cigarettes until he is sure that Gergana has already left for her job in Borovetz. He is very grateful that she has a job but feels ashamed. He hates that he has to spend the day watching television with his parents while she is working. In all of the new television dramas, imported from the West, he watches, it is the woman who is supposed to stay home and the man who provides for his family.

On the days he does find work, he is happier. The contractors will pay him cash at the end of the day. They always deduct a few leva for transportation back to Samokov, and his total earnings are quite modest. Petar does not care so much about the money; he just wants to have work. He says that it is a man's duty to take care of his family. He tells me that it is very difficult for a man not to have work. "Not having work makes a man crazy after a while. Like me. I find myself talking to someone in my head all the time. Asking this person in my head if they can reopen the mines or build a factory in Samokov. I just want work and I think about it all the time. My mother tells me that I am praying, but I am not praying. I do not believe in God. But I see why people get weak-minded. They get weak-minded because they are out of work. They get weak-minded and start hoping . . ." He pauses for a minute, crushing his cigarette butt into

5. AN ABANDONED FACTORY IN SAMOKOV. PHOTO BY AUTHOR.

the sidewalk with his heel and spitting after it. "This is exactly why we had communism in the first place."

Petar has been swept up in the massive restructuring of the labor market that happened once the Bulgarian state could no longer guarantee full employment for all citizens. Since the economic transformation began in 1989, unemployment has been one of the biggest challenges that all of the postcommunist governments have faced. By December 2000, the national unemployment rate of Bulgaria, at 22.1 percent, still hovered well above that of its Western European neighbors.[7] This figure hides the significant regional disparities that paint a far more tragic picture of the economic situation. In March 2000, regional unemployment rates varied from a low 8.2 percent in Sofia city to an overwhelming 45 percent for both Shoumen and Turgovishte.[8]

The one in five Bulgarians who is actively looking for work but cannot find it is in addition to the over 40 percent of the population that is economically inactive (pensioners, children, disabled workers, housewives, and so on). This means that in December 2000, only 35.6 percent of Bulgarians had either full- or part-time work.[9] The high demand for jobs has not only pushed wages down; it has made it increasingly difficult for people like Petar to find work. Nationally, there are between fifty-five and seventy-five applications for each job opening, even for the most menial positions. In tourism, an opening for a receptionist in a hotel in Shumen in 2000 attracted over two hundred applications. Gergana says that today even finding work as a laundress requires extensive personal connections and sometimes bribes.

The lack of paid employment opportunities has been extremely difficult for both men and women in Bulgaria. Men like Petar have been devastated by the economic transition, even as women made up the majority of the registered unemployed throughout the 1990s.[10] The situation for women has been made worse, however, by reemergent patriarchal attitudes; men's high unemployment has started to push women out of many previously feminized economic sectors of the economy.

Environmental groups that protested the high levels of pollution caused by both Bulgarian and Romanian industrial enterprises in the city of Ruse spearheaded the opposition to the communist regime in Bulgaria.[11] These concerns allowed the postsocialist governments to close loss-making manufacturing enterprises that polluted the environment and drained the state coffers. The first wave of redundancies was made up primarily of men employed in these facilities. These workers were redirected to jobs in the light industries and services, which during communism were largely the domain of women. At the same time, Bulgarian women finally had a choice as to whether they wanted to work, and many left their positions assuming that the state would continue to take care of them. Once men began to enter the labor market for women's jobs, employers preferred to hire men since men now had wives to look after, and women were now assumed to have other important duties in the home. Furthermore, the very laws that once helped women to combine their productive and reproductive roles made them less competitive than men. The possibility of maternity and childcare leave in addition to frequent absences to tend to sick children meant that women were viewed as unreliable and expensive compared to their male counterparts.[12]

The post-1989 restructuring eventually hit many sectors where women were the most vulnerable to redundancies, primarily the bloated public sector. Employment in this sector experienced a steady downward plunge; in just two years, from 1997 to 1999, it decreased by 12.9 percent.[13] The market reevaluation of many professions in Bulgaria, however, made certain jobs, which had been considered "women's work" under communism, increasingly prestigious. Although some men attempted to find employment in what were traditionally women's professions, many, like Petar, preferred unemployment to accepting a traditionally female position in the early years of transition. There was no specific national data available on the percentage of men and women in different sectors of the economy before 2000, but observations, interviews, and popular sentiment during the 1990s suggest that women still made up the majority of the labor in the "prestigious" professions according to the new capitalist paradigm: law, medicine, banking, finance, and public administration. Under communism these were all feminized professions in which women had large stocks of cultural capital. As the demand for services and wages in these professions began to rise, women were the primary beneficiaries.

The problem was that most of those professions were still concentrated in the ever-shrinking public sector. Those women who could successfully relocate to the same jobs in the private sector were initially offered decent wages and good opportunities by Bulgarian standards. Teachers and doctors who worked in private schools and health clinics could make up to five times the wages of their colleagues still employed by the state. Even maids and dishwashers experienced a slight increase in salary when they moved out of government jobs, at least in the early stages of the transformation. And although private-sector employment offered few benefits, budgetary cuts meant that once-generous public-sector perks were disappearing. Unfortunately, new employment generation in the private sector was also incredibly slow in most professions, and certainly not fast enough to absorb those who had lost their public positions. Two notable exceptions were garment and footwear manufacturing and tourism.

Table 1 in appendix A demonstrates the number of jobs gained or lost in six traditionally feminized sectors of the economy between 1996 and 1999, the three-year period after the real privatization of the Bulgarian economy began. Over 70 percent of the new jobs created in women's sectors were in sweatshops for European and American clothing and shoe manufacturers. Although the World Bank has officially applauded the increase in export revenues from this sector, it also admits in public documents that the wages and working conditions in the factories are among the worst in the country.[14] Eighty percent of those working in these factories were Bulgarian women, many of whom had been displaced from public-sector employment.[15]

The only other significant generator of employment for women in Bulgaria was tourism; this sector was responsible for 25 percent of the new jobs created for women between 1996 and 1999. In contrast to garment and footwear manufacturing, tourism jobs are among the most desirable in the Bulgarian economy, as my own research has helped to show.[16] In the context of high unemployment for both men and women and changing expectations about the family and who "should" work, it is rather remarkable that women dominated this sector throughout the 1990s and continued to dominate it in the early years of the twenty-first century.

One anecdote from an interview I did with a young woman in Sofia highlights this continued feminization of the tourism sector. Katina was a twenty-three-year-old travel agent in Sofia who wanted to own her own sightseeing agency. Both of her parents worked in tourism, and she was studying to get a master's degree in international tourism in the geography program at Bulgaria's most prestigious institution of higher learning—Sofia University. She was tall and slim, and her bobbed hair curled in around her prominent jawbone. She was dressed in a skirt suit with a cream blouse under her well-pressed jacket. Her shoes were three-inch classic pumps, and she carried a high-quality knockoff of a Gucci handbag. She was the picture of feminine professionalism.

When I asked her if she always dresses so nicely to go to work, she lowered her voice to explain that she works in an office with eleven other women and only two men. "The women in my office dress very chic. We all like to shop and talk about fashion. But there is a kind of competition among us, too. I think that is what happens when you work with all women."

The gender composition of Katina's travel agency is indicative of the tourism sector as a whole. Despite the lack of data on the gender composition of different economic sectors in the Bulgarian economy from before the late 1990s, there is evidence to support the claim that men seeking alternative employment opportunities in a shrinking job market have not displaced women in tourism. This is a very important finding, given that tourism jobs in Bulgaria were relatively lucrative and sought-after in the postsocialist period.

Table 2 in appendix A (based on data collected from a variety of different studies) demonstrates that about 65 percent of those employed in tourism are women. The National Statistical Institute in Bulgaria reported that women made up 58 percent of those employed in the category "hotels and restaurants" in March 2000. By March 2003, women made up about 61 percent of the employees in hotels and restaurants despite the fact that employment in hotels and restaurants had officially increased from 79,854 at the end of 1999 to 120,600 at the end of 2002.[17] This significant expansion in tourism employment—a 66-percent increase in just three years—occurred in the context of widespread unemployment for both men and women. The fact that the percentage of women employed increased even as new jobs were created demonstrates that women were not being pushed out of the sector by men. This may also help to explain why registered unemployment for men finally surpassed that for women in 2001.

In earlier research, I examined the gender composition of employment in the resorts, and found that the longer a resort had been privatized, the larger the percentage of women employed there (table 3 in appendix A).[18] This suggests that privatization and marketization favored women more than men in the Bulgarian tourism industry. Tables 4 and 5 in appendix A use data collected from two surveys (the International Tourism Survey and the Seaside Survey) to demonstrate that Bulgarian women employed in tourism have more education and more years of work experience in the sector than men, and thus dominate the top positions, particularly at the managerial level. Their continued presence in the sector is very much the result of their revalued cultural capital.

Of course, one could argue that tourism jobs are so bad that men do not want them. Tourism sectors in many countries are feminized because tourism is often viewed as unstable, low paid, and menial employment that women accept because they have no other opportunities available to them. Could this also be true in Bulgaria? Are Gergana, Dora, and Katina just happy to have a job that pays?

There is a large body of scholarly literature that examines the relationship between gender and tourism.[19] Most studies focus on whether tourism employment exploits women or whether it gives them valuable opportunities in economies with high rates of unemployment. Few of these studies, however, specifically look at women in a socialist or postsocialist context where women dominate white-collar service professions such as education, health, and law.[20] Despite the realities of gender segregation under communism, there is no evidence to disprove that jobs in the tourism sector in Bulgaria offer opportunities and alternatives for younger women looking for prospective careers and older women hoping to preserve their careers.

One study conducted by Edith Szivas and Michael Riley specifically examined employment in the tourism sector during the economic transformation of Hungary.[21] The authors initially hypothesized that tourism was a "refugee" sector where workers displaced from other sectors of the economy found employment and subsequently suffered from lower incomes and lower job status. Although they did not intentionally disaggregate by gender, their sample of surveyed workers included 58 percent women. The authors surveyed people who had moved into tourism from other sectors of the Hungarian economy, and found that a majority of respondents felt that they had greater job security, career prospects, and social status when they moved into tourism. They also said that they enjoyed their physical environment more, that their standard of living had increased, that their working hours were more flexible, that they were more satisfied with their jobs, that they felt that their education better matched the job requirements, and that they were paid more.

Thus, the character of tourism employment is culturally specific and formed in relation to the other opportunities available in the host economy. The Hungarian study supports the idea that negative Anglo-American stereotypes about tourism employment may not apply to transitioning countries.[22] Furthermore, the value of employment in a particular sector within an economy will determine the relative importance of women's dominance of that sector. If the sector is desirable in terms of wages or other benefits, women's employment therein may translate into substantial economic opportunities not otherwise available to them in the larger economy. In other words, if the jobs are good jobs, women usually do not get them.

The idea that the attractiveness of tourism jobs is relative to the other economic opportunities available is important, especially in countries like Bulgaria where unemployment is high and finding work has become increasingly difficult. It is well recognized that much of the work in the tourism sector internationally is low skilled, poorly paid, and inherently unstable.[23] The tourism industry as a whole has also been criticized for promoting environmental and cultural deterioration in the host societies and for bringing very few economic benefits to the workers and citizens of the tourist destinations.[24] Tourism is a mixed blessing for countries that can become entirely dependent on tourist fashions and the economic or political circumstances of the tourist-generating nations.[25] Furthermore, tourism promotes an unequal international distribution in the consumption of leisure between citizens of the developed and developing worlds.[26] Finally, the phenomenon of sex tourism represents people from the developed world "screwing" the developing world both figuratively and literally.

By 2003, the tourism sector in Bulgaria was not without its own growing problems, though sex tourism was not one of them.[27] Most importantly, as Bulgarian tourism attracted more foreign visitors, ordinary Bulgarians were unable to enjoy their own coastline. Few but the most privileged Bulgarians could afford to go to the Black Sea resorts during the summer, and many were bitter at what they saw as the recreational imperialism of the Western European tourists. Additionally, there is the untold environmental damage that mass tourism inevitably brings, although this was not yet a concern among the Bulgarian officials to whom I spoke in 2003.

It would be false to claim that tourism itself can save the Bulgarian economy or single-handedly restore the nation's GDP to pre-1989 levels. In the early part of the twenty-first century, however, it was one of only a handful of functioning economic sectors in Bulgaria, and its importance could not be underestimated. As the largest generator of foreign exchange, tourism was essential for maintaining Bulgaria's balance of payments and macroeconomic stability. Similarly, employment in tourism at that time must be considered in the context of the endemic lack of employment opportunities. Some Westerners might consider that work in tourism is demeaning to both Bulgarian men and women, but job satisfaction could still remain high because Bulgarians considered any job better than no job. This question of job satisfaction was one that came up in almost every interview I had with tourism employees.

TOURISM JOB SATISFACTION

The resort of Albena is an isolated oasis, away from the confusion and deprivation of day-to-day Bulgarian life—one elderly Dutch visitor I met called it a "tourist concentration camp." With steep, graduated steps toward the Balkan sky, the architecture of the central four-star hotel and the smaller hotels along the shoreline is reminiscent of the stone pyramids of the Aztec and Maya Indians of Central America. The beach itself is two kilometers of sugary-white sand; it is the longest stretch of unbroken coastline on the Bulgarian Black Sea coast and is bookended by high cliffs. Just above the beach, a second line of hotels emerges out from the thickly wooded landscape. Everywhere in the resort, there are wide green lawns and carefully sculpted gardens.

Unlike Desi, who lives in Varna, most of the employees in Albena live in Dobrich. Dobrich is in the far northeastern corner of Bulgaria, cradled in green hills that roll away into the Black Sea. The bus station is in the center of the city. Each morning between May and September, there are hundreds of locals boarding the long, blue-and-yellow employee buses that carry them to the resort. As they wait, many of them read the national newspapers, *Labor* and *24 Hours*, catching up on the latest scandals involving Bulgaria's politicians and celebrities. Others grab a quick breakfast from the little kiosk at the station. This consists of *banitsa* (a pastry made of flaky dough, eggs, and a white cheese similar to the Greek feta) and *boza* (a slightly sweet, fermented, barley drink with the viscosity of an American milkshake). Most of those waiting, however, simply sip thick espressos served in tiny plastic cups and puff away on the sweet-smelling tobacco of Bulgarian cigarettes that cost about one-fifth of the imported brands.

These men and women of Dobrich are very fortunate to have any employment at all. In April of 2000, Dobrich was a city of roughly 100,000 people with a 20 percent official unemployment rate, although the unofficial rate was most likely much higher.[28] In the rural areas surrounding Dobrich, there were 29,000 more Bulgarians, and about a third

6. A BULGARIAN WAITER IN BOROVETZ. PHOTO BY AUTHOR.

of them did not have jobs.[29] At the beginning of each tourist season, over 10,000 people in Dobrich apply for about 2,000 temporary jobs in Albena. Although there are no guarantees, former Albena employees are given preference over those who have never worked in the resort.

Hristo is a bartender in Albena, one of a few men in Dobrich who graduated from an English-language high school. He works murderous hours even by American standards. The tourist season in Albena lasts roughly from the middle of May to the middle of September, with a peak of six weeks from 15 July to 31 August. Because Hristo is unemployed for the other eight months of the year, he works 120 consecutive days in the summer without a break. Seven days a week, Hristo arrives in Albena around 8 A.M. and leaves to go back to Dobrich around 3 A.M. His evening shift at the bar lasts from 5 P.M. until the last customer leaves—sometimes as late as 4 A.M. There are no more employee shuttles at that time, so Hristo shares rides with bartenders in other hotels because he does not own a car.

It is difficult to coordinate with the other bartenders, so Hristo often has to wait more than an hour after his own bar closes before he can go home. A good bartender keeps patrons in his bar as long as possible. Since Bulgaria has no laws prohibiting alcohol sales after a certain hour, it is always in the bartender's interest to sell more drinks. The management judges the ability of a bartender based on how many drinks he sells over a certain period of time. The tourists love the decadence of staying up as late as possible. Hristo never used to mind the hours, but now getting home at 3 or 4 A.M. means that he has not seen his wife or five-month-old son for three months.

Even though his shift doesn't start until noon, he arrives in Albena at 8 A.M., because there is only one employee shuttle before 4 P.M. He spends his morning hours studying English or German in a cafe. Half of the time he studies from textbooks, and other days he just practices with the tourists. Some mornings the maids give him an empty room to sleep in. The resort management does not allow operational employees to take up even vacant hotel rooms, in case of last-minute bookings. Hristo works a three-hour lunch shift in the bar starting at noon. The traffic is light; Hristo uses this time to stock his bar and clean up things from the night before. At 3 P.M., he usually heads down to the beach for a short nap before getting ready for his evening shift.

Every Friday night is Hristo's "birthday." The seven-day package tourists leave Albena on Saturday around noon, and Hristo always gives them a farewell bash in his honor. Hristo knows that the tourists drink more if there is a special occasion. If they drink more, they spend more money, especially since they want to get rid of all their local currency before they depart. The "birthday boy" also enjoys considerable tips, and some tourists bring him small presents. Hristo spends the entire week telling each individual guest who wanders into his bar that he is having a birthday party on Friday. Some weeks he distributes little invitations. He makes the tourists feel special, inviting them personally and telling them not to tell too many people because he only wants to invite the tourists he really likes.

Hristo knows how to throw a great party, even though the hotel bar he tends is small and ugly compared to the big new beach bars on the sand. I have been to four of Hristo's birthday parties. The evening always begins in the same way. Hristo waits until there are about thirty tourists mingling in the bar after 9 P.M. The lights suddenly turn off, and two women from the kitchen come into the room carrying a small cake with thirty blazing candles. One of the women—usually Desi, who has been serving the tourists all week in the restaurant—explains to Hristo in a purposefully loud voice that several of the tourists asked the kitchen to make Hristo a special cake for his birthday. Desi then begins to sing "Happy Birthday" in English or German and all the tourists in the bar join in. Hristo beams and feigns surprise, thanking the tourists profusely for the special cake.

Every week Hristo pays the kitchen from his own money to bake the cake and gives Desi a share in the night's tips for going along with the ruse. The tourists are always happy to believe that the cake was their idea, and they even feel a little guilty that they were not the ones to think of it. This slight guilt makes them give even bigger tips. When Hristo blows out the candles on the cake, the beginnings of tears are noticeable in his already misty brown eyes. Each week, he looks around the room and thanks each of the guests by name. "My dear friends," he says, "thank you so much for coming to my birthday party. I am so happy to be sur-rounded by so many good friends. I can't thank you enough for coming to my party when there are so many other things you could be doing on this, the last night of your holiday in Bulgaria. Because you've made me feel so special I want to do something special for you all."

At this point, he has everyone's attention. As if the idea just came to him, he reaches under the bar and pulls out a corked glass bottle with no label. "This morning my grandfather gave me this bottle of special home-made plum brandy that he distilled especially for my birthday. This is the most traditional Bulgarian drink in my village. It is called rakiya. My grandfather is one of the best brandy makers in the village, and I was planning to save this bottle for a special occasion. But this is most defi-nitely a special occasion, and so I would like to invite you all to share with me my grandfather's special plum brandy."

Almost instantaneously, Hristo starts lining up small brandy glasses on the bar. The tourists press forward for their free drink. At the same time, Desi presses play on the bar's sound system and the voices of John, Paul, George, and Ringo fill the room. Hristo shouts the lyrics, bobbing his head up and down almost violently, as he hands the tourists their glasses of rakiya. "You say it's your birthday! It's my birthday too, yeah!" he sings.

Everything is well rehearsed: Hristo does not live in a village; the rakiya is store-bought and simply poured into the unlabeled bottle to look homemade. Yet every week Hristo gets the party started in the same way, and the music blares and the drinks flow until 2 or 3 A.M. On most Fridays, the music and the crowd attract about one hundred tourists, many of whom are not even part of the package tour. Hristo is so happy that he even manages to convince me that it really is his birthday.

If the party is a good one, which it almost always is, the package tourists leave on Saturday slightly hungover but full of fond memories of the resort. Some of them later come back to spend another summer holiday in Albena. Others go home to Western Europe and tell their friends what a great time they had in Bulgaria. This means more tourists in Albena, and more birthday parties for Hristo.

Hristo tells me that he loves his job. Even though he works very long hours, he is happy to tend the bar. "Working in Albena is perfect for me because I can study and practice my English everyday. There is really nowhere else that I could work in Dobrich where I could speak with native English speakers. I can learn new vocabulary and improve my pronunciation. I can learn jargon and slang, things I cannot learn from books. Plus, I get paid and make good tips."

Desi echoes Hristo's opinion and says that she would hate working in an office. "In the hotel, I can walk to a window and look out to the sea at any time. I can walk down to the beach on my breaks. When you work in tourism, you are also working with happy people who are on holiday. If I were a doctor, I would have to work with sick and worried people all the time. If I were a judge, I would have to work with people who have problems. Tourism is good for the psyche. You are surrounded by happy children and sunny days."

In Golden Sands, Dora tells me that the most important reason that she likes to work as a chef is that she loves to meet and cook for new people. Under communism, she was forbidden from being too friendly with the tourists. Dora was never able to form friendships with the Western Europeans, even the ones who came back year after year. Dora had always longed to talk to the people from the Western countries, to find out what their lives were really like under capitalism and to get new recipes. "Talking to foreigners is a little bit like traveling abroad even though you are still in the same place. You can learn so many new things, new perspectives on life. I always loved to meet new people. The more people I met, the more 'international' I felt." After 1989, Dora was able to be much more open with the Germans who visited Golden Sands. She now has seven pen pals in Germany, and she hopes that she will get the opportunity to travel to Germany in the winter.

Katina says that the most important reason for working in the travel agency is that she hopes to have the opportunity to travel abroad. With one of her first paychecks at the travel agency, Katina went out and bought herself two brand-new, matching, red suitcases and a red carry-on bag. Although she has not yet had the opportunity to use them, her chosen career path in tourism is fueled largely by an insatiable desire to see the world. "Of course, I want to go to America and Western Europe. Those are the first places, and everyone has to go there. But I also want to travel to more crazy places. Like Zanzibar. Have you ever been to Zanzibar? Or Tierra del Fuego in Argentina. I love the name. It means land of fire, you know. I also want to visit Papua New Guinea. I read something somewhere about tribes there where the women form groups and go out and rape men. Isn't that strange? And I also want to climb Mount Kilimanjaro, too. Even though I know that it is full of tourists, it just has to be done. And, of course, the Pyramids. Have you seen the Pyramids?"

I had seen the Pyramids, and Katina's enthusiasm for travel swept me up into a long conversation about the different places that I had visited. With many Bulgarians working in tourism, I had the same conversation about the places where they wanted to travel. Even with maids and gardeners whose prospects for business-related travel were quite small, their proximity to people from other countries fired their imaginations about the world beyond Bulgaria's borders. Practicing foreign languages and meeting new people also appeared over and over again as explanations for why people enjoyed their work in tourism. Most people, however, felt like Desi, and believed that tourism work was simply more pleasant than work in other professions.

To be able to generalize from the comments and thoughts of Hristo, Desi, Dora, and Katina, I included questions about job satisfaction on both of my survey questionnaires. Table 6 in appendix A demonstrates the findings of these surveys. Of the 828 men and women who responded to the first survey, around 84 percent of them believed that their "professional goal" was a career in tourism, indicating that there are many people working in tourism because they want to work there and not because they could not find a job anywhere else. The survey also found that both men and women in the International Tourism Survey agreed that they have opportunities to meet "new and interesting people" and the ability to practice foreign languages in tourism. About 95 percent of those surveyed also agreed that tourism was more pleasant than other jobs, while approximately 55 percent said that they had actual opportunities to travel.

Perhaps the most important factor to be considered when comparing tourism jobs to other jobs available in the Bulgarian economy is the question of money. I knew from the very beginning of my research project that this would be important, but pinning down just how much tourism employees earned was a difficult task. According to the National Statistical Institute, employees under a labor contract working in hotels and restaurants had among the lowest average annual wages and salaries in the economy.[30] The NSI data directly contradicts a commonly held belief among the tourism workers I interviewed that tourism jobs were quite well paid. The discrepancy may have stemmed from the fact that 43.8 percent of the total number of people employed in tourism in 2000 were not under a labor contract, according to the National Statistical Institute.[31] The wages and salaries of this 43.8 percent were not included in the statistics. It is very difficult to know how accurate the numbers are. Furthermore, tips and gratuities are not included in the figures, and this omission may also skew the average annual salary downwards. Finally, because employers must pay 37 percent of their employees' gross salary for social insurance, many labor contracts may report a much lower salary than the employees actually receive. Bonuses and "under-the-table" salaries may considerably supplement the tourism employee's wages, especially since the seasonal nature of employment in tourism and the high employee turnover make it very difficult for the government to regulate the sector effectively.

In order to untangle the truth about salary levels, I tried to gather this data through a second survey by asking more specific questions about the extra benefits of working in tourism. Table 7 in appendix A shows the results. The survey showed that about 63 percent of tourism employees believed that tourism jobs were better paid than other jobs and that 53 percent believed that tourism had more "fringe benefits" than other jobs, although I had a very difficult time translating "fringe benefits" into Bulgarian. Forty-two percent of employees said that their employers fed them while they were on the job, and 33 percent said they received tips.

The shortcomings of this survey data, however, were made obvious to me during subsequent interviews. For instance, Gergana pointed out that the question on employers providing food did not properly distinguish between employers who provide free food and employers who provide subsidized food. She explained that the question was most likely read to mean employers who provide free food. Since most Bulgarian hotels do provide some form of subsidized meals, my results probably underestimate how many tourism employees rely on their employers for some of their meals. A second problem that appeared on both the International Tourism Survey and the Seaside Survey was the formulation of the question regarding tourism wages. I asked if tourism wages were higher than those of other jobs in Bulgaria, and only slightly more than half of the respondents in the first survey said that they were. However, when I asked Dora, Hristo, and Gergana if tourism jobs paid better than jobs in Varna, Dobrich, or Samokov—the cities and towns where resort workers lived— the response was an overwhelming yes. Many Bulgarians believe that jobs in Sofia and Plovdiv are better paid because they are in the cities, and "Bulgaria" is taken to include the bigger cities. With the benefit of hindsight, a better survey question would have read, "Tourism jobs are better paid than other jobs available in your region." In this case, I am sure that the positive response rate would have been much higher.

In my informal conversations with tourism employees who eventually became my friends, I was able to breech the delicate subject of money. Although the figures I quote are not representative of wages in the sector as a whole, they do show that there is considerable money to be made in tourism, and that many tourism employees are paid unofficially in order to avoid Bulgarian income taxes.

Many men and women working in lower operational positions such as maids and groundskeepers in private hotels confided that their labor contracts stated that their wages were 110 leva a month in 2003. One hundred ten leva was the national minimum wage and the maximum amount that an employee could earn without having to pay income taxes.

However, they often received cash-in-hand payments of an additional 40 or 50 leva on top of the 110 base salary. These additional payments were the result of verbal agreements between the employer and employee at the time of hiring.

Most of the workers preferred this system since it allowed them to "legally" avoid paying taxes, and employers preferred this system because it allowed them to make smaller employer contributions to the national insurance and pension funds. Many employees had no labor contracts at all for the same reasons. The problem was that if an employer decided not to pay the additional salary, there was nothing an employee could do legally to demand it. There was never anything in writing about the extra money; employees always worked at the risk of not being paid the full amount. Gergana told me of several cases in Borovetz and Pamporovo where workers were not paid their wages for an entire tourist season. At the end of the season, they were paid only the minimum wage and subsequently laid off. In particular, the Mafia-run hotels had a bad reputation for this practice. They were always able to find replacement employees, however, because unemployment was so high, and 110 leva a month is better than nothing at all.

The few remaining state-run hotels and the handful of internationally managed hotels preferred to do everything legally. After much investigation, I found that one of the major hotels in Sofia began their wage scale at 150 leva a month in 2000. The maids and laundresses received 150 leva a month, although the laundresses and dry cleaners received five extra days off a month because of the difficulty of their work. For all other employees in the hotel, the salary range started at 200 leva and went up to 450 leva. Four hundred fifty was the top salary for all of the high-level operational positions, such as the receptionists and head waitstaff. All of the salary levels between the 200 and 450 leva were negotiated individually with employees based on their education and experience. To give a basis of comparison: in June of 2000, the minimum wage in Bulgaria was 75 leva and the average wage in the country was 229 leva a month; in the summer of 2003, the average wage in the country was 272 leva, and Gergana was earning a net salary of 200 leva a month as a maid in a state-owned hotel. The higher-level staff in her hotel earned up to 500 leva a month.

During the winter of 2001, the official salary of a ski instructor employed in Borovetz was 200 leva a month. While I was in Samokov, Gergana introduced me to a neighbor of hers, Pencho, who had worked as a ski instructor in the resort. According to Pencho, most ski instructors could earn as much as 1,200 leva a month. The additional 1,000 leva was from tips and commissions for organizing excursions and parties for the tourists. Pencho told me that he had worked for four months and earned about 5,000 leva, an impressive sum, and more than enough to live on in Bulgaria for the entire year. In 2003, he was working in a tourist agency in one of the larger hotels. Again, his official salary was only 200 leva a month, but he hoped that he might have the chance to go abroad if he was working in a more "official" capacity in tourism. He also hoped to help organize more excursions and parties during the high season, and make some extra money on commissions.

In 2003, receptionists in private hotels in Borovetz earned approximately 180 leva a month. On the Black Sea coast, the wages in the big resorts were approximately 200 leva a month, according to the friends of Dora and Desi that I interviewed in Golden Sands and Albena. Their wages could also be supplemented by commissions on excursions and currency exchanges. As head chef, Dora earned 450 leva a month. Waiters, waitresses, kitchen staff, and bartenders received an average wage of about 150 leva a month. In all-inclusive hotels and for the kitchen staff, this wage was rarely supplemented by tips, and was therefore rather paltry. This was not true for the majority of waiters and waitresses in the resorts.

In regular restaurants (not all-inclusives), the tips can be considerable. Desi explained to me that the German and Dutch tourists will always leave a standard 10 percent tip. Other nationalities are slightly more or less generous, so that the waitstaff consider 10 percent a good average. The price of the bill depends on the size of the party, but the waitstaff say a reasonable average is 25 leva a table. At the height of the season, Desi can work as many as ten tables at a time and can have as many as thirty tables a day. Most waitstaff work five-day weeks, although many waiters and waitresses, like Desi, choose to work seven days a week during the high season in order to earn extra money. With an average tip of 2.5 leva (about $1.50) per bill times thirty tables, Desi can earn about 75 leva a day in tips. If she works only five days a week, this will add up to 375 leva a

7. A KIOSK VENDOR IN GOLDEN SANDS. PHOTO BY AUTHOR.

week or 1,500 leva a month. Even if Desi works only for the two months of the peak season, she will have earned 3,000 leva in tips above her base salary. The tips are nontaxable, and are often in hard currency. It is not surprising that Desi feels lucky to have her job.

It was even more interesting to calculate the earnings of the men and women who sell ice cream, corn on the cob, and fresh fruit to the tourists on the beach. One day, on the beach at Sunny Day, I watched a man selling fresh fruit walk up and down the beach for about eight hours. Each time he sold a tray with twenty-four fruit cups, averaging a price of about 1.5 leva per cup (the price varied depending on the buyer). If he sold five trays of fruit cups a day (which I saw him do in about four hours) he would earn about 180 leva a day, minus the cost of the fruit (which is negligible in Bulgaria, especially if it comes from his own garden). If he works five days a week for two months, the fruit-cup seller will earn 3,600 leva for the high season. In reality, he probably earns much more than this because he works every day, and the demand for fresh fruit on the seaside is very high. On the other hand, he probably pays a bribe to the hotels to allow him on the beach, and so 3,600 is probably a reasonable figure. If you divide this 3,600 by twelve, the fruit-cup seller has a higher monthly salary than the average monthly salary of the country (300 leva a month versus 272).

All throughout the tourism sector, there are artists, entertainers, souvenir venders, masseuses, beauticians, and so on who make enough money during the tourist season to sustain themselves throughout the year. It is difficult to get the exact amounts of their earnings because they are afraid of the tax collector. The roughest of calculations points to the fact that people employed in tourism, whether officially or unofficially, have the possibility of earning much higher salaries than are available in other sectors of the economy because of the massive inflow of tourist euros.

Other Bulgarians also felt uncomfortable discussing their salaries, because many enterprises had recently made salaries a matter of confidential negotiation between the employer and the individual employee, a new system in Bulgaria. The new system encouraged secrecy, and many interviewees told me outright that they did not want to discuss their earnings.

Despite the difficulties in getting real numbers, the anecdotal and survey evidence does suggest that the overall salaries in tourism are better than in many other professions, particularly considering that other professions have seen an erosion in their earnings. Dora explained the theory of salary relativity to me one day over a coffee. "Maybe it's because other industries in Bulgaria are not so well developed under the new system. They are not paid as well. For example, doctors are not paid so well in

8. SELLING ICON REPLICAS TO TOURISTS IN ALBENA. PHOTO BY AUTHOR.

9. MAKING BULGARIAN LACE FOR TOURISTS IN BOROVETZ. PHOTO BY AUTHOR.

Bulgaria. Everywhere else in Western Europe, they are considered to be from the upper-middle class. The same is true for teachers and for professors. But I think that they are very badly paid in Bulgaria. And other jobs, too. I know that in Western countries if you work in some industry as an engineer, you are also very well paid. But in Bulgaria it's just the opposite. All the engineers are staying at home without a job, or if they find a job it is not so well paid. Maybe that is why people in Bulgaria consider that tourism is so well paid compared to other sectors. Because it really is."

Another potential source of personal revenue for tourism workers was even more difficult to discuss than salaries, and almost impossible to include on a survey. Tourists around the world are targets for every conceivable trick to relieve them of a little bit more of their money. In 2000, the issue of "corruption" was all over the media, and Bulgarians considered it to be one of the biggest problems facing the development of the country. As an American, I never felt comfortable directly asking a question about employee dishonesty, but the topic came up in a variety of different contexts. Desi and Hristo both were embarrassed about their own weekly birthday party, but delighted in talking about how careless most tourists were with their money. "I need it much more than they do," Hristo told me in his own defense.

Desi first breached the topic with me by telling me that many waiters and waitresses would add a leva or two to each bill for "service." "Most of the bills are written in Cyrillic and only the Russian tourists can read them. Most tourists never check. Of course, I would never do this, but I know that it is done."

This practice of overcharging the tourists manifested itself in many different ways, and had its roots in the double pricing system that existed during communism. Before 1989, all Western tourists were supposed to pay for their hotel and restaurant bills in hard currency instead of in Bulgarian leva. This functionally set up a system where tourists were charged much higher prices in the resort than Bulgarians. This system largely remains in place to this day.

In the large resorts, and even in some of the smaller hotels across Bulgaria, foreigners continue to pay a rate that is two or three times the rate for Bulgarians. Even if the Bulgarian and the foreigner are a married couple sharing a bed in the same room, the rate for the Bulgarian will be thirty leva and the rate for the foreigner will be ninety leva. On the beach, the fresh fruit and corn vendors charge the Western tourists twice the price they charge Bulgarians. Because I look like a local, I was once told to go back to my own umbrella when trying to buy corn on the cob on the beach in the resort Sunny Day. "The price is different for you," the vendor said under his breath in Bulgarian as two British tourists picked out their cobs. Similarly, when my husband took our daughter on a little children's ride in Albena, he was given two extra tokens for being a Bulgarian. Throughout the resort, tourism workers set their prices high for the Western tourists, allowing them to realize a much higher profit. For the most part, the tourists do not realize this because the prices are still relatively low.

Another common trick is shortchanging the tourists. Since foreigners are unfamiliar with the Bulgarian currency, it is easy for the waiters and bartenders to just keep an extra lev or two without the customers noticing (and without having to put it on the bill where the restaurant manager might find out). The amount is insignificant to the tourist, but over time, it can add up to a tidy sum for the tourism worker. The same thing can be done in the exchange bureaus and reception desks when tourists are changing money, or at the souvenir stores. Again, the tourists rarely notice.

10. A BULGARIAN CHAMBERMAID. PHOTO BY AUTHOR.

Finally, tourists can also be subject to a wide variety of special "fees" and "fines." Any small misstep or misfortune can be seized upon by an enterprising employee as an excuse to suck a little bit more cash out of the unwary tourist. A broken glass at lunch, which the employee will replace for two leva, can cost a tourist ten leva. If the tourist is drunk and clumsy in a bar—perhaps even simply spilling a drink on the carpet—a special "cleaning" fee of twenty leva may be charged. If for some reason a guest needs medical attention, the fees for seeing a doctor are considerably inflated. Particularly in the Mafia-owned hotels and restaurants, the staff can invent small fees and fines for almost any "infraction." Most of the tourists pay the fines to avoid any trouble with the locals.

Given all of the legitimate and shady opportunities to make money in the tourism sector, it should be no surprise that tourism jobs are highly coveted by Bulgarians. Remembering the context of a stagnant economy and high unemployment rates, the fact that tourism is one of the few sectors of the economy that is still creating jobs is also very important. Almost all of the tourism workers I interviewed felt that tourism was a dynamic and important sector, and that tourism continued to have the best economic prospects in the Bulgarian economy. Hristo says, "There is nothing in Bulgaria for Bulgarians anymore. All that we have, we will be giving to people in other countries from now on. Tourism will always be good in Bulgaria because the Western Europeans have to come here to enjoy our beaches. They cannot take our beaches with them back to Germany or France. Until they figure out how to do that, I will always have a job if I want to."

Back in Samokov, Gergana and I board the employee bus to Borovetz. As the bus pulls away from the station that reeks incessantly of sulfur and urine—Gergana tells me that she loves working in tourism because she can escape from Bulgaria. She chats for the entire fifteen-minute drive through the towering pines to that other world that is the tourist resort. "In Borovetz," she says, "the streets are clean and the wide lobbies of the hotel are filled with happy people enjoying their holidays."

She knows that the British that stay in her hotel are from the more humble classes, and she takes pleasure in seeing the varied possessions they leave scattered about their rooms. They have Walkmans, nice new clothes, sweet-smelling shampoos, shaving creams, and body lotions. Their children have expensive toys and the pocket computer games with which Mitko would love to play.

"Maybe someday," she says as we pull into the parking lot, "Bulgarians will live in a good world again. Maybe Mitko's world will be good again. I cannot do anything to change anything. But I can try to make sure that he is tall."

3

The Red Riviera

"The reception is like the command center of the hotel. Everything goes through the front desk. We are the first to greet the guests on their arrival, and the last ones to say farewell when they depart. We hear all of the complaints."

Sonia has been working as a receptionist in the Hotel Transcontinental in Golden Sands for thirty-six years. Over half of her career in tourism was under communism, when the Bulgarian seaside was known as the "Red Riviera." Although she admits there are many things that have changed since 1989, she claims there are more things that have stayed the same. Receptionists in the four-star hotels in Bulgaria are very high in the employee hierarchy in most of the resorts. As under communism, they must have a university-level education in tourism, which, in Bulgaria, is a serious academic degree in either geography or economics. They must also speak at least two foreign languages in addition to perfect Bulgarian. The only difference today is that Russian is no longer required. Sonia says proudly that she still uses hers almost every day, but most of the younger staff speak no Russian at all.

Receptionists in Bulgaria still work in two-day shifts—two days on and two days off. On the first day, they work from 8:00 A.M. to 5:00 P.M.; on the second day, they work an all-night shift from 5:00 P.M. to 8:00 A.M. Then they have a forty-eight-hour break before they start their next day shift. In the high season, there are two receptionists for every shift, but Sonia works alone in the low season. Behind the reception desk, there is a little office with a bed, a bathroom, and a television for the night shifts. The nights are usually very quiet, expect when there is a transfer of new tourists during the high season.

The mechanics of managing package tourists has also changed little since the communist times. The charter flights of tourists from England, Germany, or Scandinavia arrive at the Varna airport on Saturday evenings. They are transferred by bus to the Golden Sands resort where they are dropped off at their hotels. Then begins the long process of check-in and the inevitable complaints about the lack of rooms with an ocean view. Sonia is convinced that the tour operators tell all of the tourists that they will have an ocean view, when in reality only half of the rooms in any hotel can have such a view. This was a problem under the old system and is still a problem today.

Sometimes the tourists get very upset. One of the receptionist's hardest jobs is to try to judge which tourists will not mind a "park"-view room in the hotel. Sonia tells me that couples with very small children and pairs of single male or female friends will usually accept a park-view room. Young couples with no children, unmarried couples (you can tell by the last names), and elderly couples will usually demand an ocean view. The trick, she says, is always to get as many people as possible to accept park-view rooms first. The younger staff always want to give the ocean-view rooms away first, thinking it will make it easier to get the remaining tourists to accept park-view rooms if the others are already full. Sonia knows that some tourists can get so angry over the room issue that it will ruin their whole holiday. It is much better to give the ocean-view rooms away to the tourists who are willing to complain for them. After standing in line, checking in, and hauling the luggage up to their rooms, only the tourists who really care will come back down to complain once they find that they have been given a park-view room. It is always good to have rooms available to accommodate these guests.

As the tourists settle in there will be a barrage of phone calls to the front desk. Is there room service? Can we have more towels? Can someone bring up an iron? Can we have an extra bed? What time does the pool close? Do you have any aspirin? What time does breakfast start? Do we need tickets? When are the excursions? Is there a pharmacy? What time is it in Bulgaria?

Sonia tells me, "Of course, all of the answers to these questions are in the information booklet in every room. But tourists do not like to read. Why read, when you can just call the front desk?"

Most package tourists spend seven days in Bulgaria, although some come for fourteen. First, they will have to change money. The receptionists will get a small commission if the tourists do this at the front desk. The receptionists always recommend to the tourists that they change money only in the hotel to avoid being cheated. The currency issue and the rate of exchange is one thing, Sonia says, that has changed a lot since the end of the old system. Before 1989, the tourists had to change their money in the hotel, but now there are change bureaus everywhere. One thing that has not changed is that the receptionists still have to explain Bulgarian money to the tourists who have never been to Bulgaria. Bulgaria has always been very inexpensive for the Western European; Sonia says that they treat the lev like play money.

Almost all of the tourists will spend the first few days on the beach, eating in the all-inclusive hotel restaurant, and drinking in the local bars in the evening. After a few days, either because they are bored or sunburned, some tourists will want to go on an excursion. Sonia explains that excursions are where the real money is made in Bulgaria. The local representative of a tour operator will organize three or four excursions during the week. These excursions are to cultural monuments and museums, other towns in the region, craft markets or shopping areas, and, from the Golden Sands resort, to the Varna Opera. The tour operator organizes the trip and transportation and acts as the interpreter for the day. The cost for these excursions is not included in the price of the package, and is paid by the tourists in hard currency (not in leva) to the tour operator or to the hotel. The tour operator takes a huge commission from these excursions, and receptionists may also make a small percentage if they help encourage tourists to join the trips.

Under communism, the only way for a tourist to leave the resort was with an organized excursion. The hotels and tour operators were assured a steady flow of customers, although the repeat tourists tended not to want to go on the same excursion more than once. Changing one or two of the excursions every year solved this problem. After 1989, however, tourists could leave the resort when they wished and the number of those interested in excursions decreased. "Today," Sonia complains, "tourists can rent cars and drive anywhere they want to go. Only the first-time tourists will go on the excursions, and even some of them will prefer to organize their own trip because they have been told that it is cheaper."

For Sonia and thousands of the older employees in Bulgaria's international tourism sector, the differences between the communist and capitalist ways of organizing leisure are the subject of endless discussions. Even the younger employees with no work experience under the old system have been convinced that there were some redeeming qualities of the command economy. Indeed, the particular shape and organization of tourism under communism, and the unique way in which labor in the sector was gendered, have helped women maintain their dominant positions in the sector after 1989.

The development of tourism in Bulgaria was unlike the development of tourism anywhere else in the world.[1] In contrast to many developing countries where hospitality industries were built from scratch by foreign investors and tourism consultants flown in from abroad, Bulgaria developed the vast majority of its tourism infrastructure under communism. The physical and human capital of the tourism sector in Bulgaria was developed under very different conditions and for very different reasons than that of its competitors in advanced capitalist or developing countries. The rebuilding of the tourism sector under new market imperatives was very path dependent on the socialist forms of tourism. The success of the tourism industry in Bulgaria after 1989, and the success of the women employed therein, is in part a direct consequence of the factors informing the historical development of the sector under communism between 1944 and 1989. At the same time, the privatization process reshaped ownership and power structures in particular ways. This allowed some Bulgarians, particularly women like Sonia, to adjust their "portfolio" of stocks of economic, social, and cultural capital in response to the new institutional changes. Finally, like tourism in many other countries, tourism labor was distinctly gendered, but the implications of this gendered division of labor were somewhat atypical, in that it did not produce or reinforce the economic marginalization of women.

SOCIAL TOURISM

The Russian communists' attitudes toward the unequal distribution of leisure under capitalism heavily informed the development of tourism in Bulgaria. In the late nineteenth century and early twentieth, when the first sparks of social revolution began to ignite across the European continent, tourism was very much a privilege of the aristocracy and the bourgeoisie.[2] Restorative trips to the seaside and medicinal stays at mineral spas were far beyond the means of the working classes. It is not surprising that the Bolsheviks were fervently committed to radical changes in the social distribution of leisure. The early socialists were convinced of a direct link between tourism and health. Marxist-Leninist doctrine stipulated that leisure was an inherent part of the productive process. Thus, the communists reduced the working day and gave all workers the right to annual holidays. To support this program, Lenin nationalized all resorts and spas in Russia and converted them into public sanatoria in March 1919. In addition to appropriating those facilities, which would henceforth see to the medical needs of the proletariat, the Bolsheviks embarked on an ambitious campaign to increase the number of leisure facilities during the 1920s and 1930s.[3]

With Lenin's death, however, the Soviet Union began a mad drive toward industrialization at all costs. Stalin's leadership encouraged suspicion and mistrust not only among the country's leaders, but also toward all Westerners. The forces of capitalism were construed as an ever-present, external threat to the survival of the revolution. Soviet citizens were galvanized by their collective xenophobia and dreams of industrial might. Stalin used propaganda to divert attention from the general decline in living standards that accompanied rapid urbanization and economic transformations.

The development of tourism, even social tourism, was at odds with this Stalinist vision of the proper organization of society. First, there was no time to rest. The glorious future of communism required the labor of all citizens; men and women of all ethnicities were mobilized in the collective effort. Second, all resources were to be funneled into the development of industrial capacity. The construction of nonproductive assets such as hotels and resorts was postponed indefinitely. Finally, the insular and autarkic nature of Stalin's Soviet Union relied on feeding the popular belief that all foreigners were spies and counterrevolutionaries. The emphasis on the development of industry and the paranoia toward potential foreign visitors were at least partially inherited by Bulgaria when it became a People's Republic after World War II.[4]

11. POSTCARD OF THE BEACH AT VARNA IN THE 1920S.

12. POSTCARD OF THE BEACH AT VARNA IN THE 1940S.

Bulgaria had received tourists since the early twentieth century, but tourism infrastructure was minimal when the communists took power. Like the Soviets before them, the Bulgarians constitutionally enshrined the right of every worker to annual paid holidays. They, too, began converting nationalized buildings to serve as holiday houses. From its inception, the Bulgarian tourism industry revolved around the provision of "social" holidays for the domestic labor force. In 1948, the state tourist organization, Balkantourist, was formed on the model of the Soviet Intourist set up in 1929. Balkantourist began the development process for tourism facilities in Sofia and in the major cities on the Black Sea coast.[5] The vast majority of early social tourism infrastructure took the form of *pochivni stantzii* (holiday houses). These holiday houses were most often affiliated with a specific trade union or owned by an industrial enterprise. For instance, the military's holiday houses were sprinkled around the country, most often on the seaside, in the mountains, and near a balneological center. Other enterprises such as the National Television Company had their own holiday houses, as did the Central Committee.[6] Holidays in the holiday houses were heavily subsidized for all workers. Holiday packages given to workers often included the cost of the accommodation and three meals a day.

As social tourism expanded, so too did the number of state organizations that supported it. Balkantourist was created to oversee the entire Bulgarian tourism industry, becoming the largest single owner of Bulgaria's tourism infrastructure. In 1966, the Committee on Tourism was formed. This committee was directly accountable to the Council of Ministers, and Balkantourist became its operational body. Beneath Balkantourist, and working alongside the trade unions, were four smaller organizations that specialized in social tourism provision. The first was Cooptourist, a travel organization that covered the leisure needs of those Bulgarians not part of the trade unions or belonging to a specific enterprise or government agency. In practice, this included Bulgaria's agricultural laborers and producers of small handicrafts. Although Cooptourist owned some of its own holiday houses, its main role was to coordinate with the other social tourism organizations.

The second organization was Orbita. Controlled by the Komsomol, Orbita specialized in tourism for young people and students.[7] This or-

13. POSTCARD OF THE HOLIDAY HOUSE OF THE BULGARIAN POSTAL WORKERS UNION.

ganization owned a wide variety of youth hostels, youth camps, small hotels, discos, and recreational facilities around the country. Pirintourist was the third agency; it focused on mountain tourism, mostly trekking. Pirintourist owned a number of small mountain chalets throughout Bulgaria and organized specialized hiking tours. Lastly, Shipka was the Bulgarian version of the American Automobile Association. Shipka provided information to Bulgarians who wished to spend their holidays using a private car. Shipka was a centralized distributor of information about roads, accommodations, and restaurants in Bulgaria.

Most Bulgarians had the right to fourteen days of paid holidays a year in addition to the numerous state holidays. Before 1989, at least 50 percent of Bulgaria's hotel capacity was reserved for domestic tourists.[8] The goal of social tourism was not only the rejuvenation of the workforce, but also the fostering of national solidarity among the historically and culturally different regions in Bulgaria. This was particularly important for the ethnically Turkish strongholds and in Bulgarian Macedonia.[9] Various schemes were designed to encourage Bulgarians to travel around their country, but in a controlled way, organized by the communist state. Sonia remembers that one of the most popular of these devices was the social tourism "passport." Each time she visited a site of social or historical importance in her country, she was given a stamp in a small booklet. Since most Bulgarians, like Sonia, did not have real passports and could not travel abroad, these token passports were well received. Most of the Bulgarians I interviewed who are old enough to remember these social tourism passports still recall them with fondness.

COMECON SPECIALIZATION

In the 1940s, the Bulgarian communists had no real intention of diversifying the country into an international tourist destination. Most improvements in tourism infrastructure were for the expansion of domestic tourism in line with Marxist-Leninist doctrine. It was a legal disagreement with Czechoslovakia that first pushed Bulgaria into the international tourism market.[10] Prior to World War II, Czechoslovakia invested in several sugar refineries and electricity production facilities in Bulgaria. When the Bulgarian communists subsequently nationalized them, Czechoslovakia demanded reparations in hard currency. Unable and unwilling to meet the request, the Bulgarians refused. After protracted legal wrangling in Paris, Czechoslovakia agreed to accept a barter-style payment: vacation packages on the Black Sea coast. The restless Czechoslovak intelligentsia was accustomed to taking its holidays on the coasts of Spain and France, but the country's new communist leaders feared that the intellectuals would flee. The Czechoslovak state refused to grant them exit visas to the West, but it deemed the Bulgarian coast a suitable (and politically safe) vacation alternative.[11]

Peter Doitchev was one of the first Bulgarians to work in tourism under communism. He officially greeted the first 800 Czechoslovak tourists in 1948, and remembers that there was little infrastructure on the seaside. By his account, all of the tourists were housed with Bulgarian families. The Bulgarian "tour guides" had to requisition blankets and sheets from the military. They were delivered to the private homes on the backs of mules because there were only two automobiles in the entire city of Varna.[12] By 1951, tourists began to trickle in from the socialist brother countries Poland and Hungary. Not too long after, sunseeking Soviet citizens began to make the pilgrimage south to Bulgaria's shores. Al-

14. POSTCARD OF VARNA, WHICH WAS BRIEFLY RENAMED "STALINE" IN THE 1950S.

though Bulgaria was slowly building infrastructure, demand from both domestic and foreign tourists vastly exceeded the meager supply.

After Stalin's death in 1953, many socialist societies experienced a general relaxation of dogma. This coincided with a gradual increase in living standards, a greater emphasis on the international goals of socialism, and a push toward more intrabloc tourism. Yugoslavia was a potential competitor for Eastern bloc tourists, but its defection from the Stalinist fold in 1948 caused its tourist industry to focus on Western European tourists to the exclusion of its Eastern "brothers." Bulgaria was particularly suited to become the so-called "Red Riviera" because it had a relatively long summer season, and its Black Sea coast was clean and free of dangerous sea animals.

In the 1960s and 1970s, Sonia tells me, Bulgaria's coast became the most fashionable place to be for the elite of all Eastern bloc countries—a kind of socialist St. Tropez. Artists, writers, dancers, politicians, and communist luminaries from all fields summered in the resorts of Golden Sands, Sunny Beach, and Albena. In the hotel lobby or on the beach one might catch sight of Yuri Gugarin (the first man in space) and his entourage, or the latest prima ballerina of the Bolshoi. The leaders of Western-country communist parties also holidayed on Bulgaria's shores. And, on a more humble level, workers and farmers from all of the Eastern bloc countries congregated there. Russian and Ukrainian tourists in Sozopol and Sunny Beach in the summer of 2000 told me that they still return to Bulgaria not only because it is affordable, but also because of their fond memories of the socialist times.

Most of the holidays during the socialist period were arranged through bilateral barter agreements. Even though Bulgaria was inexpensive, an excursion to Bulgaria still cost three or four times the price of a similar holiday on the Baltic coast or on Hungary's Lake Balaton. This added to Bulgaria's exclusivity. Holiday excursions were traded among socialist nations, to the great advantage of Bulgarians who might not otherwise have had the opportunity to travel abroad. Young people were encouraged to travel within the Eastern bloc on student excursions organized by Orbita and its counterparts; many of these excursions were essentially free. By 1989, Bulgaria was dependent on the socialist countries for 70.9 percent of its incoming tourists.[13]

The facilities offered to intrabloc tourists were essentially the same as those available to Bulgarian workers. Depending on the social status of the guests, the accommodations consisted mainly of one- and two-star hotels, holiday houses, youth hostels, and campgrounds. Bulgaria had little in the way of a service culture and socialist guests were treated essentially the same as Bulgarians: not as customers or clients but as fellow workers who were fundamentally equal to those who served them. This basic lack of customer service would later become one of the greatest constraints on the development of international tourism.

A great benefit of the intrabloc tourists was that, because they were centrally allocated to accommodations throughout the country, their presence helped to fill Bulgaria's resorts and tourist complexes through-out the year. During the off-season, seaside hotels could be given to student groups or other tourists on "friendship" exchanges. Despite their numbers, however, these incoming tourists contributed little hard currency to the Bulgarian economy. Only with the arrival of tourists from the Western European countries did Bulgaria begin to realize its full tourism potential.

The turning point for the Bulgarian tourism industry came in 1955 and 1956 when the first West Germans came to the country's resorts.[14]

Since the two Germanys had been divided, family members separated by the Iron Curtain had searched for a place where they could reunite for holidays. Bulgaria was the ideal destination because both East and West Germans could travel there with relative ease. The West Germans began paying the cost of the holidays for both families in hard currency. It was then that the Bulgarian government took notice of tourism's potential economic contribution.

In 1957, a train full of imported Hungarian porcupines arrived in Varna to help clear the swamp snakes from what eventually became one of Bulgaria's largest and most developed resort complexes: Golden Sands.[15] By the early 1960s, Bulgaria was threatening to divert wealthy tourists away from the French Riviera. Bulgaria was incredibly cheap by Western standards; the brand-new facilities were strikingly modern and chic. But Bulgaria's socialist mentality undermined any chance that Bulgaria had for usurping the fashionable resorts of the West. Peter Doitchev recalls that as early as 1961 Golden Sands began attracting guests who usually summered at Cannes and Nice. By his account, a very wealthy French woman and her family rented an entire floor of the Hotel Astoria one summer. After a pleasant week's stay, the woman suddenly decided to cut her visit short. When asked to give an explanation, she said that while she was dining in one of the resort's more "exclusive" restaurants, a young Bulgarian woman waved to her from across the room. When the French lady realized that the young Bulgarian was the very woman who had done her hair not less than four hours previously, she was scandalized. She did not want to share her meals with the people she paid to serve her. For this offense, the woman promptly left the resort, abandoning an entire floor of rooms at the height of the summer season.

Socialist egalitarianism obviously had trouble accommodating the class divisions necessary to cater to wealthier Western tourists. As a result, Bulgaria's appeal to the Western elite eventually faded. The country did gain popularity among the Western working classes who were attracted by the affordable prices and did not mind the poor quality of service and lack of social boundaries. Other Western tourists were ideologically motivated—trade unionists, democratic socialists, or those who simply wanted to see life behind the Iron Curtain.[16]

Throughout the 1960s and 1970s, visitor arrivals to Bulgaria steadily increased from both the socialist bloc and Western European countries.[17] In 1973, the Zhivkov government finally began committing serious resources to building tourist infrastructure in order to bring in the hard currency needed to bail Bulgaria out of a severe oil crisis.[18] That same year, the Bulgarian government signed contracts for the construction of four five-star hotels by foreign companies.[19] By 1974–75, one-fifth of Bulgaria's foreign exchange was coming from the tourism sector.[20] The early 1980s saw the development of Bulgaria's mountain tourism with the addition of the two downhill-skiing resorts of Borovets and Pamporovo. In 1985, international tourism in Bulgaria was the third largest generator of net hard-currency income among all other industries.[21]

A tour operator in Sofia named Krassimir calls the period around "the changes" in 1989 "a golden time for tourism in Bulgaria."[22] Balkan Holidays London, a subsidiary of Balkantourist, was one of the three top tour operators in the United Kingdom at that time. They arranged chartered flights from over twelve airports in Great Britain on Balkan Airlines, Bulgaria's former flag carrier.[23] The airline had no less than a hundred charter flights a week from the UK, Germany, and Scandinavia.[24] Balkantourist also owned a fleet of long-distance buses that brought tourists from Germany on a weekly basis. According to one estimate, Bulgaria spent the equivalent of 20 million dollars on international promotion in 1989 and 1990.[25]

Administratively, Balkantourist was responsible for the central coordination of all international tourism. The organization owned not only hotels, but also restaurants, bars, buses, sports facilities, ski lifts, etc., and had an extensive network of representative offices across the globe. By the late 1970s, Balkantourist was the seventeenth largest hotel chain in the world.[26] It was the largest of the Eastern European tourism agencies, and became one of the most powerful state-owned enterprises in Bulgaria. Because consumer goods were scarce and many basic amenities were in short supply, Balkantourist also owned huge storage facilities in which goods were stockpiled for the high tourist seasons. Balkantourist had priority when it came to the requisition of many otherwise unobtainable commodities such as imported foodstuffs and beverages.

Tourism expansion in Bulgaria was not without its problems. Ideologically, tourism was always at odds with socialism's core goal of industrial expansion. It is interesting to note, for instance, that precisely in the middle of the tourism boom, the importance of the sector was officially and publicly unrecognized. In Todor Zhivkov's report to the Eleventh Congress of the Bulgarian Socialist Party, he painstakingly outlines the "Guidelines for the Development of the Economic Sectors" by reciting a laundry list of key industrial, agricultural, and infrastructure developmental priorities.[27] Yet nowhere in the 120-page transcription of his speech does the Bulgarian leader spend any significant time discussing the success of the tourism sector.

CENTRALIZED CONTROL VERSUS SATISFYING INDIVIDUAL NEEDS

Communist centralization in tourism meant that all important decisions were made by a handful of people at the top of Balkantourist. The central office in Sofia controlled all of the hotels, restaurants, and tourism facilities around the country. The Balkantourist administration fixed salaries for different job categories and made all decisions regarding the amount of resources to be invested in the "human capital" of the personnel. There was little local control over reservations or infrastructure improvements. Even within the individual resorts, the resort directors concentrated power in their own hands. Hotel and restaurant managers had their staff hired for them by the central office; they had little say in who worked for them or in what capacity. This centralized control of Balkantourist allowed the state to manipulate the tourism sector to its own ends.

While the tourism sector enjoyed special privileges, former senior Balkantourist employees claim that the Bulgarian state consistently drained hard currency out of the sector and redirected it to other parts of the ailing Bulgarian economy.[28] On the one hand, this meant that the revenues from tourism were redistributed more equally to the Bulgarian population and did not serve only the interests of those fortunate enough to be employed by Balkantourist. On the other hand, it meant that there was little money available for infrastructure maintenance and improvement. Many tourist facilities in 2000 had not been changed or upgraded since they were built in the 1970s and 1980s. In some hotels, even small items such as lamps and blankets had not been replaced for over twenty years.

The mechanism the Bulgarian government used to take hard currency out of the tourism enterprises was the system of fixed exchange rates. Balkantourist made contracts with foreign tour operators for amounts denominated in Western currencies. Those monies were then remitted to the Bulgarian Foreign Trade Bank that converted the hard currency into the local lev at a fixed, and extremely unfavorable, rate. Thus, the tourism enterprises received only a portion of the real value of the contracts they fulfilled. The Bulgarian state artificially manipulated the exchange rate to attract tourists. COMECON tourists had a fixed rate of 1.12 leva to the convertible ruble, while the rate for Western tourists was manipulated by the state in order to attract more visitors and discourage the black market.[29] Many Western tourists were also allowed to change money at well over the official rate in hopes that the low prices would make up for the poor quality of both the service and infrastructure. The state's ability to adjust the exchange rate ensured that the tourism sector never received its fair share of the revenues it generated.

If Balkantourist or a specific hotel or resort needed to import supplies of equipment from abroad, they had to apply for a special hard-currency loan from the foreign trade bank. These loans, even for essential capital goods such as elevators, had to be approved by the bank and carried high interest rates. What little profits the tourism enterprises generated were often transferred back to the state in the form of interest on these loans.

The difficulty in obtaining hard currency forced hotels to buy their supplies from Bulgarian or COMECON sources. In practice this meant that hotel and restaurant managers were constantly improvising with whatever supplies they could find. Interior design was an impossibility. Diliana, a former Balkan tourist manager in Borovetz, told me that buying two or three hundred lamps for new hotel rooms was a Herculean feat for the procurement department; pleasant lampshade design and matching color schemes were the very least of their concerns.[30] Tablecloths and silverware were often mismatched within the same restaurant. Ivanka, a food and beverage manager in Albena, told me of a broken waffle iron that could not be replaced until a kindly tourist brought one as a gift to the hotel when he returned the following year.

In spite of the steady erosion of infrastructure and the bleeding out of profits, many older Bulgarians like Sonia still feel today that Balkantourist was an organizationally efficient enterprise, partially because the system continues to rely on centralized package tourists from abroad.[31] Because everything was centralized under the old system, organizing tours through Bulgaria or stays in the resorts was extremely easy. Accommodations could be organized throughout the country by a central reservation system, and overbookings could effortlessly be diverted to empty hotels nearby. From a marketing perspective, Bulgaria was one "product." Promoting the country as a whole maximized the resources allocated for advertising.

There were financial advantages, too, to the state's monopoly on flights and accommodations. In international tourism, foreign tour operators try to capture as much profit as possible from a tourist-receiving country. These profits are inevitably repatriated out of the country, or, in the case of package tours, the tour operators are paid in full in the country of origin, and very little money ever makes its way to the host country.[32] Under communism, the foreign tour operators had to negotiate charter flights and itineraries directly with the Bulgarian state, which assured that the maximum amount of profit was retained in the country.

The negative side of centralized tourism management was the bureaucratic inertia that characterized the socialist economy as a whole. Lack of competition between different hotels and resorts, guaranteed occupancy rates, and little or no profit retention contributed to a situation wherein there were no incentives to improve or expand tourist services. The lack of a customer-service–oriented work ethic exacerbated the rift between Western tourist expectations and the actual conditions in Bulgaria's resorts. The government's security concerns regarding the "contamination" of the country by capitalist holidaymakers overshadowed any interest the Bulgarian state might have developed in improving the quality of its product.

TOURISM AND ESPIONAGE

The Bulgarian equivalent of the Soviet Union's KGB was the Darzhavna Sigurnost, or Committee for State Security, popularly known by its own acronym: the DS. The DS was modeled on its Soviet predecessor and was perhaps the most loyal to Moscow of the Eastern European security organizations.[33] The Soviets, and hence the Bulgarians, were wary of the expansion of tourism for two significant security reasons. First, the DS and the KGB were concerned about the demonstration effect of Western holidaymakers on the Bulgarians with whom they had regular contact. Government and security officials were (perhaps rightfully) concerned that Bulgarians who interacted with tourists would become attracted to Western lifestyles and ideas and begin to doubt the moral superiority of scientific socialism.[34] This was particularly true with regards to the varied personal consumer goods that the Western tourists brought with them— the clothes, shoes, cameras, hairdryers, and so on. Second, the innocent, sunseeking tourist provided the perfect cover for Western intelligence agents wishing to infiltrate Bulgarian territory. Consequently, tourists to Eastern Europe were strictly controlled by the state.

All of the major resorts in Bulgaria (Golden Sands, Sunny Beach, Albena, Borovets, and Pamporovo) were geographically disconnected from Bulgarian cities and villages, and were largely inaccessible to the local population. In addition, middle managers in many of the hotels and resorts, often women, were usually DS collaborators or informants. Anyone taking a trip outside of the resort or independent tour around the country had to be accompanied at all times by a Bulgarian tour guide prearranged by Balkantourist. Several of these guides (again usually women) told me that they would have to meet with a DS agent after each tour to answer a list of questions about each member of the group. All independent itineraries had to be preapproved, often by DS officers. Restaurants and hotels authorized to accept foreign guests were linked in some way with the DS and equipped with surveillance equipment. Any personal contacts between foreigners and Bulgarians had to be immediately reported, with the exception of the sanctioned contacts between tourism employees in the resorts and their Western guests.[35]

Bringing up the subject of surveillance and internal security matters with Bulgarians was even more difficult than asking them about their salaries. Gergana, Desi, and Katina all said that they knew that the security agents used to be there but did not know if they still were. Bulgarians like Sonia who were employed in the resorts prior to the end of the communist period volunteered even less information (I suspected that Sonia had probably collaborated with the DS on at least one occasion). Although few tourism employees would discuss the topic directly, in the course of informal interviews and conversations they often alluded to the role of the secret police. On occasion, a person I was interviewing would pantomime two gentle taps on his own shoulder or surreptitiously turn out his lapel to allude to informants or the secret police. Tapping on the shoulder referred to someone's invisible epaulets, and meant that someone was suspected of being a plainclothes police officer or someone from the Ministry of Interior. The turning out of the lapel was a reference to the practice of DS and KGB officers planting small microphones in the carnations on their dinner jackets. If you turned over their lapel, you would see the wires and be able to expose the spy. These nonverbal signs were sprinkled randomly throughout conversations to refer to workers who were suspected of having been collaborators with the DS under communism.

The only people who spoke openly about the DS were Dora and Desi, who knew of particular employees who were "relocated" out of the tourism sector after becoming too "friendly" with a Western tourist. Dora said that she remembered a tour guide who had spent the night in a West German tourist's room. After that night, Dora never saw the woman in Golden Sands again. Another receptionist was caught trying to smuggle a letter to the West with a departing tourist. The tourist was not punished, but the receptionist lost her job, and "who knows what else." Other waiters and waitresses were warned by the DS that they should not talk with the tourists for too long when taking their orders.

The DS also went to great lengths to make sure that the tourism employees never doubted the superiority of communism. The local leaders of the Communist Party told Desi about the terrible stresses the tourists from the capitalist countries were escaping. She was told that they did not have any guaranteed employment and that each of them was always teetering on the brink of absolute poverty. Those tourists to whom she brought lunches in the restaurant were really no better than slaves to their employers who could toss them out at any time for any reason. Desi's supervisors in Albena told her that she should feel sorry for the tourists, because the only relaxation the tourists had all year was in their short trip to a socialist country where they would be valued as fellow workers and treated with respect. Their lives were miserable and dull, and they all secretly longed to immigrate to the Eastern bloc, but their governments would not let them.

As a waitress, Desi often overheard the conversations of the Western tourists even though she was afraid to talk to them about political matters. In each restaurant, Desi knew there was always an agent of the Bulgarian security service dressed as a tourist. She told me that she often played a game with herself trying to figure out who the agent was, but it was very difficult for her since she knew that they often dined together with the other tourists. To Desi, the tourists always seemed to be happy. They were so rich and had so many nice things compared to Bulgarians. How could they be as unhappy as her supervisors said? Their children were healthy and their women were so fashionable and well dressed.

Once, Desi mentioned these observations to a local secretary of the Communist Party. He told her that it was all part of Western propaganda. He told her that some of the tourists were given special clothes and travel allowances when they came to the Eastern bloc. They were told that they would be watched, and if they said anything bad about capitalism they would be reported and not allowed to travel again. This made a lot of sense to Desi, and from then on she did honestly feel sorry for the tourists who lived in such an unequal and unfair capitalist world.

What was strange to Desi was how often she felt that it was the tourists who were feeling sorry for her. Something about their eyes and the way they tipped her so generously filled her with doubt. At least they got to travel, she thought, as she brought them their meals and counted her tips at the end of the day. And she often watched them as they boarded their buses back to the airport after their week in the resort was over. They did not look so sad to leave.

Like Dora and Desi, many tourism employees wanted to practice their foreign languages, but they never knew if the tourist was a real tourist or a secret agent working for the Russians who was posing as a Western tourist. Dora says that this was a problem particularly because so many Western tourists asked her what it was really like to live under communism. They were genuinely curious, as many Western tourists in Bulgaria were attracted by the promises of socialism. Dora had many criticisms of her government, but out of fear of secret agents, she always told the tourists that she loved her country and that communism was good for the people.

Beyond Desi and Dora, it was quite difficult for me to obtain any empirical evidence on this topic. The files of the DS had not been declassified when I was doing my fieldwork in Bulgaria. Over time, however, it became clear to me that Bulgarians who had worked in tourism under communism considered the presence of these undercover informants to be a real threat, which shaped the character of work in the sector perhaps more than any other extraneous factor.

Suspicion of tourists and foreigners was common throughout the communist world. No doubt the Bulgarians were only following the lead of their Soviet comrades to the east. All tourists to the USSR were closely scrutinized and encouraged to travel in large, easily controlled groups, much like the Bulgarian excursions.[36] The DS and the KGB were diligent about collecting information on anyone who might prove useful to their intelligence activities in the future. Perhaps the most insidious way the tourism sector was abused by the socialist secret services was through what David Lewis called "sexpionage." In Lewis's study into the use of sexual entrapments by Soviet intelligence, he shows that most of the operations took place in hotels where important foreigners were staying as tourists and guests.

Once the state decided to blackmail a particular foreigner, the preapproved itineraries were used to determine the most opportune time and place. Usually the target tried to check into a preapproved hotel where he or she (but usually he) had a room reserved. When he arrived at the reception desk, the staff informed him that he had no reservation. The flustered tourist then usually produced some kind of documentation proving the existence of the reservation. The staff apologized profusely, claiming some sort of mix-up and upgrading the guest to a "special" suite thoroughly equipped with state-of-the-art Soviet surveillance equipment. At this point, the "raven" or "swallow" (male or female sexual agent) then arranged to meet the target.[37]

Perhaps the most reliable sources on the use of tourism for the purposes of espionage and sexual entrapment are the actual notes on KGB files smuggled out of Russia in the early 1990s by Vasili Mitrokhin. According to the KGB's own files, the Bulgarian seaside was considered an excellent site for espionage activities. Soviet agents deployed within the Eastern bloc were sent "to cultivate Western tourists or to monitor contacts between Soviet citizens and Westerners."[38] In 1966 and 1967, for example, a number of agents were sent to Bulgarian Black Sea resorts to mingle with Western holidaymakers and to look for possible recruits.

The KGB files document several cases of sexpionage centered on the Black Sea. In one case, a male Soviet agent, posing as a Western tourist, seduced female Soviet agents planted there in order to see how easily these female agents would have sex with foreigners without prior KGB approval. Perhaps the most interesting case was that of the British "Romeo" spy, John Symonds. Symonds, a London policeman who fled persecution in the UK after being accused of taking bribes from local criminals, spent eight years working for the KGB. The handsome British policeman was trained as a "raven" and deployed to Bulgaria to "cultivate suitable targets" among the hordes of sunseeking secretaries and bored housewives of the West.[39]

The extent of the infiltration of tourism by Bulgarian, Soviet, Western, or other agents is impossible to gauge accurately. It is certain, however, that a feeling of danger and suspicion permeated the tourism industry in Bulgaria, and this had implications for those Bulgarians employed there. Working in tourism was considered perilous: one careless comment to the wrong "foreigner," and a Bulgarian could easily lose her job, or worse. This, however, changed with time. By the 1980s, prohibitions on contact with foreigners were more lax. Bulgarians working in tourism had to communicate with Westerners in order to serve them, and extended conversations with tourists could be justified by the need to provide good customer service, which many foreigners complained was lacking among the Bulgarian staff. Friendliness could result in foreign-language practice, a better tip, or even a small gift. Although the DS was always watching, and you never knew if the supposed tourist was actually a KGB spy, for many Bulgarians the benefits of working in tourism and talking with the tourists far outweighed the risks. These conversations and interactions with Westerners were an important part of the tourism work experience, and a very valuable form of cultural capital that accrued largely to women during the communist period.

In the infancy of Bulgarian tourism, communist leaders considered tourism a bourgeois and unimportant sector because it fell outside of the core communist goals of rapid industrialization. In the late 1940s and 1950s, many of the first employees in tourism were members of the bourgeoisie or former fascist sympathizers because these two groups were the most likely to speak foreign languages. In either case, the communists considered work in tourism as an appropriate punishment for the multilinguists' ideological crimes. In the 1960s and 1970s, however, as tourism grew in importance and the number of Western tourists increased, the communist regime and the DS began to worry about the "ideological purity" and political "trustworthiness" of the employees. Increasingly, tourism jobs were only given to members of the communist party.

At the same time, Bulgarian women came to dominate Balkantourist. Although the very highest positions in the enterprise were given to politically well-connected men, women held the vast majority of the technocratic and middle managerial positions. This was true for a variety of reasons unique to the command economic context and communist gender relations. Among Bulgarians, jobs in tourism were becoming very desirable. In the 1980s, it is said that Todor Zhivkov actually had to prohibit men from being hired in tourism positions in order to concentrate more male labor into the factories and mines that were still considered the most vital sectors in communist ideology.[40] This division of labor was based on an underlying assumption that most men were physically stronger than most women and should therefore do the work that required physical strength. Women were concentrated in the professions like law, medicine, finance, and tourism, which required less physical labor and also allowed them to more easily combine their productive and reproductive duties to the state.

Desi explained to me why tourism jobs were highly valued under communism. "We were so isolated under communism. It was so difficult to leave the country; you had to have hundreds of invitations and bank guarantees and things. It was our only chance to see life behind the [Berlin] Wall, to meet people from other countries. And, of course, there were all those tips in hard currency. We made more money than even the miners and engineers because of the tips. People perceived then that working in tourism was really a bit pink [privileged]."

Receiving tips was perhaps the most important benefit of tourism employment. Most Western tourists felt obliged to tip despite low levels of service. In fact, the practice of tipping was accepted, even encouraged, by the state. A tourist information board in the Hotel Samokov in Borovets during the 1999–2000 ski season still posted the following advice: "It is customary in Bulgaria to leave a 10 percent tip to waiters, bartenders, tour guides, ski instructors, hairdressers, etc. even if he probably doesn't deserve it."

Those employees in tourism who did not receive tips could easily sell leva to tourists on the black market. The artificial rate of exchange imposed by the state meant that the market value of dollars was often several times the official one. Because Bulgarians were hungry for dollars, those employed in tourism were in the ideal position to capitalize on the situation, buying dollars cheaply from the tourists and selling them dearly to other Bulgarians.

Access to foreign monies allowed Bulgarians access to the hard-currency or Korekom shops that stocked imported goods for the tourists and foreigners. These stores carried consumer electronics as well as Western clothes, perfumes, tobacco, and alcohol. Imported Western cigarettes like Rothman's or Kents, only available in these stores, became the commodities that defined personal success in socialist Bulgaria. This division was maintained by the fact that goods in these stores were sold only for dollars to which ordinary Bulgarians did not have access. Only high-ranking officials, those involved in foreign trade, and those who had regular access to foreigners could purchase dollars with any regularity.

Thus, the largely female workforce in tourism during the communist period had constant access to precious "economic capital" in the form of this hard currency. As in Desi's case, this bolstered their position after 1989 by gaining them some financial security in a time of wild economic fluctuation. Several interviewees hinted that tourism workers often had hard-currency "mattress" savings stashed away for emergencies.[41] This is important for two reasons. First, anyone with hard-currency savings would have started the transition with more flexibility and opportunities for travel abroad than those with savings in leva. Hard currency could purchase rationed goods in the dollar stores when there were shortages in the years immediately following "the changes." Second, the hyperinflation that wracked the Bulgarian economy and devalued the lev would have made those holding hard-currency reserves incredibly rich over night. Even if a worker had no hard-currency savings, she might have had continued access to hard currency from the tourists during the periods of hyperinflation. In either case, many tourism workers were better insulated from the "shock therapy" than other Bulgarians. Thus, economic capital (in the form of foreign currency or a position which allowed access to hard currency) gathered during the socialist era could be converted into greater stocks of human/cultural capital (in the form of education, training, or experience abroad) or into more economic capital (in the case of hyperinflation of the local currency).

In addition to the possibility of earning hard currency, resorts and tourist facilities that were always well stocked provided access to basic amenities even when there were shortages in the rest of the country. Although the stockpiles were kept under tight control, a certain amount of attrition was inevitable. Many women were able to ensure that their families always had access to basic goods by "borrowing" supplies from the hotels. There were also gifts from tourists of small items such as toiletries, cosmetics, feminine hygiene products, magazines, and/or cigarettes that were very valuable to the workers who received them. Many of these objects acquired cult status, and could be sold to other Bulgarian collectors.

Another reason tourism was so desirable was that tourism jobs were either on the seaside or in the mountains—these were beautiful geographic settings far preferable to the insides of factories and offices. No matter how much communism attempted to glorify the miners and steel workers, working outdoors in the sunshine still had definite appeal in what was traditionally an agricultural society. Most importantly, Bulgarian tourism was a seasonal job, and Dora, Sonia, and Desi had all benefited from advanced professional training courses and longer holidays in the off-season. Learning new skills or studying new languages was considered part of their responsibility as a tourism worker. As a result, the tourism labor force in Bulgaria was far more qualified than both the labor force in other sectors and the tourism labor force of other countries. In addition, the acceptable unemployment of the low seasons made tourism an attractive opportunity for women, allowing them to more easily combine paid employment with family responsibilities. Since housewives were stigmatized as bourgeois and work was considered a social obligation, tourism jobs were among the few available that could ease Bulgarian women's double burden.

Bulgarians working in tourism under communism also had more opportunities to travel abroad and to learn and practice foreign languages with native speakers. Although foreign travel was unlikely for anyone but the highest-level managers, the mere possibility of foreign travel was enough to raise the social status and respectability of those employed in tourism. Most importantly, jobs in tourism gave Bulgarians like Dora access to Westerners. In tourism, Dora could get information about the nonsocialist world. She could hear Western music, smoke Western cigarettes, observe Western fashions and mannerisms, perhaps even read Western books and magazines. She could witness the realities of capitalist culture first hand.

Because the socialist state severely restricted the access that Bulgarians had to foreigners from capitalist countries, a familiarity with Western tourists became an important form of social and cultural capital for those employed in the sector. Not only did foreigners bring ideas and information about the nonsocialist world, they could often be useful contacts for Bulgarians who were willing to take the risks associated with maintaining a connection. Dora explained to me the value of her Western friends. "You know that I graduated from the German gymnasium. So I wanted to speak German which meant that I had to have contact with Western people . . . I was able to talk to them, and I learned about their way of life. It was not as they [the communists] said it was. As they tried to tell the Bulgarian people it was. I knew that they were lying. So when 'the changes' happened, my eyes were already open because of my contacts with the tourists. It was easier for us [people working in tourism] because we had that contact with Westerners. We already knew how the West worked. We knew how the people lived. This helped me a lot."

Sonia, the receptionist, also felt that having worked in the tourism sector under communism gave her certain advantages in the postsocialist period, particularly with regard to foreign travel. "Contact with foreigners was very important. I have a cousin in England, and it was very difficult for me to visit her. If I was someone higher up in Balkantourist I would have been able to travel without a problem. Even for me, because I was a receptionist in a big hotel and a member of the party, they trusted me a little bit. So I could go once or twice to England. But it [foreign travel] was really a problem for most people. It was the only forbidden thing at that time, so officially forbidden. Because if you had to travel somewhere, you had to get your exit visa. This was a problem for most people."

Under communism, any Bulgarian wishing to travel abroad had to apply for an exit visa that had to be approved by the Ministry of Interior. The process was long and difficult, because anyone who made it to the West could declare political asylum. During my time in Bulgaria, I heard many sad stories of families torn apart by defections. If one member of the family left the country illegally, the rest of the family was held responsible. They lost their jobs and were often subjected to intense scrutiny by the DS. Any communication between the family members on either side of the Iron Curtain was confiscated by the police. In one case, the mother of a friend of mine in Sofia had waited years to get an exit visa for a two-week visit to her family in Greece. The visa was finally approved. A week before she was to leave, she asked her boss for the time off from work, and the request was denied. When she tried to explain her situation, her employer reported to the DS that she was planning to defect. Not only was her exit visa to Greece rescinded, but she faced a lifetime ban on all travel outside of Bulgaria that ended only with the demise of communism in 1989. Thus, the exit visa requirement was essentially a ban on all foreign travel except to socialist "brother countries."

Contact with Westerners and travel experience outside of the socialist bloc could create valuable international networks for the Bulgarians who were able to maintain them. After "the changes," these networks provided possible business partners, contacts with Western universities and colleges, or, most importantly, foreigners willing to write the letters of invitation needed for most Bulgarians to obtain visas to visit Western countries. In this respect, the social/political capital of having contacts with foreigners during the socialist times could translate into opportunities to accumulate both economic and cultural capital after 1989.

Another avenue open only to tourism workers in the years just after "the changes" was the opportunity to go for further education or professional training abroad. After 1989, "study tours" for Bulgarian professionals were available through many international and nongovernmental organizations, including the Open Society Institute, USAID, and the European Union's PHARE program.[42] These tours brought professionals from the former socialist countries to the West to show them "how things are done" in a capitalist economy. Because tourism was such a strategic sector of the economy, many of these programs were designed specifically to retrain tourist personnel. Many managers and especially marketing specialists (who were almost exclusively women) were sent abroad at the expense of foreign agencies to participate in practicums or short internships in Western enterprises.

Of course, these programs were very popular among Bulgarians and hence quite competitive. Successful candidates were generally those with already high levels of cultural capital: a university education, relevant professional experience, and the ability to speak foreign languages almost fluently. Interviews for these competitions were often conducted with local Americans or Europeans, and Bulgarians who had worked with foreigners and practiced their foreign languages with native speakers had a great advantage.

Foreign study or experience gained in the postsocialist period was quite common among most of the higher-level operational and managerial workers in tourism. A marketing assistant in the Sofia Sheraton was sent to Seoul for an M.B.A. in tourism paid for by the foreign owners of her hotel. A former tour guide and an "expert" in tourism in the Bulgarian Ministry of Economy went to Japan at the expense of the Japanese government for a six-week training program in tourism. Two receptionists in Albena went to Holland for practical training as part of their coursework at the Bulgarian-Dutch College of International Tourism. One of these women eventually went on to work in a South African hotel for another year. Several of Dora's colleagues in Golden Sands have been granted "guest worker" visas to work in tourism in Germany.

Even those who were not lucky enough to go abroad could take advantage of the many new private universities and colleges specializing in tourism. These colleges gave scholarships to professionals interested in "retraining" themselves. Many receptionists took advantage of computer training programs to learn new reservation software. Even Bulgarians who had been working in tourism for decades felt that continued education was necessary to survive the changes. Diliana, a marketing manager in Borovetz with thirty-one years of experience in tourism, received her university degree in tourism almost two decades after she started working in the sector: "I went back to university when I was fifty years old, after my son was grown and nobody was making a hassle in my house. Things were changing so quickly, points of view were changing, so I decided to go back to school. First, I would have a chance to improve my education, and second, I could become familiar with the new expectations and the new realities."

Diliana's experience is confirmed in studies that show that older women in general had an easier time being reemployed than younger women immediately after "the changes."[43] Work experience and knowledge of foreign languages were very useful in securing places in these new programs. These new degrees and the experience gained abroad increased the competitiveness of tourism workers even further, giving them access to many of the new jobs created by the institutional restructuring of the sector. In sum, access to new programs and coveted jobs was very much dependent on the education and position one had before 1989.

Thus, tourism workers before 1989 had the skills and attitudes that could greatly enhance their ability to survive as workers in the soon-to-be-liberalized labor market. An interesting mystery of this process is *why* this cultural capital was so suddenly revalued after 1989. How did general education and work experience become the new arbiters of success, particularly for women in the tourism sector? Why would cultural capital be valued differently under different economic systems?

If we return to the work of the sociologist Pierre Bourdieu for a brief speculative interlude, we can explore some of the theoretical implications of this process. In Bourdieu's own work there is not much of an explanation for the varying values of cultural capital under different economic systems. The only time he discusses the matter, he argues that social differentiation happens using whatever kind of capital is useful for the particular society in which people live, even in what he calls the "least differentiated societies," meaning the socialist countries.[44] In October

1989, however, in a lecture in East Berlin,[45] Bourdieu did introduce the concept of political (i.e., social) capital as the primary organizer of socialist social differentiation: "When other forms of accumulation are more or less completely controlled, political capital becomes the primordial principle of differentiation, and the members of the political 'nomenclatura' have hardly any competitors in the struggle for the dominant principle of domination which takes place in the field of power . . ."[46] Bourdieu sets up a model wherein political/social capital suppresses other significant forms of capital, namely economic and cultural capital, in order to shore up the privileges of the communist elite.[47] But this does not explain *why* cultural capital (or economic capital) did not necessarily translate into class privilege under socialism or how the political-capital–bearing elite was able to prevent this from happening.

In terms of economic capital, the problem was easily solved. All of the economic capital was simply nationalized. The communist state owned everything and no one had access to private economic capital. The opposite was true for cultural capital. The communist state had as one of its core ideological goals the "uplifting" of the workers and peasants, and the imparting of cultural capital evenly among the population. One of the original Russian revolutionaries, Leon Trotsky, considered access to culture for the masses one of the driving forces behind the revolution.[48] These communist ideals would ultimately create a system that allowed the children of village peasants to earn university degrees.

To guarantee the equal distribution of economic capital, the state had to centralize the means of production. To guarantee the equal distribution of cultural capital, however, the socialist state provided ready access to education, credentials, skills, and "discerning tastes" to as many people as possible. In some ways, the state compensated for the scarcity of economic capital with access to cultural capital. In 1977, adult literacy rates in most socialist countries equaled or surpassed those of the advanced industrialized countries.[49] In Bulgaria, primary-school education was almost universal, and between 1960 and 1978 the percentage of youth enrolled in secondary school increased from 55 percent to 90 percent. In 1977, 22 percent of those between the ages of twenty and twenty-four were enrolled in higher educational institutions, a higher percentage than in the United Kingdom, Switzerland, Finland, or Austria.[50] Even the critical

American anarchist, Emma Goldman, grudgingly acknowledged one Soviet success in her book, *My Disillusionment with Russia*. She writes that "so far as quantity is concerned, the Bolsheviki deserve credit for their educational work and the general diffusion of education."[51]

Relative to capitalist subjects, members of socialist societies as a whole also had greater access to bourgeois culture. The socialist state subsidized the ballet, the opera, symphonies, theaters, and the arts for the purposes of making these available to the masses. Organizations such as Proletcult, set up to promote culture for the proletariat, were generously subsidized even during times of famine and civil war.[52] Indeed, many former socialist subjects (at all levels of society) prided themselves on being infinitely more "cultured" than their capitalist counterparts. In Bulgaria, Lyudmila Zhivkova, the Oxford-educated daughter of Todor Zhivkov, pursued the cultural enrichment of the masses with an almost religious zeal. We have seen that the cultural capital of tourist workers like Desi, Dora, Sonia, Gergana, and Hristo was extensive: their education, their knowledge of foreign languages, and their familiarity with Western tastes. But this capital translated into "class" privilege only after 1989 with the introduction of capitalism.

Perhaps the kernel of the problem is Bourdieu's use of the term *capital*.[53] For Marx, *capital* refers specifically to economic capital and is based on a model of scarcity (as is all of modern economics).[54] Thus, economic capital is finite in quantity and is allocated according to class position wherein the capitalists accumulate the wealth at the expense of labor. It is intuitive that economic capital is scarce because there is a fixed quantity of natural resources and labor power that can be converted into commodities and money in the long run. When Bourdieu extends the analogy to "cultural capital," he implicitly assumes that the total amount of cultural capital is also fixed.[55] As with economic capital, a scarcity of cultural capital means that those who have it can translate it into specific privileges at the expense of those who do not. Indeed, in 1970s France (or the United States or Japan) this was probably the case.

Under a command economy, however, cultural capital may be far less scarce. Again, one of the central socialist ideological goals was to extend it to as many people as possible.[56] It may be precisely because cultural capital was not scarce under communism that it could not translate into social differentiation. Cultural capital could translate into class privilege only when it became scarce after the onset of capitalism (quality education is no longer paid for by the state). Thus, capitalism not only deals "efficiently" with scarce resources in terms of its distribution of (naturally limited) economic capital, but it creates a scarcity in cultural capital by lowering the salaries of teachers, closing rural schools, introducing or raising school fees and tuitions, not enforcing child labor laws, and so forth. This new scarcity of cultural capital justifies and reproduces class privilege.[57] Under socialism there was no direct link between higher education and privilege. This was particularly true because wages in the mining and manufacturing sectors under communism were higher than those in most of the "professions" like law and medicine that required postsecondary degrees. Thus, scarce economic capital was not necessarily allocated disproportionately to those with higher education, a fact that irked the socialist intelligentsia considerably.[58]

One key question is whether or not cultural capital is "naturally" scarce. One could argue that education, training, and promoting "high culture" cost money (which is finite). Yet education can be extended to a large number of people for relatively little monetary cost if there is the political will, as we know from the brigades of youth in communist countries around the world that participated in widespread literacy campaigns and from the work of Paulo Freire in Brazil.[59] Furthermore, one person's education does not take away from another's education in an economy that guarantees full employment for all. In this sense, education is almost a perfect public good (i.e., a good that is difficult to exclude someone else from using: one person's use of it does not deny someone else's use). There is not a finite amount of education and training out there that must be allocated efficiently because it is scarce. It is only capitalism that makes it scarce. It introduces a competitive market system wherein individuals compete for scarce employment opportunities and where differences in education and ability determine employment prospects, and, ultimately, class privilege.[60]

The same can be said of the "scarcity" of political capital in the communist context. Party membership was not finite in quantity. Theoretically, everyone could have become a member of the Communist Party, but party membership was intentionally made scarce (through a variety of prohibitions) in order to justify the privileges enjoyed by the socialist political elite.

The implication of this argument is that all forms of symbolic capital become valuable in terms of social differentiation only when they become scarce for some externally imposed reason like a sudden change in the economic system from communism to capitalism or vice versa. The scarcity of symbolic capital is not "natural." It is always constructed by those who want to protect and increase their own privileges, whether under a command or market economy. But cultural capital specifically translates into privilege only when there is a commodification of education (such as under capitalist regimes of accumulation) that makes it scarce (i.e., higher education is expensive, not only in terms of direct monetary outlays but also in terms of the opportunity costs of leaving the labor market to study full-time).

The trajectory adjustment theory of Gil Eyal, Ivan Szelenyi, and Ellen Townsley also supports this idea. They, too, claim that Bourdieu's model may not be applicable to their case of Central Europe. They find that cultural capital becomes the most important determinant of class differentiation after the end of socialism, even more important than economic capital, but they do not completely give an explanation for why this is the case.

The question then becomes: if so many socialist subjects had access to cultural capital before 1989, why were so few of them able to translate this capital into class privilege after the onset of capitalism? Here is where gender enters the argument in fascinating ways. Cultural capital was allocated to socialist subjects along specifically gendered lines. Women like Desi the waitress were concentrated in the universities, where they got a more general education, whereas men like Desi's husband were concentrated in the more technical colleges, where they learned skills specific to the communist command economy. During communism, these technical colleges were conduits for students into the industrial sector, a kind of vocational training. Most of the students were men, so there was a gendered division of labor in favor of the men who primarily worked in this sector. This changed rapidly after 1989. Desi and other women in tourism like her suddenly found themselves holding the type of cultural capital valuable in the new global capitalist context (i.e., general education, foreign-language ability, etc.). They were then able to reallocate stocks of capital in their portfolios and adjust their trajectories toward gaining privilege under the new system.

But of course not all women in Bulgaria possessed the same amounts of cultural capital. There were many women who had not pursued higher degrees at the universities, but had instead pursued technical degrees or chosen not to study in foreign-language secondary schools. Much of their capital under the old system was social capital that had little value under the new system. The difference in access to cultural capital among Bulgarian women as a whole explains why women in tourism might be doing relatively well after 1989 while many other women struggle. Tourism in Bulgaria had a very high concentration of women with large amounts of the "good" cultural capital.[61]

A WOMAN'S PLACE IS IN THE HOTEL?

The gendering of this cultural capital both before and after 1989 would play an important part in preserving women's dominance of tourism after the economic transition began. Since the majority of workers were women, the skills and attitudes necessary for tourism work came to be associated with certain stereotypical "feminine" characteristics. By the late 1980s, Bulgarian women were imagined to be more "biologically" suited to tourism work. As one older male hotel manager in Sofia explained to me, "Before 1989, it was not polite for a man to work in tourism."

The sudden changes in the economy that followed the end of communism began to drastically reshape the social expectations and discourses about what was "naturally" men's and women's work.[62] Communist ideologies had advocated for the emancipation of women and the equality of the sexes, but in reality there remained a gendered division of labor between men in the factories and women in socialism's less prestigious areas—law, banking, finance, medicine, and tourism. In the immediate postsocialist period, many Bulgarian women willingly withdrew from the labor force. No one in Bulgaria understood the concept of unemployment, least of all the women who thought their husband's prestigious jobs in the factories would be secure forever.

At the same time, there was a new "democratic" concept of femininity appearing in the popular culture, a new gender paradigm for women. Working women were associated with communism, and women's emancipation was considered a relic of an oppressive regime which had tried to destroy the Bulgarian family. In newly available Western women's magazines and on billboards around the major cities, cosmetic companies like Clarins were offering up the image of the well-dressed and glamorously "kept" woman as the new feminine ideal. In the music videos of the ubiquitous "pop-folk" music called *chalga*, sultry Bulgarian vixens glorified a brand of predatory femininity where a woman's "love" could be gained only in exchange for expensive cars, clothes, and jewelry.

Professional women who had not left their jobs after 1989 were destabilized by the new discourses of appropriate "femininity." Men displaced by the crumbling of Bulgaria's industrial base began competing for jobs in traditionally feminized sectors. The rhetoric about communism's distortion of women's "proper role" helped to justify the displacement of or discrimination against many working women. Furthermore, work in these sectors began to be recharacterized as "men's work," using popular images borrowed from Hollywood and the Western media.[63] Slowly, as new jobs in banking, law, finance, and medicine began to appear in the private sector, men began to move into these professions.

The character of work in the tourism sector, however, remained distinctly feminine in the popular imagination. Privatization, employment expansion, and the sudden popularity of tourism degree programs for both young women and men had done nothing to change the socialist measure of tourism as a woman's sector. In all of my interviews and conversations, I asked different Bulgarians why tourism has remained so distinctly feminine. Time and time again, men and women in all different positions, from the laundresses to the hotel managers, fell back on a communist ideology that tourism was somehow naturally suited to women's labor. Although it was clear that women were obviously the most educated and experienced for their positions due to their revalued cultural capital, I was always surprised by the extent to which women justified their domination of the sector based on their role as mothers.

Hristo felt that because women had to deal with very small children they were simply more patient and polite with foreigners. Desi thought that it was because women in Bulgaria are expected to take care of the house: "Women in Bulgaria must cook and clean and make things comfortable for her family. She has the mentality of always thinking about the needs of other people, her husband, her children, sometimes her parents. Men think much more about themselves and their own needs. Women cannot do this. In this way, it is natural for women to work in the hotel. Almost all of the hotel managers in Albena are women. They are all wives and mothers too, and that is why they can manage a hotel without too much extra effort."

In Golden Sands, Dora also believed that women have a greater intuitive understanding of the tourist's needs. "Everybody in the world cares about food, all of our lives revolve around it. This is the same if you are Bulgarian or American or German or Japanese. We all want our food to be well prepared, to taste good, and to be served by someone nice. As a mother, I know that food is very important, and it is my responsibility to make sure that I feed my family well. As a chef in the resort, I know the tourists will be unhappy if their food is not good or if they do not get their food exactly as they like it. They are really just like children in some ways."

At the reception desk in the Hotel Transcontinental, Sonia explained that Bulgarian women just work harder than men because of their dual roles. "Under communism we had to work and to take care of our families. We became very organized in order to do this. This makes us more efficient workers which is what the new [hotel] owners like."

In Borovetz, Gergana felt that much of the work in tourism was just considered "women's work" in Bulgaria. Even if there were extra jobs open, many men would not accept jobs as chambermaids or in the laundry. "A man has too much pride," she said. "Boyan would never clean a toilet or make a bed. Not in his own house and certainly not in a hotel. This is a woman's job. In the restaurants and at the reception desk, there are some men working. Even this is women's work. Those men cannot find jobs anywhere else."

In almost all of the conversations I initiated about why there were so many women working in tourism, the explanations somehow drew a direct connection between women's work in the home and women's work

in a hotel or resort. This "naturalization" of tourism as a mere pro-
fessionalized extension of women's domestic duties certainly originated
under communism and may have protected many of these jobs from an
influx of unemployed male labor after 1989. So many of these comments
came from the women themselves that it was clear to me that they truly
believed that women were simply "better" at dealing with tourists than
men. Interestingly, there was no class differentiation among women in
higher and lower positions in tourism. At all levels, even in the managerial sphere, women claimed that tourism work is feminine. The fact
that many of these women had university degrees, years of work experience, and spoke foreign languages was secondary to the biological advantage of being a woman. Women's cultural capital had been distinctly
gendered under communism, and it was this gendering of cultural capital
that had prevented men with similar qualifications from entering the
sector and displacing women.

Thus, women already employed in tourism before 1989 were protected
by the gendered distribution of cultural capital under communism, and
the sudden reevaluation of that capital in the early 1990s. Because tourism jobs were so desirable, however, just cultural capital alone would not
have been sufficient to secure women's position within the sector. Communist discourses about women's natural suitability to tourism (or the
discourses of the communist gender regime) were deployed against displaced men clamoring for work in one of Bulgaria's most dynamic sectors. The gender ideology of communism refutes the idea that women are
less suitable to capitalism in general, but instead posits that certain work
could *only* be performed by women. This notion that only women could
work in tourism also continues to skew new hiring decisions in favor of
younger women hoping to start careers in the sector. Gergana explained,
"You know, even if a man applied for a job as a maid, he would not be
hired. Nobody in Bulgaria would believe that he could do a good job
cleaning anything. And he would quit the minute he found another
position."

Sonia, too, told me that the hotel manager had had several bad experiences with male receptionists in the Transcontinental: "Tourists can be
very stupid and annoying, but you always have to be nice to them no

matter what they ask you for. Sometimes they treat us very badly, like we are uncivilized. There was once a receptionist here in the Transcontinental who lost his temper and started yelling at a drunken tourist. They started to fight and the police had to come. It was very embarrassing for the hotel. I think they [the management] are very careful when they hire new receptionists after that. Men just go crazy, and that is not good."

Desi in Albena confided that many of the male waiters tamper with the food of return customers who did not tip on their previous visit to the restaurant. "You know some of the waiters spit on the food. I think this is disgusting, but they think it is funny. The tourists never notice, but if the [food and beverage] manager finds out they will be angry."

The seasonality of tourism also continues to gender tourism work. For most employees, tourism work lasts only through the tourist season: December to April in the winter resorts and mid-May to mid-September in the summer resorts. Although there are some Bulgarians who work both seasons in different resorts, this requires employee accommodation in the resort that is not near their homes. Some employers have started doing this in order to keep their best employees on the payroll all year, but most workers can count only on four months of work out of the year.

This system is still discursively constructed as particularly suited to women's "natural work" because the extreme flexibility of tourism allows many Bulgarian women to combine their household responsibilities with work in tourism. Although Gergana was employed all year, Sonia, Dora, and Desi all said that they use the off-season as a time to spend with their families. Dora said that she almost never sees her son during the season, and is thankful to have so much time off to spend with him in the winter months. The women also need this time for "household duties," including private farming and the preparation of foodstuffs both for sale and for family consumption. This is important since so many Bulgarian families survive on food that they grow and process for themselves. In Samokov, the potato-growing season falls during the tourism off-season. The majority of workers in Borovets, unlike Gergana and Petar, own private plots of land, which they can farm for profit. Desi, Dora, and Sonia also use the downtime in tourism to preserve vegetables for the winter. And seaside tourism is the perfect job for university students like Katina's classmates since they can work in the summer and study through the rest of the year.[64]

The seasonal nature of tourism allows many Bulgarian women to withdraw from their official jobs for months at a time, providing the opportunity to dabble in other sectors of the economy when interesting or lucrative opportunities arise.[65] Of course, these other jobs are really available only to the most educated of the tourism workers, and therefore those with less cultural capital (maids, kitchen staff, and laundry workers) have more difficulty finding temporary jobs outside of tourism in the off-season. Receptionists and tour guides with language skills—and so with much higher stocks of cultural capital—can sometimes find work as translators or interpreters.

I also found that a long off-season is one of the factors that attracts women to tourism in the first place. When asked if they were "employed in another sphere" outside tourism during the off-season, about 26 percent of men said yes versus only 16 percent of women.[66] Slightly fewer women than men said that they *wanted* to work all year round: approximately 59 percent of men compared to 54 percent of women.[67] What tourism workers *actually* do in the off-season, however, is less important than people's perceptions about what they do. Because of the double burden women had under the old system, Bulgarians still believe that women have something to do in the off-season (i.e., take care of their families and household responsibilities). Men are perceived as having "nothing" to do when the summer or winter season ends. This stereotype is particularly relevant because the majority of women working in the tourism sector are, in fact, married with children. The Seaside Survey found that about 52 percent of the male respondents were married versus 65 percent of the women. Furthermore, 57 percent of the women workers said they had children compared to 46 percent of the men. This majority of women tourism workers with families may further reinforce the idea that tourism is a sector particularly suited to women's "natural capabilities" as mothers and wives. When the advent of capitalism began to shift the gender regime under which Bulgarian women lived, discursive legacies of the communist notion of women's biological suitability to tourism combined with their relatively high levels of cultural capital to solidify women's employment opportunities at a time of rapid institutional changes and economic restructuring in the sector. Thus, the "gender capital" of communism was also revalued with the sudden emergence of free-market competition.

ONE WEEK UNTIL SVETLA'S
UNIVERSITY ENTRANCE EXAM

Je bous
>*tu bous*
>*il bout*
>*nous bouillons*
>*vous bouillez*
>*ils bouillent*

Je bouillais, tu bouillas, il bouillait, nous bouillions, vous bouilliez, ils bouillaient

Simple conjugations, compound conjugations, être verbs, regular -er verbs, stem-changing verbs, irregular -re verbs. Svetla plans to conjugate one hundred French verbs every night for the next week before the exam. Her hand is cramping from writing, and it is already one o'clock in the morning. Twenty-two more verbs to go, each in at least four different tenses, and then she will go back and check them for mistakes.

Je bouillis, tu bouillis, il bouillit, nous bouillîmes, vous bouillîtes, ils bouillirent . . .

4

To the Wolves: Tourism and Economic Transformation

In the summer of 1989, Prolet was working in the reservations office in Golden Sands. She and her one colleague were responsible for coordinating all contracts for English-speaking tourists. This was a very good job under the old system, and she had been allowed to travel several times to the United Kingdom to meet with British tour operators. Prolet had a university degree in tourism economics and spoke Russian, English, Dutch, and passable Danish. When "the changes" happened in 1989, she was still employed in Golden Sands. It was November, and contract work for the following summer would go on until January. There was so much uncertainty about what would happen in the Eastern-bloc countries that Prolet worried about the coming tourist season. She also worried about her job. The first few years of the 1990s were uncertain for everyone employed at Golden Sands, and there were whisperings about privatization of the resort.

In 1993, a British tour operator that Prolet had met while visiting England asked her to work as a local representative of their firm in Bulgaria. This would entail a considerable salary increase and the chance to travel several times per year to the United Kingdom. It also meant leaving her job in the reservations office at Golden Sands and becoming the employee of a foreign company with little or no job security. Prolet took the risk.

She worked for the British tour operator for five years, and made many contacts with professionals in the tourism business in the United Kingdom. She also had the opportunity to attend several international tourism conferences in Spain and Australia. While on a business trip in

London, she learned of a correspondence course through the Open University that would allow her to get an M.B.A. while she was working. In 1998, Prolet and two of her former colleagues from Golden Sands began to think of setting up their own tour operation in Bulgaria. After 1989, many new private hotels were built along the Black Sea coast. These hotels were mostly family-owned and had no way to market themselves to tourists from Western Europe.

Prolet had the idea of becoming an intermediary between British tour operators and these small Bulgarian hotels. She was able to use a contact she had made at the tourism conference in Australia to get a small amount of start-up capital to rent an office and buy a secondhand computer, a desk, a telephone, a fax machine, a telex machine, and a small assortment of office supplies. For the first year of her business, she kept her job with the British company and worked after hours in the rented office in Varna. After only one year, she had already brought over one hundred British tourists to Bulgaria. The Bulgarian families were happy because they could rent their rooms out at higher rates, and the British tourists were happy because they were glad to save a little money, be out of the resort atmosphere, and have the chance to experience a more "authentic" Bulgaria. Prolet took a commission on each tourist, and also organized special excursions for the tourists, lead by local university students studying English philology.

Prolet's British employers were not displeased when she finally quit her job to focus on her own business. In fact, they offered to invest further in her business by concluding contracts for their excess demand exclusively with Prolet's new firm. At the peak of the season, Prolet's former employer always had more tourists wishing to travel to Bulgaria's resorts than there were places available. For several years, they had been turning last-minute tour bookings away. They offered to conclude contracts with Prolet for these last-minute bookings as long as she could guarantee that the accommodations provided would be up to the standards required by the British firm, standards with which Prolet was extremely familiar because of the five years she had spent working with them. After her first year as a full-time entrepreneur, Prolet was making a decent profit and enjoying her success. Polishing off her Danish language skills, she began diversifying into the Scandinavian market. In addition to a steady stream of British clients, Prolet's firm started bringing Danes, Swedes, and Norwegians to the Black Sea coast.

By 2003, Prolet was a successful businesswoman. She had seven employees working for her year-round, and five students that she hired in the summers. But the long hours and the stress were starting to tire her. The business was no longer a challenge. When a more established Bulgarian tour operator offered to buy her business outright, she sold it for a considerable amount of money by Bulgarian standards. The last time I heard from her, she had accepted a new position as the director of marketing for a brand-new German-owned hotel in Golden Sands. Her old colleague from the Golden Sands reservations office in 1989 was the hotel manager, and Prolet told me that she was happy not to be in charge for a change. She had saved the money from the sale of her business, and said that someday she might build her own hotel. In the meantime, she said, she was studying German.

Although Prolet's story is certainly exceptional, it does demonstrate how some individuals in Bulgaria were able to use skills and education gained under the communist system to adjust to the institutional changes that accompanied the economic transformation. Prolet was exceptional under the old system; she had all the right education and training and a very good job in one of Bulgaria's premier resorts. She was able to use her contacts and her skills (her portfolio of stocks of cultural and political capital) to adjust her trajectory in response to the changes reshaping the economy in Bulgaria. Because she had the right mix of capital, and a little ingenuity and perseverance, she was also able to be exceptional in the postsocialist period. This is not to say that all Bulgarians with Prolet's position and education were able to adjust their trajectories in the same way. Prolet's entrepreneurial success was a unique function of the new business possibilities open to her after 1989, her own individual choices on whether to pursue those opportunities, and her preexisting skills, contacts, and experiences from the pre-1989 period.

As in Prolet's story, both the character of tourism in Bulgaria before 1989 and the effects of the economic transformation on the sector are the building blocks for the story of how Bulgarian women came to and continue to dominate tourism. Any understanding of how women were able to maintain their dominant positions in tourism despite overall

15. THE BEACH AT VARNA (NOW CALLED ST. KONSTANTIN
AND ELENA) IN 2003. PHOTO BY AUTHOR.

declines in women's employment in the 1990s must take into account the
specific historical circumstances of tourism in Bulgaria: how and why
communism gendered employment in the sector. Yet, it is also essential to
understand that the collapse of communism had widely varying ramifications for different sectors of the postsocialist economy. These differences created distinct combinations of setbacks and opportunities for the
sectors. This often led to drastically diverse consequences for the sector's workers, depending of course on their different portfolios of stocks
of capital.

When considering the transition from one economic system to another, it is important to keep in mind that communist tourism was
working quite well. There was a steady stream of middle- to lower-class
Western Europeans who happily returned to Bulgaria's shores every summer for inexpensive fun in the sun, pouring much needed hard currency
into the local economy. Of course, some hotel managers and employees
were disgruntled by the state's redirecting of tourism's immense profits to
the industrial sector, but this was an ideological wrinkle. Economically,
centralized tourism in Bulgaria was very successful.

The implosion of communism in 1989 and the triumph of global capitalism forced the restructuring of all command economies. All state

monopolies, even successful ones, were forced into privatization by free-market governments under pressure from the international financial community—most notably the International Monetary Fund and the World Bank. Tourism in Bulgaria, like all other sectors of the economy, was caught up in this maelstrom of economic transition. The form of privatization in the tourism sector was partially informed by the unique characteristics of the sector during the communist period. In order to understand how it is that Bulgarian women employed in tourism came to be the ultimate beneficiaries of the restructuring, however, it is also essential to understand the factors that influenced the marketization of tourism after 1989.

DISMANTLING COMMUNISM
THROUGH PRIVATIZATION

One evening at the bar of the Hotel Dionisia, Desi comes in and asks Hristo to lend her a lighter. I am sitting at the bar writing notes in my journal. Hristo pulls out a box of lighters, offering it to Desi.

"Here, take one," he says.

"Where did you get all these?" Desi says.

"From the tourists," Hristo says in Bulgarian. "I privatize two or three of them every night."

It is the first time I have heard the word *privatize* used this way. I laugh. "You privatized them?" I ask in English.

"Yes." Hristo smiles, obviously pleased at his own wit. He also switches to English. "They belonged to someone else, and now they belong to me."

"How is that different from stealing?" I say.

Hristo leans toward me over the bar. He shakes his head and makes two "tch tch" sounds as if to emphasize how little I really know about things.

"It isn't," he says.

In the minds of many Bulgarians like Hristo, the word *privatization* became synonymous with theft. State socialism was always about being "social." The state prohibited the ownership of the means of production in order to prevent individual capitalists from exploiting their workers and extracting surplus value. Bureaucracy, stagnation, and inefficiency in the economy were justified in terms of the hegemonic communist ideals of equality and a "classless" society. These beliefs structured everyday life in Bulgaria for over forty-five years; two generations of Bulgarians knew no alternative. The sudden and unexpected collapse of communism could not erase entire lifetimes of belief. The idea of taking the "worker's property," entrusted by the proletariat to the Bulgarian state, and placing it in the hands of private "entrepreneurs" flew in the face of all established Marxist doctrine. Thus, privatization required not only the physical transfer of assets from the state to the market, but also the accompanying psychological processes that would make these transfers successful.

Economic reform and political change were always slow to happen in Bulgaria. Throughout the 1980s as perestroika and glasnost spilled over into the Eastern bloc, Bulgaria stubbornly remained an orthodox, Soviet-model, communist country.[1] It made very few market-oriented economic changes. In 1989, 95 percent of the Bulgarian economy was still controlled by the state.[2] Although Bulgarians and foreigners alike perceived 10 November 1989 as a huge milestone, in reality the Bulgarian Communist Party (BCP) remained functionally in power, albeit under a new name: the Bulgarian Socialist Party (BSP).[3] The first real economic reforms were not implemented until February 1991, over a year after Todor Zhivkov's resignation.

Before 1989, the 4.9 percent of the Bulgarian GDP contributed by the private sector mainly came from small touristic businesses, especially handicraft production.[4] At the time, private businesses were restricted to one-person "enterprises" and/or artisan cooperatives. Decree 56, the law that set the stage for the liberalization of the Bulgarian economy, was then retroactively applied from the beginning of 1989. It allowed private firms to be registered in any sector. These new firms were allowed up to ten full-time employees and an unlimited number of seasonal employees.[5]

Additionally, Decree 56 required that state-owned enterprises be broken up into either joint-stock companies or limited liability companies.[6] The legal owners of these new entities were to be other enterprises or public institutions. This allowed enterprise directors to subdivide their enterprises and to appoint themselves, their friends, or their relatives as directors of the newly created "entities." Between these two new possibilities for the formation of "private" enterprises, 342 corporations, 1,643 partnerships, and 9,231 one-person firms were registered in 1989 alone.[7] It is difficult to measure accurately how many of these were legitimate businesses, because many were most likely shells set up by state bureaucrats and enterprise directors to illegally convert public property into private assets. These "spontaneous privatizations" were ubiquitous; an enterprise director or a state bureaucrat would set up a subsidiary of his own enterprise and sell it to himself.

The privatization of these state-owned assets was an institutional change, but even this institutional change was path dependent.[8] The structural constraints that Bulgaria inherited from the communist period were crucial factors in determining its privatization strategies. This was particularly important since Bulgaria was a relative latecomer to privatization. It was the last Central or Eastern European country to pass a privatization law, in part because Bulgaria initially wanted to repudiate its considerable external debt.[9]

Bulgaria's leaders had accumulated a sizeable hard-currency debt during the 1980s. From 1985 to 1989 Bulgaria's gross foreign debt grew from 3.9 billion dollars to 10.2 billion dollars.[10] This money was largely unaccounted for, and accusations were leveled at the Zhivkov government for its hand in the debt accumulation. Much of the money, however, was probably drained in the immediate aftermath of 1989. The disintegration of the COMECON in 1991 drastically reduced Bulgaria's exports, and a lack of hard-currency reserves precipitated a debt crisis. In March 1990, the Bulgarian government declared a controversial moratorium on the repayment of its foreign debt. This prompted the keen interest of the International Monetary Fund and the World Bank in Bulgarian affairs, fearing that the Balkan country would set a dangerous precedent in the East.[11]

Czechoslovakia had little external debt in 1989 and could afford to implement a privatization program based on the essentially free distribution of shares in the state's assets to the population at large.[12] But Bulgaria needed hard currency to pay its international creditors. Privatization was like the World Bank foreclosing on the country. Assets like state-owned enterprises could not be directly seized by the bank, but the World Bank could withhold loans until the government agreed to privatize its assets and service their existing debts with the proceeds. This constraint initially led Bulgaria to embark on a privatization course based on the idea of market privatization: cash bidders were sought for state-owned enterprises with the goal of maximizing state revenues.[13] There was little initial concern for a "fair and equitable" distribution of resources, which served to turn many enterprise directors against the state. After all, Bulgaria's external debt had been most likely accumulated by politicians who siphoned the borrowed funds from the state budget into their own Swiss bank accounts. Enterprise directors were understandably angry that their enterprises should be sold to pay the IMF and World Bank for the corruption of Bulgaria's political elite.

Thus, the scramble for the state's assets was filled with uncomfortable economic and ideological uncertainties. Enterprise directors and state functionaries felt threatened by the imminent corrosion of their personal positions. As the post-1989 governments changed in rapid succession, many enterprise directors were hired and fired based on their political affiliations. This created personal instability for those in charge, and they sought to enrich themselves before they lost their positions.[14]

Furthermore, because market privatization required that all assets be paid for in hard currency, few domestic investors were able to participate in the privatization program. The idea that their enterprises would be taken over by foreigners created an atmosphere in which the directors and employees could easily rationalize their "spontaneous privatization" of their enterprises' physical assets. While the "borrowing" of enterprise assets for personal use was a common "fringe benefit" of the communist workplace, blatant theft from the enterprises began only after 1989 when the extended surveillance web of the DS started to fall apart.

Bulgarians created endless variations on how to drain state assets long before the official privatization process began.[15] Directors often intentionally led their own enterprises into bankruptcy in order to discourage other potential buyers. This not only increased the director's personal wealth, it also lowered the value of the enterprise so that the director or one of his friends could acquire it at a drastically reduced price. In Bulgaria's uncertain climate, it was almost impossible to determine the value of an enterprise. In lieu of market valuations, administrative determinations of prices were made. This further concentrated power in the hands of the enterprise directors who, in many cases, were the only people with accurate information about an enterprise's assets and debts. The process was further complicated by the rampant inflation that characterized much of the early transition period in Bulgaria. Enterprise valuations constantly had to be revised. The uncertainty regarding the worth of any enterprise meant that many of Bulgaria's former communist elite could acquire assets for little money (trading in social capital for economic capital).

Decree 56 also allowed these same individuals to create private firms or joint-stock companies "owned" by their enterprises. These enterprises could then be leased out to newly established "private companies" on favorable financial terms, and the leaseholders would be granted preferential treatment when the enterprise was sold off. In other cases, contracts with foreign parties previously mediated by a state organization (such as the Foreign Trade Bank or Balkantourist) were rerouted through newly formed private intermediary companies like Prolet's tour agency, which absorbed all of the profits of a transaction. Or, employees simply took home an enterprise's assets (small machines, tools, supplies, etc.) and kept them for personal use or sold them for cash. In Golden Sands, Sonia told me that lamps, mirrors, blankets, towels, dishes, pots, pans, and silverware began to disappear.[16] Former Bulgarian Prime Minister Reneta Indzhova estimated that approximately 50 percent of state enterprises had been spontaneously privatized by the end of 1994.[17] The Bulgarian government was forced to consider alternative methods of privatization or to continue hemorrhaging assets.[18]

In response to this situation, the Bulgarian government increased the priority of management-employee buyouts (MEBOS) and introduced a mass privatization program in 1995.[19] The management-employee buyout (MEBO) was a more efficient way to privatize state assets for which there were no cash investors. After all, an enterprise's own employees would know best how to run the newly privatized enterprise. Plus, it was politically popular to redistribute the state's assets to the Bulgarian people in whose name the state had technically "owned" the means of production. Before 1995, enterprises for which there were outside buyers could not be privatized through MEBOS, effectively antagonizing the managers and employees and encouraging the internal sabotage of the enterprise. After 1995, however, MEBOS were given priority over cash bidders for the first time. The government treated MEBOS favorably in that they had to pay only 10 percent up front of the bid they submitted. After that they would pay an additional 10 percent of the total each year for ten years, interest free, which discounted the bid price significantly.

In the hierarchy of the forms of privatization most conducive to corruption, MEBOS rank second only to spontaneous privatizations.[20] MEBO privatizations were opaque by nature in that the managers and employees negotiated the terms of the deal directly with the state with little outside supervision. Furthermore, once MEBOS were given priority over other investors, the management-employee teams increasingly became fronts for money-laundering operations. It was also popularly alleged that BSP politicians used the MEBO strategy to reward friends and political allies with part of the state's assets on preferential terms.

Until 1997, 50 percent of the employees of an enterprise had to participate in a MEBO in order to bid for the enterprise. After the new democratic government took power in 1997, only 20 percent, or one-fifth, of an enterprise's employees were necessary to form a MEBO.[21] After that, multiple groups of employees could form their own MEBOS, find their own financial backing, and compete for the enterprises. The official reasoning behind this change was to create more competition for the assets in question. Many average Bulgarians and the media, however, felt that this change was another example of state corruption. The new law allowed the leaders in the Union of Democratic Forces to pay off and reward *their* supporters, some of whom had alleged links to both the Bulgarian and the Russian Mafias. Of the total 1,101 enterprises privatized by the end of 1999, just under half were concluded with MEBOS.[22]

In addition to the MEBOS, a mass-privatization scheme based on the Czechoslovak model was implemented in Bulgaria after 1994.[23] This form of privatization involved the essentially free distribution of investment "points" to all adult Bulgarians. Each Bulgarian received vouchers that could then be traded for shares in any state enterprise, or handed over to an investment fund that pooled the vouchers, made the investment decisions, and later paid dividends to its shareholders. This process was overseen by the Center for Mass Privatization, a functionally separate organization from both the Privatization Agency and the individual line ministries.[24] The state would decide what percentage of an enterprise's assets would be offered for mass privatization. The center would then hold its own auctions. Thus, at any one time after the mid-1990s state assets were being privatized through three separate procedures—market privatization, MEBO privatization, and mass privatization—overseen by three different government institutions—the line ministries, the Privatization Agency, and the Center for Mass Privatization. The confusion of the privatization process manifested itself in widespread corruption.

Since 1989, everything in Bulgaria has a price.[25] Every speeding ticket or other traffic violation can be avoided with a "special fee" paid in cash directly to the officer. An envelope of banknotes will guarantee every application for a government license or permit. Tax collectors can be paid off with only a fraction of the taxes owed. It is rumored that customs officials at the borders will allow anything and anyone into the country for a bribe. There is allegedly a price list for how much it costs to buy an article in all of Bulgaria's major newspapers. Members of Parliament openly negotiate for money with different foreign companies interested in obtaining secure votes for legislation that favors their industry. The most sensationalized instances of corruption throughout the 1990s, however, revolved around the privatization of state-owned assets, and corruption in the privatization process was a ubiquitous feature of all Bulgaria's numerous governments.

There were many problems that created multiple contexts for the unbridled pursuit of personal wealth and state rent-seeking that characterized the transition from socialism. The first such problem was one of jurisdiction. The three institutions responsible for privatization fought for the right to privatize different assets. Assets under a certain value were to be privatized by the line ministry in charge while the most valuable assets had to be turned over to the Privatization Agency. Privatization transactions were lucrative to the bureaucrats who handled them, because generous bribes and kickbacks were an expected part of the process. One of Bulgaria's most notorious politicians, a former minister of industry, was known colloquially as *Gospodin Decet Protzenta* (Mr. Ten Percent) for the 10 percent he supposedly skimmed off the top of every privatization deal.

All of this was going on at the same time that the government was dealing with an onslaught of restitution claims returning all previously nationalized property to its original owners or the owners' heirs. When the communists came into power after World War II, the government nationalized almost all of the private property in the country, including the factories of Bulgaria's industrialists. After 1944, apartments, stores, and private homes had also been nationalized along with most of the country's agricultural land.[26] When communism collapsed in 1989, giving back this property to the "rightful owners" was one of the first tasks of the postsocialist state.

A friend of Sonia's in Golden Sands was hoping to be restituted an apartment in the now-fashionable center of Varna because her grandfather had once owned a small bakery there. In Sofia, I met a twenty-three-year-old woman whose grandfather had been one of the wealthiest industrialists in Bulgaria before 1944. After the communists took power, he spent much of his life in a work camp. His granddaughter was restituted three apartments, two factories, and the largest contiguous piece of land allowed by the government for the settling of restitution claims. Also, in the capital, the Sofia Hotel was plagued with restitution claims. The American investors who bought the hotel had to involve the American ambassador before the Bulgarian government agreed to settle the outstanding claims.

These claims were made not only by individuals, but also by municipalities seeking to reclaim their "traditional" lands.[27] The verification of these claims was a difficult, time-consuming, and contested process. Many false or unverifiable claims were made. An overwhelming number of enterprises were subject to these restitution claims. According to the Ministry of Industry, by the end of 1994 there were over 12,000 claims against industrial enterprises.[28] Many of the state's tourism assets were also built on previously nationalized land and were included in restitution claims. Although there was no official number available in 2000, experts suggested that restitution claims made against tourism enterprises were numerous.[29] Troublesome as the restitution claims were for the tourism sector, the real problems would start with the privatization process.

The road to full marketization in tourism was twisted and full of obstacles and challenges. Tourism in Bulgaria was developed for the workers of world communism: ideologically the entire sector was predicated on social justice and egalitarianism. Tourism-sector employees did not consider themselves service personnel, but comrades doing their part to build the socialist future. Consequently, it was very difficult to take one of the only profitable sectors of the economy left by the end of the 1980s and transfer ownership of it to private individuals. In the end, the breakup of tourism was one of the most fiercely contested battlegrounds of the post-1989 period.

On the one hand, the decrease in traditional manufacturing exports and the dire need for hard currency gave the state many disincentives for the privatization of its profitable tourism assets. On the other hand, tourism managers and employees of Balkantourist were tired of state control after years of having their profits taken from them and redistributed elsewhere. Tourism had never been given proper recognition for its contribution to the Bulgarian economy; it had always been the "hidden export."[30] The tension this created between the state and the tourism sector informed the development of Bulgarian tourism throughout the postcommunist period.

Tourism was also one of the first sectors to see an explosion of private businesses immediately following "the changes."[31] Once the exit-visa requirement was abandoned and the general population received passports in 1990, traveling abroad quickly became a national obsession. The services of travel agents were in high demand. Furthermore, Decree 56 allowed for an unlimited number of seasonal employees, which boded well for the seasonal nature of tourism enterprises. By 1994, there were approximately 4,500 small private travel agencies in Bulgaria started by people like Prolet.[32]

The success of tourism under communism had been highly dependent on the centralized authority of the state tourism authority, Balkantourist. Centralized tourism managed to survive the first two years of transition almost unscathed. The election of the Union of Democratic Forces in 1991, however, began the erosion of Bulgarian tourism's centralized organizational structure. As minister of finance, Ivan Kostov (the future prime minister of the 1997–2001 UDF government) worked with the World Bank and the International Monetary Fund to begin the implementation of "shock therapy" in the Bulgarian economy.[33] Kostov cut tourism promotion out of the national budget altogether. The budget cuts also required the closure of many of Balkantourist's overseas representative offices. Between 1990 and 1992, Balkantourist had to close seventeen of its twenty-seven offices abroad.

It was this uncertainty about the future of Balkantourist, even from as early as 1989, that prompted Prolet to quit her job and work for the British tour operator: "At that time, I just did not know what would happen in the future. I still could not believe that communism was really finished. I expected that the Russians would come with their tanks again in Eastern Europe. They never did, and it looked for sure that Balkantourist would be broken into small pieces. I was a member of the party, and I thought maybe they would not keep me if the democrats came to power."

Ultimately, the economic transition from communism required the total restructuring of the tourism sector. After eighteen years of working in various capacities at the Council of Ministers's Committee on Tourism (COT), Nedyalka Sandalska became the interim president of the COT and was charged with the monumental task of demonopolizing Balkantourist. In accordance with Decree 56, Balkantourist was broken up into eighty-nine regionally based, state-owned tourist companies, which accounted for almost all of the state's tourism assets.

The breakup of Balkantourist separated out functionally independent units that had previously been subsumed under one economic structure. Hotels and restaurants became individual companies, as did auxiliary services such as tourism transport, tour operators and travel agencies, suppliers and retail services, and construction and engineering departments.[34] These tourism companies were later transformed into subsidiaries under the sole proprietorship of the state. Balkan Holidays, the international branch of Balkantourist, was split off from its mother company and became an independent tour operator. Only one of the tour operators was allowed to keep the name *Balkantourist*, and its managers did everything possible to decrease the value of the company so that it would be sold (hopefully to them) at a lower price. For example, the few Balkantourist offices left abroad falsely claimed that the resorts were booked and refused to accept reservations from potential tourists.[35] More complicated than the dismantling of Balkantourist's tour-operator functions, however, was the fracturing of the resort complexes.

The state believed there would be more potential investors if the large resorts were broken up. Not only would smaller pieces be easier to sell and generate more revenue for the state budget, smaller pieces also meant more privatization transactions, which equaled more opportunities for bribes. The process for deciding how resorts were to be broken up was utterly opaque. Ministry bureaucrats assigned the value of the individual pieces and could adjust the prices upwards or downwards for a fee. An investor could buy a state enterprise valued at five million dollars for two million dollars if he paid a one-million-dollar bribe. The decisions of the Privatization Agency were discretionary, and minute procedural errors could be used to disqualify bidders who were not the "favored" investors.

Another important factor affecting the demonopolization of the tourist sector was the draining of human/cultural and social capital. Almost immediately after the changes, many long-term Balkantourist employees like Prolet set up their own private firms. Using their personal knowledge of the business (cultural capital) and their contacts with tour operators and travel agents abroad (social capital), former workers easily established viable and competitive enterprises, which further reduced the value of the state's tourist organizations. In addition, newly built Mafia hotels created tough competition for the old, run-down, state-owned hotels. The explosion in private auxiliary services such as bars, restaurants, and shops also threatened the low-quality state-run equivalents.

The *Slanchev Brag* (Sunny Beach) resort presents one example of the difficulties of marketizing enterprises built under a command economic system. Sunny Beach was a huge resort with a capacity of approximately 27,000 beds in over thirty-five hotels. Ten architects, each responsible for three or four buildings, designed the whole resort.[36] Many of the structures shared utilities such as water and electricity lines, and some were physically connected to one another. The resort also centralized many services. There were centralized laundries, centralized groundskeepers, centralized reservations, and centralized marketing for the whole resort. Most importantly, stockpiled goods were kept in one centralized warehouse that supplied all of the hotels and restaurants.[37] Because of the prohibitive cost of privatizing the resort as a whole, the state decided to dissect Sunny Beach into more manageable and marketable pieces.

The solution ultimately broke the resort into ten hotel companies, one restaurant company, one sport company, one supply company, and one transport company. One holding company was responsible for the joint marketing and infrastructure.[38] Sunny Beach was restructured without any prior notice, publicity, established rules, auctions, or participation of the trade unions.[39] Authorities claimed that there was no privatization law and therefore no rule to guide them in the mid-1990s. Soon after the breakup, however, rumors abounded that the restructuring had been intentionally organized in such a secretive manner to stymie any competition from the outside. The managers of the new companies were accused of ruining the resort's infrastructure and image in order to reduce its value in hopes of acquiring the assets at more favorable prices, which, in fact, many of them later did.[40]

The loss of both physical, cultural, and social capital, the pressures of the private sector, the perceived prevalence of spontaneous privatization, and the relatively low cash value of the assets involved all ensured that tourism was one of the first sectors (after agriculture) to be targeted by the government's privatization program. But the market-privatization strategy brought forth few buyers, least of all the coveted foreign investors. Only the newly established Mafia could afford to buy the assets from the state. In the initial stages of privatization in tourism, many of the "crown jewels"—luxurious four- and five-star hotels—were indeed sold off to so-called "domestic investors." The handful of foreign investors who did venture into Bulgaria were mostly Turks and Greeks who bought hotels and then stripped them for spare parts. The combined value of the sinks, toilets, beds, lamps, and other fixtures was often higher than the value of the hotels as businesses. These foreign "investors" quickly bankrupted the hotels and left the empty shells behind as monuments of emerging capitalism gone awry.[41] Only 25 percent of the assets were in private hands by the end of 1995.[42] Speed became the new concern of the state.

Due to the failure of market-privatization strategies, many hotels were also privatized through MEBOS. These MEBO privatizations in tourism often failed because the managers and employees had little extra capital available for the much-needed renovation of hotel facilities. With the exception of MEBOS supported directly by political parties or "semilegitimate" investors, most of the new owners of the hotels made no reinvestments whatsoever, and their infrastructures continued to age and decay. At the same time, the MEBOS raised prices in order to increase their own salaries. This paradox of decreasing quality and increasing costs essentially made many of the MEBO-run hotels uncompetitive in the new tourism market, and began undermining Bulgaria's reputation as a tourist destination.[43]

Official information from the Ministry of Economy in April 2000 claims that only 31 of a total of 340 privatization deals (9 percent) it made in tourism were with manager-worker teams. There is no similar number available from the Privatization Agency that was responsible for the privatization of the most valuable assets in tourism. Experts believe, however, that MEBOS acquired the next best tourism assets after the Mafia.[44] Indeed, whole resorts such as Albena and Elenite were acquired through MEBO privatization.

Tourism was also a popular sector for both individual voucher investors and mass-privatization voucher investment funds. In 1996, 25 percent of the shares in the state's joint-stock companies of all of the major resorts were offered for mass privatization.[45] Although voucher privatization did indeed speed up the privatization process, it also opened up new avenues for corruption and criminal activity. While it is impossible to measure the extent of the practice, it seems that many investment funds were organized by Mafia affiliates and used as fronts for laundering money made by trading with Serbia during the United Nations embargo on Slobodan Milosevic.[46] Daniel Kaufmann and Paul Seigelbaum consider voucher privatization in general the least conducive to corruption.[47] But Bulgaria's experience with mass privatization met with mixed success.

One rare example of a successful voucher privatization was Albena.

The privatization of Albena, the newest and third-largest of the Black Sea resorts, combined a MEBO with vouchers. Albena was the only large summer or winter resort privatized as a whole. Unlike Sunny Beach, which had been designed by ten architects, Albena was the product of a single designer. The resort's entire infrastructure was integrated and interdependent. For instance, the water supply of the four-star Hotel Dobruja passed through the pipes of the two-star Hotel Maastrict. Many hotels shared electricity and common facilities. Breaking the resort up into smaller pieces would have required significant amounts of state investment even before the privatization process could begin.

Furthermore, Albena, like all of the seaside resorts, encompassed a wide variety of accommodations to satisfy everyone from moneyed Westerners to Bulgarian factory workers. There were the so-called "front-line" hotels right on the seaside, the less attractive "second-line" hotels in the hills above, and the bare-bones "tourist villages" further away from the seashore. The management of Albena argued that if the resort was broken up into pieces, only the most attractive hotels on the front line would be bought by investors (most likely by organized crime), while the second-line hotels would remain neglected or be left to the cash-starved MEBOS. The character of the resort as a whole would suffer, they argued, because of the vast disparity between the qualities of accommodations. This had already begun to happen in Sunny Beach and Golden Sands.

Albena's management was absolutely committed to the privatization of the resort as a whole and staunchly fought the state's attempts at "reorganization." The general director of the resort, Krassimir Stanev, was a former high-school teacher who had started in the resort as a tour guide and worked his way up the hierarchy. Stanev firmly believed that the division of Albena would cause irreparable harm to its international competitiveness. For its part, the state was skeptical that an investor could be found to purchase the resort in its entirety and believed that selling off smaller pieces would generate more revenue.

In 1995, Albena employed 7,000 people, including the seasonal workers. Both Desi and Hristo remember vividly that Stanev personally went to every hotel, restaurant, and shop in the resort to ask the workers and their families and friends to contribute their privatization vouchers to a mass-privatization fund. Over 150,000 people eventually gave their vouchers to

16. A BEACHFRONT HOTEL IN ALBENA IN 2003. PHOTO BY AUTHOR.

the fund; at that time it was the fourth-largest mass-privatization fund in Bulgaria. To obtain an even larger share of the resort, the managers and employees of Albena organized a MEBO which eventually secured French financing of approximately 50 million dollars for the completion of the cash privatization. The management acquired a solid majority of Albena's shares in 1997. Since then, the resort has remained under the centralized control of General Director Stanev, who oversees all resort operations. Despite the slightly anachronistic management structure, Albena is one of the most successful examples of tourism privatizations in Bulgaria.[48]

Privatization was the key institutional change that unequivocally revalued women's cultural capital in tourism to their benefit. During the communist period, the managerial structure of Balkantourist looked like a pyramid with a handful of politically appointed men at the very top and masses of educated technocrats beneath them doing the actual work of running the tourism sector. Women filled the majority of these technocratic positions in tourism—the middle-managerial core. After the restructuring of Balkantourist, many of these women became directors and high-level managers of the new tourist enterprises.

This is true for a variety of reasons. Firstly, privatization brought with it further duplication of managerial jobs at the high level. The centralized offices for reservations, marketing, accounting, and supplies were all closed down. They were replaced with new offices in each of the privatized hotels. In a resort with thirty hotels, the one central reservation office could be replaced with thirty reservation offices in each of the individually privatized hotels. This process created a bounty of new positions throughout the tourism industry. In most cases, it was only natural that women take up these positions, since many of them had already been responsible for coordinating these areas before the reorganization. For newly created positions such as the suddenly ubiquitous "marketing" jobs that appeared after the changes, it was quite common to promote receptionists, who generally tended to be women. Also, hotels recruited many young Bulgarians from tourism degree programs at the universities. The graduates of these programs were primarily women. Prolet explained the changes in this way:

> In the international department under Balkantourist, we worked together in one building. There were maybe just ten or fifteen people doing everything for the whole resort. My colleagues and I were responsible for the English-speaking tourists. There were two women who did all the reservation correspondence. There were two women for the French- and German-speaking guests, and one department for the former socialist countries. There were a few other accountants and a man who handled all the currency exchanges. Now, almost every hotel in Golden Sands has these positions. It is not better for the tourists, but we have high unemployment in Bulgaria, so it is good for that.

Graduates with master's and doctoral degrees in tourism economics or geography and former Balkantourist employees were also able to take advantage of new positions created in the many private travel agencies and tour operators that were sprouting throughout the country. But these opportunities were available only to the more educated women in the managerial and higher-level operational positions. At the lower levels, many maids, laundry workers, and especially groundskeepers were put out of work by the hotels' new owners' desire to "rationalize staffing patterns"—to shed the excess labor employed by most hotels in the communist period. Women in these lower-level positions were considered expendable. While some managed to relocate to other jobs within the sector, some (especially the older ones) were forced into an early "retirement." In this sense, there was in fact a population of women that was initially pushed out of the sector by downsizing. Overall, however, many new "professional" jobs were created in tourism after "the changes." This allowed educated women to make use of their newly revalued human capital. Education was a key divide between the workers who survived and those who did not.

Also beneficial to women workers was the tendency for the more experienced male workers to leave the tourism sector early in the transformation, feminizing tourism even further. These men started their own companies or took the opportunity to travel or work abroad. This created further opportunities for women to move up into higher positions previously held by men. In addition, the allocation of shares in the many enterprises privatized through management-employee buyouts was often based on position and years of experience in the tourist enterprise. Since women tended to have longer work experience and higher positions, they were eligible for more shares than their male colleagues. These initial gains that women made in tourism would be further solidified, ironically, by the emergence of the Bulgarian Mafia.

THE MAFIA AND "DOMESTIC INVESTORS"

In the late 1990s, they wore shiny tracksuits and gold chains. Even though they drove armored Mercedes and BMW sedans with tinted windows, they obeyed most traffic laws. Their girlfriends looked cheap, with micro miniskirts and see-through nylon blouses without bras. Their tastes were gaudy and unrefined; their neighborhoods looked like the Las Vegas Strip. They built houses like medieval castles and Roman temples—pillars, columns, and towers were the preferred architectural features. They went out to eat with handguns shoved into their belts. They wore big, gold Rolex watches and favored bright Versace prints for their shirts. They mostly stayed in their own circles—partying in chalga clubs or in special bars that were considered "neutral" territory. There were a few shootings now and again, but for the most part they kept to themselves.

By the early years of the twenty-first century, they were wearing business suits or black slacks and cashmere turtlenecks, gravitating toward the simpler designs of Armani and Hugo Boss. The jewelry was gone. They wore Ebel and Patek Phillipe watches. They drove black and silver armored Mercedes "Jeeps," and no longer stopped for red lights or pedestrians. Their girlfriends now favored the subtle tailoring of Max Mara and Krizia, and $300 brassieres from La Perla. They no longer carried their own weapons, but traveled with personal armies of bodyguards who waited by the door outside of the restaurants in which the bosses dined. Their houses became more modern and subdued as they moved in from the suburbs to the center of Sofia. In 2003, they had taken over almost every good restaurant and bar in Sofia. There was no neutral territory. There were shootings and bombings almost every week.

The police were afraid of them. The police who were not afraid of them were paid off. Prosecutors were shot. No one investigated. Journalists disappeared. No one investigated. Innocent bystanders were killed in the crossfire. No one investigated. There was no law. There was no justice. There was no accountability. The government claimed that they were trying to crack down on the Mafia, but they did nothing. By late 2003, the media was fanning fears that corruption and criminality would indefinitely postpone Bulgaria's entry into the European Union.

The sudden rise of various forms of criminality was yet another institutional change that impacted women's position in tourism. But these issues of corruption and criminality are political tinderboxes in discussions about the economic transition of the former Eastern bloc. Some scholars have argued that "moral decay" is the most powerful and relevant legacy left over from the communist period.[49] While cynicism, personal privilege, political patronage, and corruption were indeed characteristics of the late communist period, racketeering, extortion, and outright theft were introduced with the attempted marketization of the economy. The more than forty-five years of Marxist indoctrination about the evils of capitalism helped shape the post-1989 immorality. Bulgarians had been told for a long time that capitalism was inherently corrupt, and those who set out to gain from the collapse took this advice to heart.

The general atmosphere of greed and "moral decay" did indeed coincide with a growing tendency toward lawlessness throughout society. A handful of former nomenklatura and their families became fabulously wealthy overnight while the rest of the population watched on help-lessly as their standard of living plummeted. Income inequality increased sharply.[50] Commodity shortages and the rationing of goods forced Bulgarians to queue for basic things like cheese and milk while the nouveau riche drove around in their newly imported luxury sedans. The sudden and drastic polarization of incomes in a society formerly governed by hegemonic discourses of egalitarianism precipitated the need for protection. Since the police and the secret service were too busy carrying out their own spontaneous privatizations, there were no official state bodies responsible for the protection of the newly "created" private property. Under these circumstances, many newly unemployed former Olympic wrestlers and weightlifters found "respectable" jobs as bodyguards to the new rich.[51] At the same time, the billions of dollars of dirty money circulating through the Bulgarian economy created a ravenous demand for laundering services. Much of this money came from spontaneous privatizations and from profits earned by illegally exporting fuel, arms, and ammunitions to Yugoslavia during the Bosnian War. Those with connections to both domestic and foreign banks were only too happy to launder the money, albeit for a small fee. Thus, the Mafia, one of the most important players in the development of tourism in the post-1989 period, was born.[52]

Few have dared to study organized crime in Bulgaria.[53] For obvious reasons, those involved with the Mafia are unwilling to give information to outsiders, let alone agree to be interviewed for a "study." Even among Bulgarian scholars, there is marked reluctance to breach the silence surrounding these groups, perhaps due to fear. One well-known journalist investigating organized crime in Bulgaria had acid thrown in her face. She was permanently disfigured and the perpetrator was never caught. At the same time, every Bulgarian seems to be an "expert" on the Mafia, and the names of the mob bosses are as well known as the names of politicians, television stars, and chalga singers. In fact, Bulgarians can observe the so-called *mutri* in person in certain exclusive Sofia clubs and restaurants like Lipstick, Tequila, or Escape—if they can afford the extraordinary prices.

Three distinct groups make up the organized crime network in Bulgaria.[54] They evolved independently but eventually came to cooperate.

The first of these was made up of former athletes who saw state subsidies for sports disappear after 1989. In order to maintain their fairly privileged standard of living, they quickly organized themselves into gangs. Their initial activities included car theft, armed robbery, and especially racketeering of small, private businesses. As time went on, they became more sophisticated, establishing private security firms and "insurance" companies. Eventually, they began funneling their profits into the privatization of legitimate enterprises.

The second pillar of the Bulgarian Mafia is composed of former DS agents. After 1989, the dismantling of the secret police was one of the top priorities of the posttotalitarian governments, so many former officers lost their jobs. Furthermore, they were publicly ridiculed and hated by both the media and the general population. But these former policemen were extremely well connected and knowledgeable about both individuals and enterprises in Bulgaria, making them invaluable "consultants" during privatization procedures. Many of them also went into the "protection" business or formed their own private security companies. They, too, became interested in the privatization of state-owned enterprises. Since tourism was a sector with a relatively high level of surveillance by the secret police, it seems reasonable to believe that many of these "ex-cops" were particularly well positioned to acquire tourism assets.

The third group was made up of members of the former communist elite who used their positions to spontaneously privatize many of the state's assets with little or no consequences. The Bulgarian Socialist Party was accused of being "closely tied" to criminal syndicates. Politicians turned a blind eye while former colleagues drained state resources. One scholar claims that the BSP government forced the National Bank to "refinance" private banks, which then gave loans to a handful of businesses owned by "friends" of the prime minister in 1995.[55] By the summer of 1996, when the entire Bulgarian banking system collapsed, billions of Bulgarian leva had disappeared into the pockets of these "friends." At the same time, 80 percent of all personal savings were wiped out. Men and women who had saved all their lives were left with nothing.

The former nomenklatura eventually forged strategic alliances with the other two groups to defend their ill-gotten gains. In particular, the international embargo on Yugoslavia created unbridled opportunities for the expansion of organized crime in Bulgaria. All three pillars of the Bulgarian Mafia were doing business with Yugoslavia. Early on, profits were used to finance conspicuous consumption. Lamborghini cars were imported and luxury homes were built in newly created suburbs of Sofia, spawning the architectural style "mobster baroque." This was when the high-fashion designers from the West began opening boutiques on Vitosha Street. In a country where the average salary was about one hundred dollars a month, one could easily find *mutressi* (mobster girlfriends) with two-thousand-dollar handbags sipping espressos in cafes around Sofia. Even the wild consumption could not begin to make a dent in the enormous profits the criminal syndicates were generating. Large amounts of money ultimately needed to be laundered, so the Mafia began looking for opportunities for domestic investments.

The tourism sector held a special attraction for all three groups involved in organized crime.[56] Not only did the Mafia launder money through the privatization of existing tourism assets, they also heavily invested in the construction of new hotels, restaurants, clubs, casinos, and discos in seaside towns or established resorts. Many of these new "investors" may have perceived hotels and restaurants to be easy investments—those accustomed to luxury accommodations and restaurants would surely know how to run them. Hotels are also ideal venues for money laundering because there are few controls, and imaginary guests can generate the necessary "revenue" needed. The practice of money laundering in tourism was so widespread in Bulgaria that the Tourism curriculum at the New Bulgarian University actually offered a course called "Tourism and Money Laundering" in the 1999–2000 academic year.

Because the Mafia actually knew little about running tourism businesses, they relied heavily on former state tourism employees, many of whom were women. The Mafia also hired many former Balkantourist employees in their newly built hotels. What otherwise could have been a massive deprofessionalization of the sector turned out to be a relatively mild rearranging of key personnel at the managerial and higher operational levels. This aspect of the Mafia's involvement in tourism helped women hang onto their jobs and in many cases even created new jobs for them.

The Mafia was not the only source of so-called "new blood" flowing into tourism. There were also legitimate domestic capitalists who had realized profits from their private businesses. Under communism, it was common practice for enterprises to invest their "profits" into *pochivni stanzii* (holiday houses) for their employees. Successful domestic entrepreneurs continued the practice and took advantage of the remarkably low prices of the state's tourism assets. Although many of the hotels were in disrepair by Western standards, they required very small capital investments to make them suitable as vacation homes to the new Bulgarian bourgeoisie and their workers. Even if they were used as holiday houses, these hotels usually remained open to the public, and again required the expertise of the existing employees, mainly Bulgarian women.

A final inflow of tourism outsiders into the sector came from the mass-privatization investment funds. When these privatization funds invested in tourism assets, the managers of the fund would often become the de facto managers of a hotel. Despite the negative effects of the Mafia, at least they had money to invest in the renovations of the hotels. The managers of the investment funds rarely invested anything in the hotels, downsized staffs ruthlessly, and were content to suck whatever profits they could get while the hotels fell further into dilapidation. They held onto these assets, even if they were loss making, in the hopes that foreign investors would soon "discover" Bulgaria. In fact, a widespread belief that foreign investors were interested in Bulgarian tourism (but were merely waiting for the Balkans to "stabilize") may have been another reason why so many nonprofessionals flooded into the sector. They all hoped to buy low and sell high.

BULGARIA AND FOREIGN INVESTMENT

Another institutional change that happened after 1989 was the arrival of foreign investors, and the legislative changes made to accommodate them. Unlike Hungary, Poland, and the Czech Republic, Bulgaria has had comparatively small inflows of foreign direct investment (FDI) from the West.[57] By the end of 1999, foreign investors had contributed only a total of 2.8 billion dollars to the Bulgarian economy,[58] compared, for instance, to the Polish economy, which attracted about 40 billion dollars in the same period.[59] Foreign investors' disinterest may partly be attributed to the conflicts in the former Yugoslavia and a general perception of instability in the region.[60] A further explanation may be that the new Union of Democratic Forces government was uninterested in seeing tourism assets privatized by outsiders. The socialists had already pillaged much of Bulgaria's industry, and the UDF wanted tourism for itself and its political allies. There was also a strong bias against Turkish investors who showed early interest in tourism and purchased one of the more modern hotels in Sofia. For historical reasons the Bulgarians were keen to see that its hotels and resorts stayed out of Turkish hands.[61] The Privatization Agency was known to disqualify otherwise generous Turkish bids for small clerical errors and fundamentally inconsequential procedural mix-ups. There were also many problems with the privatization procedure. The privatization documentation was rarely translated into foreign languages. Finally, there was little in the way of legislation regarding the tourism sector. All of these factors forced the Bulgarian government to rethink its position on tourism in order to attract the much-coveted foreign investors. As the privatization process continued, the UDF government began to take steps to get tourism back on the right track.[62]

New laws and ordinances on tourism were drafted to help facilitate growth in the sector, not only for privatized state enterprises but also for the rapidly expanding small- and medium-sized enterprises in tourism. The Law on Tourism went into effect in June of 1998, and two ordinances on the licensing of tourist activities and the classification of tourist objects followed two months later. This new legislative framework was an ambitious attempt to codify new standards for the tourism sector. Under this new law, more than 2,500 licenses were issued by the end of 1999 including those to 243 hotel owners and 109 family hotel owners.[63]

These laws formed an essential impetus for the entrance of private businesses into the tourism sector. In an economy often crippled by its constantly shifting legislative framework for business and investment, the Law on Tourism was very resilient in its ability to regulate economic activity in the sector.[64] Many small hotels sprang up around the country, catering to a much wider variety of tastes and accommodation needs. Issues of continuing corruption aside, the laws provided a set of guidelines for standardizing the quality of hotels and restaurants throughout the country as well as setting specific standards for the educational experience of the managers. Although sometimes overly bureaucratic, the clearly set-out regulations made tourism one of the easier sectors in which to do business in Bulgaria for both locals and foreigners.

In cases where the government privatized hotels to companies and individuals without experience in tourism, especially the Mafia, these new laws indirectly protected women in managerial positions. Early in the privatization process, many Mafia investors were primarily concerned with money laundering and left most of the hotel staff in place. They had little interest in actually running profitable enterprises. As privatization proceeded, however, many more Mafiosi and other tourism nonprofessionals bought up tourism assets. The ordinance of the categorization of tourist objects placed restrictions on who could be the manager of a hotel in order to stop the new owners from placing their new hotels in the hands of inexperienced friends, family members, or "business associates." Promulgated in early 1998, the ordinance required that the manager of any hotel wishing to get or maintain a four- or five-star rating have a university degree in tourism geography or economics and speak two or more foreign languages. Managers of three-star hotels had to have a university or technical college degree in tourism and speak at least one foreign language. Similar educational requirements were explicitly laid out for all key positions in tourism from the receptionists to the maids. These requirements were also kept in the new Law on Tourism adopted in October 2002. This law regarding the mandatory education of employees effectively legislated that only those with the proper cultural capital could work in tourism.

These laws on categorization forced many of the new owners to keep the existing managers and employees in place even after the privatization. Newly built hotels wishing to receive a four- or five-star rating had to hire university graduates from tourism programs, again mostly women. Furthermore, most privatization contracts stipulated that the employees of the privatized enterprise should continue to be employed for a minimum period of time following the transaction—usually around three years. In response to the institutional changes taking place throughout the economy, the government legislated measures not only to protect workers, but also to ensure the continued viability of successful sectors of the economy. Although it was not the government's intent to preserve women's employment in the sector, these laws and contract stipulations essentially guaranteed that women would dominate the tourism sector since few men had the experience or educational qualifications to fill the positions.

In 1999, for the first time in seven years, tourism was also allocated funds for national promotion in order to help attract foreign investment. The new UDF government allocated 3.5 million leva (about 1.94 million dollars) to spend on an ambitious marketing campaign. Although not a very large amount of money, when you consider Bulgaria's fiscal constraints these funds served as an important signal that the government was serious about supporting the tourism sector once again. Furthermore, the Bulgarian government was successful in brokering international assistance to support tourism development within the country. As of July 2000, the British, Swiss, German, Spanish, and American governments had bilateral projects supporting the development of the tourism sector.

In December 1999, under increasing accusations of corruption, the prime minister reshuffled the ministries to purge the upper ranks of politicians commonly accused of wrongdoing. The privatization procedure for the Golden Sands management company was cancelled immediately under suspicion of corruption. One of the first acts of a newly appointed minister of economy was to declare that Golden Sands would be slotted for strategic privatization. This meant that only cash bids payable in full at the time of sale would be considered. Furthermore, bidders would have to disclose the source of their funds—effectively cutting the Mafia out of the procedure. The result was a successful bid for a controlling share of the Golden Sands holding company by the German tour operator Neckermann, bringing the sought-after foreign direct investment into the country. Foreign ownership marked the beginning of a turnaround in the way tourism assets were privatized. Other foreign investors finally began to take interest.

In addition to Neckermann, international tour operators such as Germany's TUI and ITS and Spain's RIU invested heavily on the Black Sea coast. The year 2001 also saw the opening of a Hilton Hotel in Sofia backed with IFC guarantees and a Radisson SAS hotel majority-owned by American capital. By the end of 1999, tourism was the fourth-largest sector for foreign direct investment after the rather ambiguous categories of "industry," "trade" and "finance." There were 142.83 million dollars of foreign direct investment in tourism that accounted for 5.14 percent of the total volume of all foreign investment.[65] In the year 2000, foreign investment in hotels and restaurants totaled an additional 20.8 million dollars.[66]

Foreign investors, too, demonstrated a strong preference for the female managers and employees who had been employed in tourism before 1989 because these women (and a few men) were much more comfortable dealing with foreigners. Expatriate stereotypes about Bulgarian men and women may have also given women a considerable edge in negotiating positions with international investors. Almost all of the foreign-owned or managed hotels I visited were staffed primarily with women. One Dutch manager told me directly, "If I could only hire Bulgarian women, I would. They are much better workers than Bulgarian men."

Most resident expatriate businesspeople are men, and they may simply prefer to work with women as Bulgarian men are often considered to be both hostile and sly. Whatever the reason, it is certainly not because women are cheaper employees. On the contrary, the generous maternity leaves still guaranteed by Bulgarian law make women considerably more expensive than male employees. That women employees still dominate the management and staff of these hotels is a testament to the strong preference foreigners have for women, despite the greater indirect expenses involved in hiring them.

Between 2000 and 2003, despite September 11th and SARS, the number of tourists traveling to Bulgaria continued to increase. About 3 million foreign tourists visited Bulgaria in 2002, an 8.6 percent increase in comparison with 2001.[67] Revenues from international tourism in 2002 grew by 11 percent compared to the revenues for 2001.[68] After the change in government in 2001, tourism once again became a focus of renewed attention, particularly when a former Albena employee, Lydia Shuleva, became minister of economy and deputy prime minister in 2003. On 1 October 2002, the government of Simeon Saxecoburgotski passed a new Law on Tourism and there was talk of giving Bulgaria's resorts special municipal status in the summer of 2003. At that time, the tourism sector was still expanding, and overbooking was one of the most serious problems of the hotels on the Black Sea in the summer. The continued expansion of tourism helped to generate employment in an otherwise dismal job market. Again, the majority of the beneficiaries were women with revalued cultural capital from the socialist period.

TOURISM AND THE THIRD SECTOR

The final institutional change that occurred in Bulgaria after 1989 was the sudden emergence of what was called "civil society" or the "third sector."[69] In tourism, all sorts of nongovernmental and "professional" associations were formed to promote Bulgaria as a tourist destination or to simply further the business interests of their members: the Bulgarian Association of Travel Agents (BATA); the Bulgarian Association for Alternative Tourism (BAAT); the Bulgarian Association of Hoteliers and Restaurateurs; the Bulgarian Tourism Chamber, etc. Most of these organizations were based in Sofia, and actively lobbied the government on behalf of the tourism industry. Since most of the members of these associations were tourism professionals, most of the members were women. It was, in fact, these organizations that pressured the Bulgarian government to pass the legislation that required educational standards for hotel employees, and thereby preserved the jobs of many women.

There were also countless regional-development organizations set up throughout the country in order to promote rural tourism, cultural tourism, ecotourism, hunting tourism, and other such niche tourist markets. These organizations often received funding from foreign bilateral aid agencies looking to promote local business initiatives. These alternative forms of tourism usually relied on guesthouses rather than traditional hotels. Many Bulgarian families won small grants to convert their homes into little bed and breakfasts, and it was usually the women in the family who were in charge of the hospitality when the visitors (if any) arrived seeking a night's shelter. There were also small tourist information offices set up in various towns and villages. These created employment for one or two locals with foreign-language training, again usually women.

These professional associations and regional-development initiatives, however, received far less funding and national attention than the many women's organizations that appeared throughout the 1990s, first in Sofia and then throughout Bulgaria. These organizations were set up with the explicit purpose to help Bulgarian women during the transition process:

to advocate for their rights and take on important gender issues. In 1998, for instance, when the USAID Democracy Network II program distributed the funding for civil-society development about a third of all of the organizations funded were women's organizations or organizations with a large gender component in their proposals. Furthermore, the availability of international funding from such international feminist organizations such as the Global Fund for Women, UNIFEM, Mamma Cash, etc., meant that groups of women or even individuals could readily form organizations for the express purpose of getting a grant. But women's NGOs or other organizations advocating for any kind of "feminist" agenda were not always met with open arms in Bulgaria.

I once made the mistake of asking Desi if she considered herself a feminist. She wrinkled her nose at me, almost sneering at the word. "Of course not," she said.

"Why not?" I asked.

She shook her head. "I live with three men, and I love each one of them. How could I be a feminist?"

"What does that have to do with it?"

"Feminists hate men."

"Feminists don't hate men," I explained.

"Of course they do. Look at all those articles in the newspaper by those feminist groups in Sofia. Always talking about men beating up their wives or bothering women."

"But it does happen . . ." I started.

"Sure, there are a few bad men, and there are a few bad women, too. Bulgarian women are strong, and Bulgarian men and women are equal. I don't know how it is in your country, but it's not like that here. Those women who write those reports just hate men."

Desi was referring to a recent spate of media coverage publicizing the findings of a controversial report that had been prepared by a feminist NGO in Sofia together with an American NGO (the Minnesota Advocates for Human Rights) with funding from the United States government.[70] The report looked at sexual discrimination and sexual harassment in the Bulgarian workplace and concluded that these were "serious and widespread problems in Bulgaria which are virtually ignored by employers, labor unions, and the Bulgarian Government."[71] The report produced a litany of complaints about how Bulgarian women were being discriminated against in hiring decisions, how they were being hired in lower positions and for less money than men, and how women candidates for jobs were judged on their age and appearance. Furthermore, the report discussed the "hostile work environment" created by Bulgarian men: the unwelcome sexual innuendo that permeated the workplace, the unwanted compliments that women received about their looks, the prevalence of sexual activity both between colleagues and between "superiors and subordinates," and the ubiquity of pornographic photos on public display. Finally, the report concluded that because Bulgarian women have such a hard time finding formal employment, they have no choice but to put up with the rampant sexism of the workplace.

Desi and her colleagues in Albena were angry when articles about the report started appearing in the newspaper. First, they felt that the description of the employment situation for women was inaccurate. In their own resort, fourteen of the sixteen hotel managers were women, and many of them knew that they earned more money than their husbands or male colleagues. From their own experience as well they felt that it was easier for women to find work in the resorts than it was for men. As for all the sexual "harassment" in the workplace, Desi felt it was ridiculous to call this a problem. In Bulgaria, it is a very common practice to have romantic relationships with people at work. Desi had met her own husband in the resort, as had many of her colleagues. And she did not understand how any woman could be offended by a man paying her a compliment on her appearance. Or how seeing a picture of a naked woman was hostile.

"They make it sound like we are intruders at work, like we don't belong here," Desi said. "But women have always worked in Bulgaria. We have no problems working with men, and men have no problems working with us. We have always worked together. Why is it suddenly a problem for women to be working with men?"

Desi's frustration with the report was echoed by many women I spoke with in the resorts, and also by professional Bulgarian women working in Sofia. While they agreed that there were some unpleasant men in positions of power, the idea that Bulgarian women were in a weaker position in the workplace did not match their own experiences. I had read a copy of the full report, and I, too, felt that its findings were insensitive to the culturally specific gender relations between men and women in Bulgaria. I understood how easily an American (with our relatively puritanical attitudes toward sex) could make these mistakes, particularly if they had written the report after staying in the country for only a few weeks. What intrigued me was that the study was coauthored by Bulgarian women working in two prominent women's NGOs in Sofia.

These same NGOs had also produced an earlier report on domestic violence in Bulgaria.[72] That report was also written in collaboration with the Minnesota Advocates and funded by the u.s. government. It had received a similarly hostile reception by many Bulgarian women. Again the report had generalized about the prevalence of violence against women, painting men as the perpetrators and women as the victims. And while there certainly was domestic violence in Bulgaria, the way the report framed men and women on opposite sides of the issue was very foreign to Bulgarian women raised under socialism.

These contradictions intrigued me, and I decided to interview the women in the NGOs that had produced the two reports. Both of the NGOs had offices in the center of the capital. All of the women I met spoke perfect English. When I asked them why they had chosen to write on these topics, I was told that they had no part in the decision. The Minnesota Advocates for Human Rights had received funding to produce the reports for a variety of postsocialist countries that included Bulgaria. In fact, the concept of sexual harassment did not even exist in the country before 1989. The local NGOs were subcontractors of the American NGO, and the Bulgarian women had been given specific guidelines about what constituted sexual harassment, how to look for it, and how to document it.

The four women I interviewed were very friendly, and thoroughly explained how they had conducted their research and reached their conclusions. Although none of the women ever said it directly, I got the impression that they each felt that they had no choice but to report the findings that the Americans wanted to hear. And in each of our conversations, the researchers were far more concerned about securing future subcontracts from American NGOs than they were about discussing domestic violence or sexual harassment in Bulgaria.

When I told them about my research in tourism and how well Bulgarian women were doing in the sector, they were not surprised. They acknowledged that Bulgarian women were very educated and flexible. They even discussed with me the possibility of doing a project with women in tourism. Nonetheless, I left their offices loaded down with armfuls of reports and working papers on the plight of Bulgarian women: their poverty, their inability to get and keep jobs, and their general incompatibility with free-market capitalism.

Of course, I brought all of the reports back to the resorts and pored over them with different women working in tourism. Almost all of them disagreed with the way the information was presented because they felt it undermined their own successes. And it was not only Desi who was hostile to the "feminists" in Sofia. More than half of the women I spoke with regarded the reports as a form of Western propaganda. When so many institutional changes had coincidentally conspired to solidify their dominance of the tourism sector, it was ironic that the Bulgarian women employed in tourism intuitively distrusted the one new institution deliberately set up to help them: the women's NGOS.

In a small living/conference room in the offices of a women's organization in Varna, Prolet has been invited to address a group of twelve women interested in starting their own businesses. The meeting has been put together by the Women's NGO with the funding of the European Union. They are giving each of the women a free lunch and a small stipend for their attendance. The NGO is paying Prolet a 100-leva speaker's fee. She has never been paid to speak before, and is quite nervous. I offered to tag along. She gladly accepted. As she is talking, I sit in the back of the room taking notes.

Prolet is wearing a conservative skirt suit, pale beige nylons, and low pumps. The two women from the NGO are also dressed in suits. One of them has her hair pulled up and wears a strand of white "pearls" and matching pearl-like earrings. The other woman has very short dark hair and wears no jewelry. The two women sit together on a low couch against the room's right wall. Prolet is sitting on a padded swivel chair in the middle of the room facing the rest of the women, who squirm on the hard plastic seats of folding chairs. She crosses her legs at the ankle as she recounts the story of her own success.

Prolet spends about half an hour outlining each detail of how she made the contacts that she ultimately used to start her tour-operating company. She then takes about fifteen minutes to talk about how to find an office, where to buy office supplies, how to hire employees and pay all of their salaries and insurances, how to set up a Web site, and how to deal with getting the licenses and permits necessary to operate legally. She finishes by explaining in brief why she decided to sell the business in the end. "It got to be too much work for me. Always worrying and working terribly long hours."

Prolet folds her hands in her lap. The woman who is running the meeting thanks her and asks the audience if they have any questions. The women jostle in their chairs, looking at each other. Thirty seconds pass.

The woman from the NGO asks Prolet if her salary was sufficient to cover all of her basic needs after she started her own business.

"Not at first, but certainly after the first year. I felt like I was making a very good salary after that."

Thirty more seconds pass.

A woman in the back of the room stands up.

"You were working in Golden Sands before 'the changes,' and you said you had a lot of connections. Do you think you could have started your business without connections?"

"No. The connections were very important," Prolet replies.

"Do you think it is possible for a woman like me to start a business without any connections?"

There is a long pause. The two NGO women frown. Prolet shakes her head.

"No," she says, "I don't think so."

A murmur spreads through the room. The NGO woman with the short hair says that everyone has some connections that they can use. Prolet sits quietly. One woman near me mumbles to another woman that the workshop was a waste of their time.

The other woman says, "I've had enough workshops. I want work."

The organizers decide that it is time to serve lunch.

5

Feminism-by-Design

Just two blocks from Vitosha Street in downtown Sofia are the offices and information center of one of the premier women's NGOs in Bulgaria. The building itself is rather humble; the stairwell is dirty and worn. I walk up four flights of stairs because there is no elevator. The office, like most in Bulgaria, is a converted apartment. The lobby/library area is the information center—a relatively large room with two modern couches and a low coffee table cluttered with brochures, magazines, and ashtrays. On one wall of the room is a floor-to-ceiling bookshelf filled with binders and books in Bulgarian, German, and English about women's issues. Against the other wall, there is an antique dining table now used as a conference table. It is also covered with papers, folders, ashtrays, lighters, and several open packs of different brands of local cigarettes. The five large windows allow the room to fill with natural light. UNIFEM charts on the status of the world's women and other women's empowerment posters provide the décor. There is an old photocopy machine in one corner.

The director's office is large, with two wide windows looking out onto the street. A kidney-shaped desk sits in the middle of the room. The desk is covered with files, newspapers, and magazines. There is a catalogue from an office supply store and a stand-up desk calendar from the British Know-How Fund. Pictures of the director's family are taped around the frame of the monitor of her desktop computer. The walls are bare save for a white board listing the names of different international organizations and what I assume are application deadlines. Against three of the walls are bookshelves jammed full of magazine files with labels written in English: "Trafficking," "Domestic Violence," "Sexual Assault," "Poverty," and so on.

The director is an attractive Bulgarian woman in her early forties with dark, curly, shoulder-length hair. She wears beaded chandelier earrings that swing as she talks. She sits across from me behind her desk gesticulating with an ultrathin cigarette. For an hour, I listen as she explains all of the projects that her organization has done in the past and how successful they have been at improving the lives of women in Bulgaria. She has complained about the ungrateful female politicians in Parliament who do not promote a feminist legal agenda and resist all lobbying attempts by her organization. When I ask about her "constituencies," she admits that Bulgarian women do not care about women's issues. "After forty-five years of 'emancipation,' women have had enough," she says. "Women now do not care about gender issues. They are too tired to care about these things. We have to care for them."

"The strength of the organization," she continues, "is networking. We belong to many networks. It is one of our main programs after the information center. We have created a large network of NGOs within Bulgaria and we belong to four international networks working on gender issues."

She proceeds to tell me about a presentation that she recently gave on Bulgarian women's issues in Helsinki. I ask her if she was in Beijing in 1995 for the World Conference on Women, and she tells me she was there. She has also been to Croatia, Poland, the Ukraine, the Netherlands, Belgium, Austria, Germany, and the United States for different gender-related conferences and trainings. Foreign donors funded all of the costs for her and a colleague to represent Bulgaria in these forums.

She spends a long time talking about the importance of forging international networks between women and women's organizations. Although she knows that I am an academic, I feel as if she believes that I am a possible source of future funding. Her presentation seems too rehearsed; her Western feminist jargon is too precise. She knows all of the right buzzwords and speaks perfect English with flawless political correctness. I feel that she is trying hard to convince me that her organization's lobbying and training activities are valuable and important. Throughout her monologue, she sprinkles comments about the difficulty of obtaining funding.

"DemNet is already gone, and USAID is graduating Bulgaria by 2006.

Many of the individual European countries are also deferring to the EU, but the EU funding has not quite started yet. These next few years will be very hard for us."

"What about funding from Bulgarian sources?" I ask.

"There is no culture of charity among Bulgarians anymore. The communists took it out of us. Even if there was, people are too poor to make donations to NGOs. As far as the business sector is concerned, the new law on NGOs gives no financial incentives for corporations to donate to us, no tax breaks. The government will not give us anything. Our only hope is the international organizations, but many of them are leaving now."

She begins to talk briefly about the political situation and the problem of corruption. I realize then that she has not quite understood how long I have been living in the country, and that I am married to a Bulgarian. Switching to Bulgarian, I give her several examples of the corruption I saw in the tourist resorts and drop the names of several high-profile politicians that I have interviewed. I also slip something into the conversation about my in-laws and the shrinking value of their pensions, and then I complain about the rising electricity prices in Sofia.

Slowly, the director's demeanor starts to change. She, too, switches to Bulgarian and uses English only for words that do not have direct translations—*gender*, *advocacy*, *lobbying*, and so forth—or when I cannot remember a word in Bulgarian. At this point, I pull out my secret weapon: Bulgarian cigarettes. I ask her for a light, and she smiles.

"Very few of you Americans smoke," she says.

Americans have the reputation of being openly hostile to cigarettes. Most Bulgarians, both men and women, smoke everywhere and at all times. American businessmen, advisors, and consultants have been known to ask complete strangers to put out their cigarettes in public places such as bars and restaurants where they are allowed to smoke. The reputation of American intolerance of smoking is such that many locals intentionally smoke twice as many cigarettes in the company of Americans just because they can. To smoke as an American in Sofia immediately marks me as different from the rest of my compatriots.

Smoking Bulgarian cigarettes, however, is always the real clincher. Imported cigarettes cost about four times more than their domestic equivalents. Most Bulgarians who can afford to buy the imported cigarettes (mostly American and French brands) do so as an act of conspicuous consumption. A handful of the intelligentsia smoke local cigarettes, not only because they are cheaper, but because of a sense of national pride. Cigarette production is one of the few remaining viable "industries" left in the country. When I smoke these cigarettes (and I always make sure I leave the pack on the table so that everyone can see that they are Bulgarian) I have noticed that people start talking to me more freely.

"What do you see as the biggest problem facing women today?" I ask, exhaling a lungful of smoke.

Without a beat, she answers, "Unemployment."

"Isn't that a problem for everyone?" I say.

"Yes, for both men and women. But single mothers, women between the age of eighteen and twenty-five, and widows are the most badly affected by unemployment today. This situation is really bad."

I pause and think back on all of the projects that her organization has been doing for the last seven years. "You don't have any projects that are dealing with unemployment?"

"No," she says.

A long moment of silence passes between us as we smoke our cigarettes. She taps hers on the rim of the ashtray, sighing.

"Nobody will fund projects for unemployment. Maybe there are some workshops and trainings for starting your own business, but the truth is that most small businesses fail after one or two months. The women are worse off after trying to start the business, because they are often in debt. I have heard of women who had to sell their apartments to pay for the loan they took to start their small businesses. Then they have no job and no home. This is not a solution. A woman is better off playing the lottery than she is trying to start a small business in this country."

"But if this is the biggest problem for women in Bulgaria, and I agree with you that it is, then somebody must be willing to fund projects dealing with unemployment," I say.

The director laughs at me, shaking her head. Her chandelier earrings swing back and forth. She crushes out her cigarette. She switches back to English.

"Look, Kristen," she says, "Bulgaria needs foreign direct investment if we are going to develop out of this transition mess. I hate that word *transition*, because it does not mean anything if you are transitioning for fifteen years. This is not transition anymore. It is just a mess. Bulgaria's competitive advantage with America and the European Union is our cheap, educated labor force. High unemployment keeps wages down and makes us more attractive to foreign investors. Neither the EU nor the U.S. has any desire to see less unemployment here, because they do not want to see wages rise."

Her telephone rings.

"Excuse me," she says, picking it up.

I stare at her for a long time. She is right, of course, but I cannot believe that she would come out and say it so bluntly. She has obviously thought about this problem before. It does not seem to trouble her too much, and she seems surprised that I do not know how these things work. I glance up at the white board of international organizations that she is applying to for funding and see that they are all in the West.

Soon after, we stand to say good-bye. I thank her for her time and promise that I will send her some articles and materials from the United States for the information center. She shakes my hand and gives me a stack of brochures about her organization in English for me to pass around to my colleagues. As I turn to leave, she calls after me. "You forgot these." She hands me my cigarettes, smiling. In English, she says, "We do the best we can."

It was this conversation that made clear to me the disconnect between the lives of women like Desi, Dora, Gergana, Sonia, and Prolet in the tourism sector and the kinds of advocacy projects being pursued by the women's NGOs in Sofia. My extended case study of women in tourism had convinced me that not all women had been negatively affected by the transition to capitalism. Bulgarian tourism under communism created a labor force with high levels of general education, extended work experience with Westerners, and fluency in multiple foreign languages. Anyone with this package of cultural capital would have had the tools to adapt to the institutional changes that followed 1989. But because women dominated and continue to dominate work in the tourism sector, it is largely women who have this unique set of valuable skills. Thus, some women were in a better position to thrive in a market economy relative to men. And if I accept the arguments of Gil Eyal, Ivan Szelenyi, and Ellen Townsley in *Making Capitalism without Capitalists* and recognize that the emerging middle class in Bulgaria is a "cultural bourgeoisie" and not an economic or political one, then women are in an even better position in the post-socialist economy because of the particular way the communist state gendered this distribution of cultural capital.

On the other hand, the phone call I received from Svetla one afternoon forced me to rethink my entire argument. I had spoken to her right after she took the entrance exam, and she told me that she thought she had done very well. She felt that all of her studying in French had paid off. Although it would be several weeks before they posted the results, Svetla started planning for the university. Knowing how hard she had worked, I too was confident for her. When she finally called me, I was completely caught off guard.

The crushing news that Svetla did not get a high enough score on her exam to get a scholarship made me realize that if women in tourism are succeeding due to the revaluation of cultural capital they gained under communism, then the next generation of women like Svetla will not have the same advantages. If, despite their talent and motivation, they cannot get the right education and training, they will fall victims to the free-market system and be unable to find work. Although Svetla still got a place in the tourism program, she does not know how she can pay for it. Svetla is devastated by her failure. She was hiccupping with despair when she called to give me the news.

I also realized that the position of women already employed in tourism was not guaranteed. One change in the law requiring a university education for high-level tourism jobs could disrupt women's tradition-ally dominant position in the sector. Therefore, despite their past successes, women in tourism still do need advocates. They need to be organized in some way, both to protect their own status and also to ensure that educational opportunities are available to all young women, not only those who can afford them. If not, tourism and other prestigious sectors in the Bulgarian economy will become places where only those who are already privileged—both men and women—can find jobs, because they have the resources to invest in their own cultural capital.

This change is already starting to happen in Bulgaria with the emergence of private tourism colleges such as the Bulgarian-Dutch International College in Albena, which offers degrees in "Hotel Management," "Marketing and Management of Tourism," and "Business Administration and Tourism." This college allows the students to actually live in the resort for three years, and gives them organized opportunities to do tourism internships in Western Europe. Alumni from the college have gone on to work for an impressive list of companies, including both international hotel chains and local Black Sea resorts. But with fees of 2,300 euros per year (about $2,800) for Bulgarian nationals and almost no scholarships available, degrees from the International College mostly go to the sons and daughters of Bulgaria's small class of new rich.

As the socialist period fades even further into the past and the generation of women that came of age under the old system slowly begins to retire, there will be fewer and fewer women in high managerial positions to resist the resurgence of local patriarchal discourse convincing younger women that they should not work. Future generations of Bulgarian women are very vulnerable to the gender disparities that inevitably seem to accompany capitalism. Continued levels of high male unemployment in the tourist regions will increase the number of men competing for jobs in what promises to be one of the most dynamic sectors of the economy. The shrinking of Bulgaria's social safety net will make it harder for women to combine work and family, and the possibility of growing wage discrimination in favor of men will make it more "economically rational" for women to leave the labor force when parents, children, or relatives need looking after. Furthermore, if fewer and fewer women are able to get the education and cultural capital that will help them to get good jobs, then the stereotype that women are less suited to capitalism will slowly be reinforced as the professions increasingly become dominated by Bulgarian men. And if these popular discourses convince Bulgarians that women are somehow biologically less suited to free-market competition, some parents will eventually begin to invest their scarce economic capital into the education of their sons before that of their daughters, since boys are supposedly more likely to succeed.

Because tourism employs so many Bulgarian women, it is a sector where one would expect women to be actively organizing to protect and increase their positions. But they are not. And despite the fact that so many women in tourism are suspicious of Western feminism, they do need advocates, and women's NGOs could play a key role in the future of organizing, but not in the way that many of them currently operate. In 2002, tourism directly or indirectly employed around 18 percent of the total female labor force in Bulgaria, and most women's NGOs completely ignored the successes of women in the sector. On the one hand, it could be that these women's organizations did not really know the importance of tourism to Bulgarian women's employment, and perpetuated the discourse of Bulgarian women's inherent disadvantages out of ignorance. On the other hand, perhaps they were forced to ignore how well educated Bulgarian women were doing in order to write grants to Western organizations which automatically assumed that all Bulgarian women were relatively worse off than Bulgarian men. It is this second possibility that is the most frustrating to working Bulgarian women.

Much has been written on NGOs in the postsocialist context, and the focus of my research has not been on civil society.[1] I did, however, work with and observe women's NGOs in Bulgaria as I was doing my research, and I knew that NGOs in general were not held in very high esteem by ordinary Bulgarians.[2] Since I studied Bulgarian women I could not ignore the steady stream of documents and reports produced by these NGOs and the reactions of the women working in the tourism sector. Like the sexual harassment report discussed in the previous chapter, statistics and "facts" about women were regularly published in the national media, and were often the subject of both fierce and friendly debates. So many women I knew in Bulgaria rejected the idea that "Bulgarian women" as a whole had unique, gender-based problems in the market economy. Instead, many felt that women were better suited to emerging capitalism because they had the right skills and were more flexible than their male colleagues in adapting to changes. In this conclusion, I want to examine three broad but interrelated ideas: the larger implications of these disparities between women, the role of revalued cultural capital after socialism outside of the tourism sector, and how importing Western ideas of gender oppression to former socialist countries might actually increase women's economic marginalization in a newly liberalized labor market.

In the late 1990s, the Sheraton Hotel in Sofia was the epicenter of foreign consultants and "experts" sent from the West to assist Bulgaria through its period of economic transition. This was before Hilton and Radisson SAS came to Sofia, and the uber-luxurious Sheraton represented the only "decent" accommodation available. The hotel actually shares a building with the offices of the Bulgarian president; its tall ceilings towering over marble columns and floors are palatial. On the velvet upholstered chairs in the lobby or in the Las Vegas–style Capital Bar and Diner, the experts would meet to share observations about the country and compare their strategies for the liberalization of the Bulgarian economy.

These consultants in the Sheraton were part of a much larger phenomenon. After the unexpected collapse of communism in 1989, billions of dollars in aid and assistance flowed from the United States and Western Europe into the former Eastern bloc. These men and women in the Sheraton were part of an army of advisors that descended into capital cities to fashion the foundations of capitalism and liberal democracy from scratch.[3] These consultants brought with them the ideological "tool kits" of capitalism—thorough, but untested blueprints for how to "transition" these societies away from communism. The proper institutions and legal frameworks needed to be put in place in order to secure the way for the eager foreign "investors" who would soon start carving up the spoils of socialism's demise. This was "capitalism-by-design" at its very best.

During this same period, many Western feminists and women's organizations also jumped on the aid bandwagon. The money was abundant. Women's organizations undertook studies and prepared reports to show that women were being disproportionately harmed by the economic transition from communism. The majority of Western scholars who wrote about gender and economic transformation (on both sides of the political spectrum) painted a very dark picture of women's position in the emerging postsocialist societies.[4] They often cited gender-disaggregated national statistics from which they could draw the easy conclusion that all women in Bulgaria were worse off compared to all men.

Although well intentioned, these statistics distorted the situation of women in several different ways. First, under communism and in the early years of postcommunism, statistics were rarely disaggregated by gender. Once the National Statistical Institute began issuing the numbers for men and women separately, it was impossible to know whether the situation of women was actually getting worse, or whether the statistics were merely showing phenomena that had existed before the transition but never been studied. Second, because the statistics looked at women as a whole, the dramatic class differences emerging between women were erased by the use of averages that showed them to be more vulnerable to income erosion and unemployment. Finally, women in Bulgaria, as elsewhere in the postsocialist world, were more likely to be involved in the informal sector of the economy.[5] Women's income and employment was much less likely to show up in the official statistics, thus making it appear that women had been more negatively affected than men. Relying on these numbers alone would paint a very dark picture of the women's position in postsocialist society.

Many Western feminist activists and NGOs really discovered the "plight" of their Eastern sisters after the United Nations conference on women was held in Beijing in 1995. Bulgarian women also became aware of the vast resources commanded by the international feminist community. Coalitions were formed between Eastern and Western women to help the Eastern women manage the transition. The capitalism-by-design model guided the solutions to the "problems" of Eastern European women. Each country was encouraged to reinvent its "national machinery" to deal with women's issues; the sections and oversight committees were formed, but they were rarely effective because transitioning countries had more pressing concerns, and women's issues were considered a low priority by postsocialist governments. The other "institutions" of Western feminism—the women's advocacy groups, the gender think tanks, the battered women's shelters, the rape crisis hotlines, the women's resource centers—began springing up everywhere throughout the former communist countries. Most of these entities were attached to local nongovernmental organizations either directly funded by large multilateral and bilateral donors or supported by Western women's organizations subcontracted by USAID or the European Union's PHARE Program to foster "civil society" in the region. Thus, donors hired professional

Western feminists to produce what I call "feminism-by-design," in much the same way as the World Bank retained consultants from the big international accounting firms to create capitalism-by-design.[6] Just like the communists who tried to abolish private property by administrative decree, the international community tried to create a new "gendered" subjectivity virtually overnight by importing the "best practices" from the West.

Interviews with the directors and employees of several Bulgarian women's NGOs in Sofia showed me just how dependent they were on external funding and how this dependence translated into their inability to set their own agendas. After 1989, "democracy-building" grants often included monies earmarked for promoting gender awareness and creating alternatives to the Communist Party–based mass women's organizations. Nonprofit organizations, think tanks, law firms, and universities in the West began to bid on "gender projects." If one of these institutions won a large contract from their government to provide democracy assistance in Eastern Europe, they could either send their own employees or hire freelance "experts" to provide the needed advice. In either case, women working in American and Western European corporations, universities, and human rights or women's organizations were subsequently subcontracted as gender "experts" even if they knew nothing about the region or its communist past. These "experts" would fly into a country for one or two weeks and make policy recommendations to the government and newly formed women's organizations. Since many of these women knew little about the local context, they came with prepackaged gender advice developed and tested in the Western countries from which they came.

Because of this, gender "consultants" who did not live in the country determined the study and documentation of the situation of women in Bulgaria. They knew what the relevant gender issues were in their own countries, and assumed that the same would be true for Bulgaria. These Western women would then make recommendations for what kind of policies should be implemented, and more importantly, which local women's organizations were worthy of being subcontracted to carry out predesigned gender projects. Thus, solutions to local problems were imported from abroad. Although some issues were culturally specific to Bulgaria, there was almost no room for the creation and implementation of homegrown projects and programs to deal with them. Because Bulgarian women's NGOs relied so heavily on their Western "sisters" for financial and logistical support, the flow of ideas was only one way. The local women's organizations that thrived were the ones that were best at doing exactly what they were told needed to be done. Certainly, not all of the Western experts were oblivious to local circumstances, and there was some valuable "knowledge transfer" done under these programs, particularly with regard to what was called "civil society capacity building," or teaching East European women how the nonprofit sector is supposed to work. But overall, it was the Western freelance "experts" who benefited from these ironically named "exchanges," raking in generous per diems and all-expense-paid explorations of Eastern European capitals.

This imbalance of resources often resulted in what has been called the "political economy of begging."[7] The concept originates in Africa where different countries receive aid only when there are natural disasters, famines, droughts, or genocides. Western countries give aid only to countries that have "problems," and it is in the interest of the politicians of those countries to play up their problems in order to secure more aid. In the world of NGO funding, countries that have the most dire "women's issues" tend to receive a larger share of the aid. Thus, it is in the interest of local women's NGOs to play up women's problems and downplay their successes.

In the early 1990s, USAID and the Open Society Institute in Bulgaria provided money for program funding to cover the start-up costs of forming an NGO dealing with one issue: gender, ethnicity, environment, health, etc. As the 1990s progressed, most new funding to NGOs became project based, meaning that the NGOs must now write grants to carry out only the specific tasks designed by gender "experts" at the grant-giving institution. Several NGO directors complained to me about the difficulty of securing funding for overhead and general operational expenses. They are always stretching their resources and capabilities in order to secure the next grant—a bureaucratic hand-to-mouth existence. The donors set the priorities, and the local women just spin the proposals out to meet those priorities. This project-based funding is one specific mechanism that creates disincentive for women's NGOs to come up with their own original solutions to local problems. Even if they think they know how to solve a problem more effectively, there are very few places they can go to get a new idea funded.

Many women's NGOS in Bulgaria have become like distributorships for Western ideas about gender. As the vast majority of the Bulgarian population becomes poorer and poorer, these women's NGOS continue to focus on gender-specific issues in an economy that, even after over a decade of transition, still has a lower standard of living than it did in 1989 when communism collapsed. For most Bulgarians the major issues are unemployment, crime, and the increasing income polarization between the politico-mobster elite and the ordinary Bulgarian people. Despite this, a survey of national Bulgarian NGOS dealing with gender in 2002 showed that their "top priority issues" were "1) Violence against women, including sexual harassment; 2) Discriminatory employment practices; 3) Limited access of women to decision-making; 4) Unequal distribution and unjust treatment of unpaid labour; and 5) Negative gender stereotypes in education and sexist advertisement."[8]

If you spent even a few weeks in Bulgaria and talked to women on the street almost none of these issues would be mentioned. Indeed, men's registered unemployment surpassed that of women's in 2001, and Bulgaria had more female members of Parliament than any other postsocialist country. You would be far more likely to hear complaints about the rising price of food and social services, the shrinking value of pensions, the stagnating of individual wages, the decreasing employment opportunities, or the growing inability of divorcées to collect their child-support payments. Outside of the offices of women's NGOS, I never once, in the almost two years that I spent in the country, heard a Bulgarian woman discuss "sexist advertisements." As they worked and struggled to keep themselves and their families fed, a few publicly exposed breasts here and there were the least of their worries.

So what is gained by focusing on these issues that pit men and women against each other and construct women as victims of capitalism? The shift from a class-based analysis of oppression to a gender-based analysis of oppression, as created and perpetuated by many women's NGOS in Bulgaria, may have actually smoothed the way for foreign governments and transnational corporations looking to take root in the Bulgarian economy by preventing any form of class solidarity and/or collective bargaining that could put upward pressure on wages. Constant attention to the supposed challenges that women face in the newly liberalized labor market may have helped discursively create a category of people who can "naturally" be excluded from it. Since 1989, the Bulgarian government has no longer been able to guarantee full employment to all men and women. The onset of capitalism created severe unemployment in Bulgaria for the first time. Theoretically, there were only two possible solutions—create more jobs or somehow find a way to reduce the number of people actively seeking work.

Since many women's NGOs in Bulgaria are informed by Western cultural feminism, they tend to view women as biologically or psychologically less competitive and more risk-averse, and therefore in need of extra help in the form of training programs and microcredit schemes.[9] Women's "lack of success" in the labor market is not explained in terms of the overall weakening of workers' rights and opportunities throughout the economy, but instead by women's own inherent incapacity to compete in a free market for labor. This attention to women's supposed marginalization erases the increasing marginalization of the majority of the Bulgarian people and undermines the possibility of class-based coalitions between men and women that might politically challenge neoliberal policies. Thus, more than being the representatives of a "civil society," the NGOs may be the unsuspecting allies of Western states in promoting ideologies that support the expansion of Western capital into the region.[10]

One good indicator of how biased many of the women's nongovernmental organizations are in favor of the ideology of Western donors is to look at the publications they produce and disseminate in Bulgaria. In one women's magazine funded by the Netherlands Organization for International Development Cooperation, the editorial content is overwhelmingly about women's antagonistic relationships with men in society. Most articles revolve around issues of domestic violence, prostitution, trafficking in women, infidelity, sexual performance, alcoholism, divorce, single motherhood, and child support. The majority of the articles focus on the struggle between men and women—the ways in which men lie, cheat, and exploit women for their own gain. Furthermore, although there was a Bulgarian version of this magazine until 1999, eventually it was published only in English due to lack of funding, and therefore became linguistically inaccessible to the vast majority of Bulgarian women.

Another example revolves around child support. Collecting child support is a major challenge that divorcées have faced since 1989. During communism child support was automatically deducted by the state from the father's wages and transferred to the mother for care of the child. The shrinking of the public sector and the relocation of many men into private-sector employment has undermined the efficacy of this system. The courts are considered inefficient and corrupt; few women have faith in the legal system. As a result, many women no longer receive support from their ex-husbands. Since 1997, the Bulgarian government and the multilateral lending institutions have vigorously promoted the independence of the market from state interference. Consequently, the government has failed to pass new legislation regarding how women should collect their support. There are a handful of women's organizations such as the Bulgarian Association for University Women that are lobbying to reintroduce the state into child-support collection since the "market" solution is obviously not working. But most women's organizations completely deny the state's role and continue to point the accusative finger at the errant fathers. Thus their ability to help women find workable solutions to their problems is constrained by the neoliberal tendencies of their donors.

In Bulgaria, many NGOs also promote microcredit schemes for women or support women's entrepreneurship, but they have met with limited success.[11] Microcredit schemes and microentrepreneurship promotion by NGOs assume that women are willing to borrow or work to pay for "basic needs," needs which were once provided by the socialist state. Under socialism, these "needs" once existed as the basic *rights and entitlements* of the communist citizen. Indeed, one of the most lauded achievements of the communist countries was the high level of human development. This was particularly true for women. As we have seen, Bulgarian women once benefited from generous maternity leaves, free education, free healthcare, free or subsidized childcare, communal kitchens and canteens, communal laundries, subsidized food and transport, subsidized holidays on the Black Sea, etc.

In the postsocialist period, these rights and entitlements have all but disappeared. The collapse of communism in Bulgaria has relegated these *rights* to the status of *needs* for the first time in many women's lives. It should be no surprise that microcredit and women's entrepreneurship projects are not welcome or useful in Bulgaria where many women have not fundamentally accepted that it is their responsibility to meet these "basic needs" in the first place. Women in Bulgaria may have incentives to work for consumer items or to save money to travel abroad, but many are resistant to the idea of taking loans to start businesses to make money to pay for things that they consider the responsibility of the state. Bulgarian women prefer to seek political solutions, which has led to Bulgarian women's dominance in the membership of the Bulgarian Socialist Party.[12] Ideologically, women may be less likely than men to accept that things such as education or healthcare can be justly provided by private, profit-seeking enterprises.[13]

A newer model is that of "social entrepreneurship," of which even the women's NGOs in Bulgaria are skeptical. One report prepared by a local NGO claimed that: "Promotion of social entrepreneurship is a new (*imported*) issue, meant as a tool for the development of a social services market, able to absorb unemployed women and men and to fill the growing gap in social service provision after the withdrawal of the State."[14] The concept of social entrepreneurship once again displaces the responsibility for what were basic rights in Bulgaria—healthcare, childcare, elder care, education, nursing, and other social services—away from the Bulgarian state and onto the "free market" (i.e., onto women), and expects that the provision of these services will be profitable for unemployed men and women. The model assumes that Bulgarian families are both willing and able to pay for these services, and that these services will be performed in the formal economy, two assumptions that do not match the Bulgarian reality. Most likely, women will have to provide these services for their families and communities for free. It is understandable that women's NGOs are hesitant to implement projects promoting social entrepreneurship even if they are desperate for funding.

As these examples show, women's NGOs that are overly influenced by Western funding, and "experts" do more to help weaken grassroots opposition to unfettered free markets and the dismantling of the social welfare state than to actually help Bulgarian women. First, they ignore the women who have been successful after 1989 and place the blame for the drastic reduction in living standards for women squarely on the shoulders of traditional Bulgarian patriarchy. They deflect attention away from the three key actors which are primarily responsible for the disappearance of the social safety net that once supported women and their families: structural adjustment policies of the World Bank, the stabilization programs of the IMF, and the complicity of the Bulgarian government.

Second, the NGOs ignore that education and cultural-capital acquisition are the keys to women's success, and that there simply are not enough jobs in the Bulgarian economy available to employ all Bulgarians who want to work. Instead, many women's NGOs focus on the technical fixes of social problems and avoid tackling larger issues of economic injustice and inequality in society.[15] Because of the project-based nature of their funding, women's NGOs emphasize individual projects, which address specific goals, narrowly defined by the project's funders. Community-based self-help projects are encouraged over national mobilizations. NGOs find it difficult to support broad-based social movements that challenge the status quo or that implicate class differences in the ever-widening gap in living standards.[16]

Third, women's rights and women's issues are once again being used as a tool to support the dominant political and economic system. Participation in NGOs that are entirely dependent on foreign funding breeds both cynicism and opportunism in the few committed women leaders who genuinely do believe that free markets and liberal democracy are more desirable alternatives to communism. In informal conversations, Bulgarian women activists have complained to me that capitalist "civil society" is really not too different from its communist counterpart. Being forced to digest the rhetoric of international organizations and proposing only those projects which support "American or European interests" is really no different from being forced to regurgitate the Marxist propaganda once required under the old regime.

Most importantly, NGOs in Bulgaria co-opt educated middle-class women who might otherwise organize a solid class-based opposition to free-market neoliberalism, the same way they once organized against the communists before 1989. Instead, these women now scramble to write grants and reports and attend international conferences in Helsinki and

Minsk. It seems that almost every other month there is some gender congress or workshop on the "problems" of postsocialist women that requires a Bulgarian feminist representative.

By focusing exclusively on patriarchy at the microsociological level, these Western-influenced women's NGOs and the middle-class women who often run them help create the perception of the victimized woman, and indirectly benefit from that perception. For some, the business of looking after women's issues has been lucrative. Middle-class women can make careers out of their "civil society"–building activities by emphasizing the problems women in their country face in order to secure the grants to "fix" them, despite the evidence that shows that some Bulgarian women are doing very well. In addition to the successes of women like those who work in tourism, almost all of the classic indicators used to show gender discrimination in a society show no problems in Bulgaria. Bulgarian women outlive men; infant mortality for boys is higher than for girls; women have higher levels of education at almost all levels.[17] Women have the right to own property and assets in their own name (which they can keep in case of divorce). Women enjoy longer paid maternity leaves than in most Western nations. In 2002, there were more female members of Parliament than in most Western European countries; there has been a female foreign minister (1997–2001), a female deputy prime minister (2003–2005), and even briefly a female prime minister (October 1994–January 1995). Nonetheless, Bulgarian women's NGOs are forced to focus on such stock phrases as the "feminization of poverty" in order to attract external donor funding. But why would foreign governments and organizations spend money to fix problems that do not really exist?

And here is where we return to the idea of revalued cultural capital. One of the purposes of NGOs in Eastern Europe is to provide employment for displaced intellectuals from the old system, to allow them to adjust their habituses to the new capitalist reality. Because capitalism is dependent on meritocracy in order to justify its unequal distribution of resources, the new system must visibly reward those with excessive cultural capital even if that capital was acquired under the old system. Bulgarians working in the NGO sector have high levels of general education. In fact, intellectuals and academics run many NGOs. As in tourism, these intellectuals had their cultural capital revalued after 1989, because they could speak foreign languages and were familiar with the West (in this case Western literature and ideas). But this cultural capital was not revalued by the unfettered international dynamics of supply and demand (such as the foreign demand for the Bulgarian tourist resorts), but instead by foreign *states* that provided funding for the creation of a civil society. In 2000, the UNDP found that "the NGO sector is growing not only because of the availability of a *solvent and low-risk market* as represented by donors, but also because of the growing unemployment among intellectuals. From its very origin this market is an *export of services*. Therefore, the NGOs sector has not emerged in a natural way, as a result of internal citizen needs; it complies with an external demand, articulated in the donors' aspiration to stimulate civic society in Bulgaria."[18] The Bulgarians working in women's NGOs have themselves admitted that one of the most important roles NGOs play is in creating employment.[19] Thus, foreign governments have essentially bought out the intellectuals. Professors and academic researchers in almost all fields have been pulled into the civil-society sector by the attraction of high consultancy fees and opportunities to travel abroad for international networking.

Meritocracy justifies capitalism's unequal distribution of resources by arguing that anyone—regardless of race, class, gender, or religion—can be successful if she has the ability and if she works hard enough. Formal education (or the lack thereof) allows people to be sorted out into the haves and have-nots in a capitalist economy. If you receive less than a "fair" share of society's resources it is because you have somehow failed to meet the requirements for being worthy enough to have that share. Meritocracy deflects blame for injustice away from the economic system and places it on the shoulders of the individual and her lack of ability. This allows the privileged to enjoy their wealth without guilt or concern for the less fortunate. The privileged believe that they achieved their wealth because they worked hard—they come to believe that they *deserve* it. Thus, in order to establish a functioning meritocracy those with education and skills must be given a higher status in the social space than those who do not have education and skills.

What the idea of meritocracy hides is that education (not just at the university level, but at all levels beginning with preschool) is a commodity under capitalism. Only those already in a privileged position in society have access to the best educational opportunities, while the children of the less fortunate have to make do with substandard schools and underpaid teachers. Capable young people like Svetla may be unable to get the right qualifications because they are economically beyond their family's means. This is particularly true in a small postsocialist country like Bulgaria where the state cannot afford to subsidize many scholarships. Certainly, this situation also holds true for many advanced capitalist countries like the United States, but what is different in Bulgaria is that this supposedly meritocratic system did not exist until the very recent past. Many Bulgarians believe that meritocracy is a lie, and they are angry at the deteriorating opportunities for social mobility for their children.

The need to prove the efficacy of meritocracy has meant creating jobs for the educated unemployed in the postsocialist period, because unemployed intellectuals are dangerous and may challenge the imposition of globalization in their country. At worst, they can be the vanguard of a new class-based social opposition to capitalism, particularly since many academics have access to large audiences of idealistic youth in their university classrooms. Moreover, if there are a lot of educated unemployed, people will cease to believe in a meritocracy, and may begin to criticize capitalism as simply an unjustified, unequal distribution of resources to those who are the most immoral (like the Mafia). The Western-funded NGO culture thus creates a new habitus among the intellectuals, one in which the tastes that mark one as privileged have steadily become Western tastes that are in line with the logic of global capitalism, especially regarding consumption. Business trips taken to Western countries, stays in nice hotels, and relatively generous per diems allow those employed in the NGO sector to acquire both the experiences and the material accoutrements of "success" under the capitalist economic system, which may dampen their opposition to it.

Under communism, cultural capital was not an asset that allowed individuals a greater share of scarce economic resources.[20] Indeed, intellectuals under the old system were frustrated with what they perceived to be a total lack of meritocracy—where political connections and age determined everything regardless of education. These intellectuals were the dissidents who helped bring communism down. According to Eyal,

Szelenyi, and Townsley, these are the inheritors of political power, with their ideological commitments to free markets and liberal democracy. However, not all of the intellectual class made it into political office, and salaries for professors and researchers steadily declined throughout the 1990s. The salary for teaching one semester at Sofia University in 2002 was 250 leva, compared to the 600 leva that a maid like Gergana made cleaning hotel rooms for the same period of time. Almost every Ph.D. or professor I knew was moonlighting at a variety of different jobs just to survive. In one case, a professor earned her entire monthly salary for attending one afternoon workshop. Many others found lucrative positions as "consultants" to the projects of international organizations or started their own NGOs. The funding was easily available in the early 1990s. For foreign governments, whether intentionally or unintentionally, funding NGOs was a way to funnel resources to members of Bulgarian society with the greatest amount of cultural capital. NGOs bolstered the structures of the meritocracy necessary for the growing acceptability of class difference among Bulgarian women based on newly scarce cultural capital. The irony is that women's NGOs may help to create the class divisions among women that their own activities as women's organizations then help to obscure.

Given these critiques, there are several things that women's NGOs can do to become more responsive to the needs of Bulgarian women, not only those employed in tourism, but also those young women like Svetla struggling to find their way in the new economy. First, these organizations must find ways to become more independent of funding from Western governments and Western organizations. Of course, this is easier said than done, but it is absolutely necessary if NGOs in Bulgaria are to gain any legitimacy among the Bulgarian people. This process may already be happening by default as foreign aid moves away from the Balkans and into Central Asia and other regions of the world that need "developing" and "liberalizing." The withdrawal of these Western donors from Bulgaria may actually give the prominent national women's NGOs the push they need to start listening to the real needs of women in their country. At the very least, the withdrawal may stop the constant stream of bad news about Bulgarian women emanating from the country in order to attract funding.

Second, women's NGOs need to become more independent of imported Western feminist "consultants" and the generic gender-project templates they support. NGO leaders must realize that projects designed in the United States or Belgium may not resonate with Bulgarian women, and could actually hinder the ability of NGOs to reach out to their constituents who reject the idea that there is anything called a "gender issue." NGO leaders must be more creative in finding homegrown solutions to local problems. Of course, there are women in both America and Western Europe who have some relevant knowledge and are committed to helping solve the real problems of women and men in Eastern Europe. Some of these women remain dedicated to work in the region even after the lucrative subcontracted consultancies have disappeared.[21] More equal coalitions between these groups should be encouraged based on mutual understanding, with women from the region taking the lead and women from abroad doing what they can to support a locally driven agenda.

Third, civil-society leaders and Western "experts" should recognize and accept the legacies of socialist feminism, and not continue to attempt to organize women as a biologically homogenous group in opposition to men. Women raised under socialism were taught to believe that working-class men and women are natural allies in their struggle against bourgeois men and women—bourgeois women and working-class women did not share similar interests. NGOs could instead organize women not only as women, but as professionals or students in sectors of the economy or areas of the educational system where women dominate. For instance, a professional association of receptionists would be a de facto women's organization without the "gender" stigma attached to it. So would an association of maids or hotel managers. In fact, a professional association of tourism employees would be largely a women's organization. Of course, there would be some male members, but the projects generated and the issues dealt with would primarily benefit women, since women are the majority of those employed in the sector.

Another example would be to create an NGO to help young people prepare for the university entrance exams in tourism by coordinating volunteers to work as language tutors, creating a library of study materials, or simply organizing study groups among students. Again, there would be a few men who would take advantage of the services provided, but on the whole tourism programs attract an overwhelming majority of women, so much so that some programs have had to create special quotas for male students. NGOs could also be formed for exams in other subjects for which a majority of young women apply.

Once the organizations are formed, they can begin to lobby the government for legislative changes or mobilize political support for certain parties. While this approach to creating women's civic organizations may not be ideologically in sync with mainstream Western feminism, it may be more successful at getting women in Bulgaria involved in shaping their own political and economic futures. In the end, this should matter most.

Finally, nongovernmental organizations and their leaders need to publicly challenge the negative effects of neoliberalism and agitate for change. If the postsocialist state can no longer interfere in the market, then NGOs must step in to address the growing imbalances in society for all Bulgarians. Women's NGOs could play a very important role in the future of the next generation of women, but only if they, too, are truly independent of the market. This means that NGO work cannot be a professional position where the leaders are the salaried employees of foreign governments. Their role should not be to justify the dismantling of the welfare state, but to work against the most egregious excesses of free-market capitalism. Particularly after Bulgaria becomes a member of the European Union, those disenfranchised by an increasingly liberalized economy will be in desperate need of public advocates. Intellectuals and activists can then use their cultural capital to become dissidents once again.

The beach is almost empty now. The sunbathers and swimmers have all returned to their rooms to shower and relax before dinner. There are only a few couples strolling together along the shore, and a handful of joggers who have waited all day for the weather to cool. The trash cans are overflowing with empty beer cans, ice cream wrappers, and corn cobs. A multicolored beach ball floats away toward the horizon.

I have given myself a day off today. I have spent the better part of the afternoon reading popular Bulgarian fashion magazines and making sand fortresses with my daughter, who is now snoring on a towel under our umbrella. I have decided to start writing tonight.

Reluctantly, I put all of my things into the beach bag, and slide my shorts over my still-damp bathing suit. Scooping my daughter onto my hip and shaking out her towel with one hand, I hoist my bag over my other shoulder and head back toward the hotel. She grumbles, but falls back to sleep immediately.

The lobby of the Hotel Transcontinental is clean and cool; my flip-flops slap noisily across the marble floor. "Hi Kristen!" Svetla calls over to me.

"How is your first day going?" I say.

"It's wonderful," she says, spreading her hands across the smooth surface of the reception desk.

After Svetla got her exam results, I told the whole story to Sonia, who agreed to interview her. Sonia was very impressed by the young woman's verbal command of French. All of the other receptionists in the Transcontinental speak either English or German, and there will be several groups of tourists from France in the hotel this summer. Sonia was able to offer Svetla only a summer position, but she promised to train her and to do what she could to find her a year-round position in another hotel in Golden Sands. Sonia knows everybody. Svetla has deferred her enrollment in the university, and is going to try and save up the money she needs to pay the first year's tuition.

Sonia hears my voice and comes out of the office. "Here's another woman in tourism for your research," Sonia says, resting her hand on Svetla's shoulder.

As we start to chat, a group of German tourists enters the lobby, walking toward the reception desk.

"That's the ITS group," Sonia says to Svetla. "Are you ready?"

"Park-view rooms to the families. Ocean views for the couples," Svetla whispers in Bulgarian.

"Good," Sonia says.

Svetla smiles, and greets the first couple with a cheerful, "Guten tag!"

"She's a fast learner," Sonia tells me, watching Svetla as she checks the German couple in and explains the amenities of the hotel. It is hard to believe that it is only her first day. "I think we just might have to keep her here," Sonia says, handing me my key. "After all, I have to retire one of these days . . ."

"I don't think so. There are a lot more Svetlas out there you need to train before you do."

"I hope so," she says, smiling. "I hope so."

Appendix A—Tables

TABLE 1 Traditionally Feminine Professions in Bulgaria
(Employed by Sector and Economic Activity Groupings)

Activity	1996	1999	Jobs Gained/Lost	Percentage Variation
Hotel and Restaurants				
public sector	28,988	12,250	−1,738	−57.7
private sector	47,467	67,604	20,137	42.4
Apparel Manufacturing				
public sector	37,866	4,404	−33,462	−88.4
private sector	46,288	92,834	46,546	100.6
Footwear, Fur, Leather				
public sector	19,381	1,555	−17,826	−92.0
private sector	9,661	20,389	10,728	111.0
Education				
public sector	252,577	225,703	−26,874	−10.6
private sector	3,243	5,236	1,993	61.5
Health and Social Work				
public sector	180,538	159,270	−21,268	−11.8
private sector	3,233	2,099	−1,134	−35.1
Cultural Activities				
public sector	16,554	16,676	122	0.7
private sector	26,996	21,885	−5,111	−18.9
TOTAL LOST:	122,413			
TOTAL GAINED:	79,526			
DIFFERENCE:	−42,887			

Percentage of new jobs created in apparel and footwear manufacturing (combined total) 72.0

Percentage of new jobs created in hotel and restaurants (tourism) 25.3

SOURCE: National Statistical Institute 1998, 2000

TABLE 2   Percentage of Women Employed in Bulgarian Tourism

Name and Year of Source	*n* of study	% female
European Union 1997	492 (in 64 establishments)	public sector 63 private sector 63
Albena A.D. 1999	2,834 (working in Albena resort complex)	66.9
National Statistical Institute March 2000	53,000 (in 21,000 non-institutional households)	58.4
Author's Survey 1999–2000	827 (in 105 establishments)	62.5
Average		62.8

SOURCE: European Union 1997, Albena A.D., NSI 2000, Author's Survey

TABLE 3   Structure of Employment by Resort*

Resort	% of Total Employed	% of Managers	Average Age	Average years of experience	% High School ed.	% College/ Tech. ed.	% Uni- versity ed.
Pamporovo							
women	58.8	58.8	30.2	8.3	55.8	22.0	22.0
men	41.2	41.2	29.6	8.3	75.9	16.7	7.4
Borovets							
women	61.5	81.2	30.9	6.6	61.1	15.8	23.2
men	38.5	18.8	32.0	6.0	80.0	6.7	13.3
Golden Sands							
women	62.3	84.0	31.3	9.3	47.4	20.1	32.5
men	37.7	16.0	27.4	6.6	71.0	11.8	17.2
Albena							
women	64.1	76.0	33.4	10.3	59.3	10.0	30.7
men	35.9	24.0	29.2	8.1	69.2	6.4	24.4

SOURCE: Author's Surveys

*At the time of the research, Albena had been privatized for the longest period of time, followed by Golden Sands, Borovetz and Pamporovo. Pamporovo is the closest to representing the labor force in tourism under the system before 1989.

TABLE 4   Selected Indicators from the International Tourism Survey

	% of Total Respondents	% of Male Respondents	% of Female Respondents
Age			
13–25	35.3	40.5	32.2
26–35	34.1	36.9	32.3
36–45	21.7	15.5	25.5
46+	8.9	7.1	10.0
Years Experience			
0–3	31.5	29.2	32.9
4–7	24.6	27.6	22.8
8–11	16.0	20.1	13.5
12–15	11.2	11.4	11.1
16+	16.6	11.4	19.7
Education			
High School	60.8	72.2	54.2
College or Advanced Technical	13.8	9.7	16.5
University	25.4	18.1	29.7
Job Category			
Managerial	12.6	8.4	15.1
Higher-level operational*	20.0	8.7	26.8
Restaurant	21.5	24.9	19.4
Bar	10.2	14.2	7.8
Kitchen	8.7	10.7	7.4
Lower-level operational**	19.0	24.3	15.9
Miscellaneous***	8.0	8.7	7.6

SOURCE: Author's Survey

*Receptionists, tour guides, cashiers, translators, etc.

**Maids, bellboys, security, maintenance, shopkeepers, etc.

***Nurses, beauticians, private vendors, artists, musicians, entertainers, etc.

TABLE 5　Selected indicators of the Seaside Sample

	% of Total Respondents	% of Male Respondents	% of Female Respondents
Age			
13–25	33.9	36.6	32.5
26–35	26.2	26.7	25.9
36–45	19.9	19.0	20.4
46+	20.0	17.7	21.2
Years Experience			
0–3	40.9	39.7	41.6
4–7	19.7	21.5	18.8
8–11	13.8	17.4	11.9
12–15	7.2	7.0	7.2
16+	18.4	14.5	20.5
Education			
Less than High School	6.5	7.0	6.3
High School	54.4	67.8	47.4
College or Advanced Technical	12.6	5.4	16.5
University	26.4	19.8	29.9

SOURCE: Author's Surveys

TABLE 6   Selected Statements from the International Tourism Survey
(n = 828, snowball sample of Tourism employees in Golden Sands,
Albena, Pamporovo, Borovetz, Hissarya and Sofia)

Statement	% Total - agree	% Women - agree	% Men - agree
Working in tourism is more pleasant than other jobs.	95.7	96.6	94.5
I can use my knowledge of foreign languages in my job.	95.9	95.9	95.9
I meet many new and interesting people in my job.	99.6	99.4	100
I have opportunities to travel in my job.	51.4	49.6	54.6
Working in tourism is easier than other jobs.*	28.5	24.9	34.5
My professional goal is a career in tourism.	83.9	83.7	84.3
Jobs in tourism are relatively well paid compared to other jobs in Bulgaria.	54.4	54.5	54.3

SOURCE: Author's Survey

*Difference between male and female response statistically significant at the 5 percent level.

TABLE 7   Selected Statements from the Seaside Survey
(n = 455 employees only)

Statement	% Total - agree	% Women - agree	% Men - agree
Compared to other professions, people working in tourism are better paid.	58.3	56.3	62.5
Compared to other working places, tourism has more "fringe benefits."	52.3	51.8	53.4
Employers in tourism provide food for their employees.	43.9	44.7	42.3
In addition to my salary, I receive tips from clients.*	24.9	21.2	32.7

SOURCE: Author's Survey

*Difference is statistically significant at the 5 percent level.

Appendix B—Formal Interviews

10-24-99
Ms. Rumiana Vajarova
Manager
Hotel Rila, Borovets

10-26-99
Mr. Mark Thomas
Managing Director
Jamadvice Travel, Sofia

11-01-99
Ms. Nadija Kutskova
Marketing Director
Pamporovo A.D., Pamporovo

11-01-99
Ms. Katya Koleva
Hotel Manager
Perelik Hotel, Pamporovo

11-02-99
Ms. Iskra Ekimova
Sales Manager
Sofia Sheraton

11-02-99
Mr. Peter Carney
Travel Writer
Sofia

11-05-99
Ms. Diliana Zarneva
Marketing Manager
Hotel Samokov, Borovetz

11-05-99
Mr. Boyan Boudinov
General Manager
Hotel Ela, Borovetz

11-05-99
Mr. Yordanka Karabeliova
Owner/Entrepreneur
Restaurant, Lawina, Borovetz

11-10-99
Mr. Thomas Higgins
Chief Investment Officer
Bulgarian-American
Enterprise Fund, Sofia

11-10-99
Ms. Aneila Dimitrova
Hotels Investment Officer
Bulgarian-American
Enterprise Fund, Sofia

11-19-99
Ms. Emelia Yanakieva
Projects Manager
British Council, Sofia

11-24-99
Ms. Gergana Mantarkova
Deputy Managing Partner
KPMG-Bulgaria, Sofia

11-25-99
Mr. Angel Giorgiev
Professor
New Bulgaria University, Sofia

11-29-99
Dr. Nikolina Popova
Professor
Sofia University, Sofia

11-30-99
Mr. Mike Hennessey
Project Manager
Grand Hotel, Sofia

11-30-99
Dr. Martin Groenendijk
Professor and Consultant
New Bulgarian University, Sofia

12-02-99
Dr. Maria Vodenska
Professor and Dean
Sofia University

12-06-99
Ms. Petya Koleva
Chief Expert
National Information and
   Advertising Center

12-06-99
Ms. Mariana Assenova
Deputy Minister of Tourism
Ministry of Trade and Tourism,
   Sofia

12-07-99
Mr. Kaloyan Tzendafilov
Expert (Hunting Tourism)
Ministry of Trade and Tourism,
   Sofia

12-07-99
Ms. Juliet Peeva
Marketing/Promotions Expert
Ministry of Trade and Tourism,
   Sofia

12-13-99
Mr. Illian Vasilev
President
Bulgarian Foreign Investment
   Agency, Sofia

01-05-00
Mr. Peter Angelov
Owner
Peter's Bar, Borovetz

01-20-00
Mr. Krassimir Kanev
Managing Director
Alder Tours, Sofia

01-26-00
Ms. Juliet Peeva
Marketing/Promotions Expert
Ministry of Trade and Tourism,
   Sofia

01-28-00
Mr. Lyubomir Pankovski
Chairman
Alma Tours, Sofia

01-28-00
Mr. Boyan Stoev
President
Magic Tours, Sofia

02-02-00
Ms. Sylvia Stoyanova
Project Manager
British Know-How Fund, Sofia

02-02-00
Mr. Lyubo Popiordonov
President and Owner
BAAT and Odessia Travel, Sofia

02-10-00
Mr. Ford Young
M.B.A Corps Volunteer
Albena Invest, Sofia

02-10-00
Mr. Evgenie Ivanov
Expert
Bulgarian Foreign Investment
    Agency, Sofia

03-06-00
Dr. Todor Radev
Chairman, Board of Directors
Albena A.D. and Albena Invest,
    Sofia

03-09-00
Mr. Stefan Katsarov
Expert
Bulgarian Foreign Investment
    Agency, Sofia

03-13-00
Ms. Nadija Kutskova
Marketing Manager
Prespa-Rozhen Hotel, Pamporovo

05-15-00
Ms. Katina Mladenova
Sales Manager
Alma Tours, Sofia

05-23-00
Mr. Krassen Roussev
Director
International Albena Tourism
    College

05-23-00
Ms. Dimi Techeva
Training Coordinator
International Albena Tourism
    College

05-24-00
Mr. Fritz Feldmejer
General Manager
Dobruja Hotel, Albena

05-25-00
Dr. Todor Radev
Chairman, Board of Directors
Albena Invest and Albena A.D.,
    Albena

05-26-00
Ms. Sonya Stoicheva
Sales Manager
Albena A.D., Albena

06-09-00
Dr. Todor Radev
Chairman, Board of Directors
Albena Invest and Albena A.D.,
	Albena

06-19-00
Ms. Judy Hafner
M.B.A. Corps Volunteer
Transcontinental Hotels, Sofia

06-21-00
Mr. Richard Miles
U.S. Ambassador
U.S. Embassy, Sofia

06-21-00
Mr. Richard Kantor
Commercial Attaché
U.S. Embassy, Sofia

06-21-00
Mr. Rick Record
Acting Director
Peace Corps, Sofia

06-21-00
Mr. Tom Bauer
President
Bulgarian-American Enterprise
	Fund, Sofia

06-21-00
Ms. Anelia Dimitrova
Hotels Loan Officer
Bulgarian-American Enterprise
	Fund, Sofia

06-21-00
Mr. Edward LaFarge
Senior Private Sector Officer
USAID, Sofia

06-21-00
Mr. Aldo Sirotica
Political Officer
U.S. Embassy, Sofia

06-22-00
Ms. Rosi Zhegova
Marketing Assistant
Sofia Sheraton, Sofia

06-22-00
Mr. Ivo Marinov
Head of Department
Ministry of Economy, Sofia

06-22-00
Mr. Hristo Hristov
Expert
Ministry of Economy, Sofia

06-26-00
Mr. Edward LaFarge
Senior Officer
USAID, Sofia

06-26-00
Mr. Nikolay Yarmov
Senior Advisor
USAID, Sofia

06-26-00
Mr. Ventislav Vassilev
Country Director
FLAG Consortium, Sofia

07-10-00
Mr. Martin Weber
USAID Consultant
Boosting Bulgarian
	Competitiveness, Sofia

07-11-00
Mr. Peter Hetz
USAID Subcontractor
Biodiversity Project, Sofia

07-14-00
Ms. Iordanka Minkova
Training Officer
Peace Corps, Sofia

07-17-00
Ms. Anelia Dimitrova
Hotel Loans Officer
Bulgarian-American Enterprise
    Fund, Sofia

07-19-00
Ms. Mira Ianova
Managing Director
MBMD, Sofia

07-19-00
Ms. Juliet Peeva
Marketing Expert
Ministry of Economy, Sofia

07-19-00
Mr. Peter Doitchev
Retiree and Author
Balkantourist, Sofia

07-21-00
Ms. Diliana Zarneva
Marketing Director
Samokov Hotel, Borovetz

07-21-00
Ms. Maya Spaiska
Front Office Manager
Samokov Hotel, Borovetz

07-22-00
Ms. Annie Janeva
Reservations
Hotel Olymp, Botovetz

07-22-00
Mr. Fuar Demirev
Marketing Manager
Hotel Olymp, Botovetz

07-24-00
Mr. Borislav Penchev
Senior Adviser
Office of the Bulgarian President,
    Sofia

07-24-00
Ms. Maria Hristova
Editor
Tourism Market, Sofia

07-24-00
Dr. Maria Vodenska
Professor and Dean
Sofia University, Sofia

07-25-00
Mr. Evgenie Ivanov
Expert
Bulgarian Foreign Investment
    Agency, Sofia

07-25-00
Ms. V. Nekova
Expert on Privatization
Ministry of Economy, Sofia

07-25-00
Mr. Phillippe Pellaud
General Manager
Radisson SAS Hotel, Sofia

07-25-00
Ms. Lydia Wisniewska
Marketing Manager
Radisson SAS Hotel, Sofia

07-26-00
Mr. Gerardo Berthin
Program Advisor
UNDP Bulgaria, Sofia

07-29-00
Ms. Katarina Shopova
General Manager
Hotel Bor, Botovetz

07-31-00
Mr. Peter Doitchev
Retiree and Author
Balkantourist, Sofia

08-07-00
Mr. Krassimir Mihov
Personnel Manager
Kempinski Hotel, Sofia

08-08-00
Mr. Rick Record
Acting Director
Peace Corps, Sofia

08-17-00
Ms. Vesislava Chiligirova
Project Manager
Swiss Interassist, Sofia

08-17-00
Ms. Donna Steiger
Volunteer
Peace Corps, Sofia

08-17-00
Ms. Svetla Bineva
Secretary General
Bulgarian Association of Travel
   Agents, Sofia

08-18-00
Ms. Antoinetta Todorova
Contracts and Sales
Balkantourist, Sofia (Multigroup)

08-18-00
Ms. Nedyalka Sandalska
Chief Executive and Chairperson
   of the Board of Directors
Balkantourist, Sofia (Multigroup)

08-21-00
Ms. Evelina Stefana
Project Manager
German GTZ, Sofia

08-24-00
Ms. Madia Stoeva
Marketing Manager
Hotel Hrankov, Sofia

08-24-00
Ms. Evelina Pavlova
Marketing Assistant
Hotel Hrankov, Sofia

Notes

INTRODUCTION

1 Unless otherwise noted, all names have been changed.

2 For example, see: Nahid Alsanbeigui, Steve Pressman, and Gale Summerfield, *Women in the Age of Economic Transformation: Gender Impacts of Reforms in Postsocialist and Developing Countries* (New York: Routledge, 1994); Mary Buckley, *Post-Soviet Women: From the Baltic to Central Asia* (Cambridge: Cambridge University Press, 1997); Barbara Einhorn, *Cinderella Goes to Market: Citizenship, Gender, and Women's Movements in East Central Europe* (London: Verso, 1993); Valentine Moghadam, ed., *Democratic Reform and the Position of Women in Transitional Economies* (Oxford: Clarendon, 1993); Nanette Funk and Magda Mueller, eds., *Gender Politics and Post-Communism: Reflections from Eastern Europe and the Former Soviet Union* (New York: Routledge, 1993); Chris Corrin, *Superwoman and the Double Burden: Women's Experience of Change in Central and Eastern Europe and the Former Soviet Union* (Toronto: Second Story, 1992); Marilyn Rueschemeyer, ed., *Women in the Politics of Postcommunist Eastern Europe* (Armonk, N.Y.: M. E. Sharpe, 1994); and Kristen Ghodsee, "Women and Economic Transition: Mobsters and Mail-Order Brides in Bulgaria," *Berkeley Center for Slavic and Eastern European Studies Newsletter* (fall 2000): 5–7, 10–13, ⟨socrates.berkeley.edu/@iseees/publications2.html⟩.

3 National Statistical Institute, *Employment and Unemployment 4/2003* (Sofia: NSI, 2004).

4 I spent twenty months doing research in Bulgaria over a period of five years using both qualitative and quantitative methods. The majority of the research was conducted while I was living in Sofia from June 1999 to August 2000, and traveling on a monthly basis to either Albena, Golden Sands, Borovetz, or Pamporovo. The bulk of the qualitative data I collected is based on more than fifteen months of fieldwork and participant observation in Bulgaria in 1999 and 2000. During this time, I also conducted over 100 formal interviews with Bulgarians employed in all levels of tourism, as well as with politicians and government officials in

charge of the sector. I made subsequent months-long research trips in 2001, 2003, and 2004. On the quantitative side, I conducted two large surveys of workers employed in the international tourism sector in 1999–2000. The first survey, which I have called the "International Tourism Survey," included a snowball sample of 828 Bulgarians employed in international tourism. It was conducted in the resorts of Borovetz, Pamporovo, Golden Sands, and Albena, as well as in the capital city of Sofia and the small town of Hissarya. The second survey or the "Seaside Survey" queried a random sample of 711 Bulgarian tourism employees and entrepreneurs in the seaside resorts of Golden Sands, Sunny Beach, and Albena, and in the town of Nessebur.

5   Gil Eyal, Ivan Szelenyi, and Ellen Townsley, *Making Capitalism Without Capitalists: The New Ruling Elites in Eastern Europe* (London: Verso, 1998).

6   David Stark, "Path Dependence and Privatization Strategies in East Central Europe," *East European Politics and Societies* 6, no. 1 (1992): 17–54.

7   For example, see: Victor Nee, "A Theory of Market Transition: From Redistribution to Markets in State Socialism," *American Sociological Review* 56, no. 5 (1989): 663–81; Jeffrey Sachs, "Postcommunist Parties and the Politics of Entitlements," *Transition Newsletter* 6 (March 1995): 1–4, ⟨www.worldbank.org/transitionnewsletter/mar95/pgs1-4.htm⟩.

8   Nee, "Market Transition."

9   Throughout the text, I use the terms "socialism" and "communism" interchangeably as they are in Bulgaria.

10   Stark, "Path Dependence."

11   *Habitus* refers to an individual's sense of the social hierarchy in which she lives and the possibilities she has for social mobility within that hierarchy. Habitus is a view of the way the world works from a specific social space in that world. Bourdieu calls his social space the *champ*, and argues that one's *champ* is defined by one's position relative to the place of other individuals who may be able to move up and down in the hierarchy. All of an individual's actions are based on her perception of her own champ compared to that of other members of her society. Different kinds of personal "capital" are used to maintain social divisions between those with a higher *champ* and those below them. *Distinction: A Social Critique of the Judgment of Taste*, translated by Richard Nice (Cambridge: Harvard University Press, 1984).

12   Ibid.

1. SHATTERED WINDOWS, BROKEN LIVES

1   Bojidar Dimitrov, *Bulgarians: The First Europeans* (Sofia: St. Kliment Ohridski University Press, 2002).

2   There are one hundred stotinki in one Bulgarian lev.

3 Manuel Castells, *The End of the Millennium*, vol. 3, *The Information Age: Economy, Society and Culture* (Malden, Mass.: Blackwell, 1998), 62–63.

4 The Croatian journalist, Slavenka Drakulic, has written extensively about the lack of basic personal amenities under communism. See *How We Survived Communism and Even Laughed* (New York: HarperCollins, 1993); and *Café Europa: Life After Communism* (New York: Penguin, 1999).

5 Katherine Verdery, *What was Socialism, and What Comes Next?* (Princeton: Princeton University Press, 1996).

6 J. Macdonald, *Czar Ferdinand and His People* (New York: Frederick A. Stokes, 1913); Will S. Monroe, *Bulgaria and Her People* (Boston: Colonial Press, 1914).

7 Mieke Meurs, *The Evolution of Agrarian Institutions: A Comparative Study of Post-Socialist Hungary* (Ann Arbor: University of Michigan Press, 2001); Gerald Creed, *Domesticating Revolution: From Socialist Reform to Ambivalent Transition in a Bulgarian Village* (University Park: Pennsylvania State University Press, 1998); R. J. Crampton, *A Concise History of Bulgaria* (Cambridge: Cambridge University Press, 1987); Bogoslav Dobrin, *Bulgarian Economic Development Since World War II* (New York: Praeger, 1973); D. Kossev, H. Hristov, and D. Angelov, *A Short History of Bulgaria* (Sofia: Foreign Language Press, 1963).

8 Vienna Institute for Comparative Economic Studies (VICES), COMECON *Data 1990* (Westport, Conn.: Greenwood, 1991).

9 Ibid.

10 John Lampe, *The Bulgarian Economy in the Twentieth Century* (London: Croom Helm, 1986), 180.

11 VICES, COMECON *Data 1990*.

12 VICES, COMECON *Data 1980* (Westport, Conn.: Greenwood, 1981).

13 Lampe, *Bulgarian Economy*.

14 World Bank, *World Development Report 1981* (Washington, D.C.: The World Bank, 1982).

15 World Bank, *World Development Report 1980* (Washington, D.C.: The World Bank, 1981).

16 Ibid.

17 Women's Alliance for Development, "Women in Bulgaria 2000" (in Bulgarian), ⟨www.women-bg.org⟩.

18 Raia Staikova-Alexandrova, "Bulgaria: The Present Situation of Women" in *The Impact of Economic and Political Reform on the Status of Women in Eastern Europe: Proceedings of a United Nations Regional Seminar* (New York: United Nations, 1992).

19 Due to declining birth rates, the Bulgarian state tried to create incentives for women to have second and third children. Despite these efforts, however, women were still overburdened by their dual roles in society, as evidenced by the continually stagnant birth rate.

20 Verdery, *What Was Socialism*.

21 Georgi Dimitrov was Bulgaria's first communist prime minister.

22 World Bank, *World Development Report 1998* (Washington, D.C.: The World Bank, 1999).

23 World Bank, *World Development Report 1991* (Washington, D.C.: The World Bank, 1992).

24 World Bank, *World Development Report 2002: Building Institutions for Markets* (Washington, D.C.: The World Bank, 2003).

25 National Statistical Institute (NSI), *Statistical Yearbook 1999* (Sofia: NSI, 2000).

26 NSI, *Statistical Yearbook 2001* (Sofia: NSI, 2002).

27 United Nations Development Program (UNDP), *National Human Development Report 1999* (Sofia: UNDP, 2000).

28 UNDP, *National Human Development Report 2000* (Sofia: UNDP, 2001).

29 Ibid.

30 Verdery, *What Was Socialism*.

31 Institute for Market Economics, *Economic Outlook of Bulgaria: 1995–1997* (Sofia: Bulgarian Academy of Sciences, 1995).

32 Keith Snavely, "The Welfare State and the Emerging Non-profit Sector in Bulgaria," *Europe-Asia Studies* 48, no. 4 (1996): 647–63.

2. MAKING MITKO TALL

1 The British who come to Borovetz are infamous for their excessive drinking.

2 National Statistical Institute, *Employment and Unemployment 1/2003* (Sofia: NSI, 2003).

3 United Nations Development Program, *Annual Early Warning Report 2000* (Sofia: UNDP, 2000).

4 Ibid.

5 Ibid.

6 *Komsomol* is a hybrid word, from the Russian *Kommunisticheski Soyuz Molodezhi*, "Communist Union of Youth." The organization served as the youth wing of the Communist Party in Bulgaria, and was the path young people took to become members in the Communist Party.

7 Ibid.

8 National Statistical Institute, *Employment and Unemployment 1/2000* (Sofia: NSI, 2000).

9 UNDP, *Annual Early Warning Report 2000*.

10 Recognizing, of course, that the number of registered unemployed is not an accurate measure of true unemployment, since it includes only people who are actively looking for work and not discouraged workers or people who decide not to register.

11 Barbara A. Cellarius and Caedmon Straddon, "Environmental Nongovernmental Organizations, Civil Society, and Democratization in Bulgaria," *East European Politics and Societies* 16, no. 1 (2002): 182–222.

12 For instance, a report funded by the World Bank claimed that labor laws protecting pregnant women and women with children under three from being fired without the consent of the labor inspectorate were an "administrative barrier to foreign investment." Foreign Investment Advisory Service, *Bulgaria: Administrative Barriers to Foreign Investment* (Washington, D.C.: World Bank, 1999), 27.

13 Republic of Bulgaria, *National Economic Development Plan 2000–2006* (Sofia: Republic of Bulgaria, 2000).

14 World Bank, *Bulgaria Country Economic Memorandum: The Dual Challenge of Transition and Accession* (Washington, D.C.: World Bank, 2000).

15 Bettina Musiolek, "How far is Bulgaria?: European Garment Industry Produces Nearby," *Frauensolidarit* (February 1998): 24.

16 Kristen Ghodsee, "State Support in the Market: Women and Tourism Employment in Post-Socialist Bulgaria," *International Journal of Politics, Cultural and Society* 16, no. 3 (2003): 465–82.

17 NSI, *Statistical Yearbook 1999*; NSI, *Statistical Yearbook 2001*; NSI, *Statistical Yearbook 2002*.

18 Ghodsee, "State Support."

19 There has been considerable research on the relationship between tourism and women's labor. For example, see: Vivian Kinnaird and Derek Hall, eds., *Tourism: A Gender Analysis* (Chichester, England: Wiley, 1994); Margaret B. Swain, ed., "Special Issue: Gender in Tourism," *Annals of Tourism Research* 22, no. 2 (1995); Thea Sinclair, *Gender, Work and Tourism* (London: Routledge, 1997); Cynthia Enloe, *Bananas, Beaches and Base: Making Feminist Sense of International Politics* (London: Pandora, 1989).

   Some scholars argue that tourism is a sector that primarily exploits women while others have claimed that tourism gives women important employment opportunities that might not otherwise be available. Evidence on either side of this debate is given in: Diane Levy and Patricia Lerch, "Tourism as a Factor in Development: Implications for Gender and Work in Barbados," *Gender and Society* 5, no. 1 (1991): 67–85; Sylvia Chant, "Tourism in Latin America: Perspectives from Mexico and Costa Rica" in *Tourism and the Less Developed Countries*, edited by D. Harrison (London: Belhaven, 1995); S. Hennessy, "Female employment in tourism development in South-West England," in *Tourism: A Gender Analysis*, edited by Kinnaird and Hall; Margaret Swain, "Women Producers of Ethnic Arts," *Annals of Tourism Research* 20, no. 1 (1993): 32–51; Gareth Shaw and Allan Williams, *Critical Issues in Tourism* (Oxford: Blackwell, 1994); Judie Cukier, Joanne Norris, and Geoffrey Wall, "The Involvement of Women in the Tourism Industry of Bali, Indonesia," *Journal of Development Studies* 33, no. 2 (1996): 248–

71; and Anna Falth, "Tourism and Gender: Opportunities for LDCs in an Intensified Global Economy," in Trade, Sustainable Development and Gender: Papers prepared in support of the themes discussed at the Pre-UNCTAD X Expert Workshop on Trade, Sustainable Development, and Gender (Geneva July 12–13, 1999): 423–34.

20   There is one interesting study in Cuba, although it is questionable whether Cuba could be considered a "postsocialist" country. See Maura I. Toro-Morn, Anne Roschelle, and Elisa Facio, "Gender, Work, and Family in Cuba: The Challenges of the Special Period," *Journal of Developing Societies* 18 no. 2/3 (2002): 32–59.

21   Edith Szivas and Michael Riley, "Tourism Employment During Economic Transition," *Annals of Tourism Research* 26, no. 4 (1999): 747–71.

22   Judith Cukier-Snow and Geoffrey Wall, "Tourism Employment: Perspectives from Bali," *Tourism Management* 14 (1993): 195–201; and "Tourism Employment in Bali, Indonesia," *Tourism Recreation Research* 19, no. 1 (1994): 32–40.

23   For example, see Sinclair, *Gender, Work and Tourism*. There are, however "pro-poor" tourism initiatives that aim to help alleviate poverty. See Caroline Ashley and Dilys Roe, "Making Tourism Work for the Poor: Strategies and Challenges in Southern Africa," *Development Southern Africa* 19, no. 1 (2002): 61–83.

24   Valentine Smith, *Hosts and Guests: The Anthropology of Tourism* (Philadelphia: University of Pennsylvania Press, 1989).

25   Lisa Mastny, "Traveling Light: New Paths for International Tourism," 1989. Worldwatch Paper #159. Washington, D.C.

26   For example, see: Smith, *Hosts and Guests*; Dean MacCannell, *The Tourist: A New Theory of the Leisure Class* (Berkeley: University of California Press, 1999).

27   Any discussion of women and tourism seems to immediately invoke the problem of sex tourism, and indeed many international tourist destinations have thriving sex tourism industries. I believe it is an important subject that must be thoroughly researched, particularly with regards to the issue of local children serving the sexual needs of foreign tourists. There was, however, no evidence of sex tourism in Bulgaria while I did my fieldwork in 1999 and 2000. Despite its long history of being a tourist destination, by the beginning of the twenty-first century Bulgaria had yet to become a host country for sex tourists. Although the trafficking of women out of Bulgaria for the purposes of sex work abroad was a recognized problem, none of the international or local nongovernmental organizations dealing with women's issues considered prostitution or sex work in Bulgaria to be a pressing issue even by 2003. In fact, it was very difficult to find any data on Bulgarian sex workers at all. Although there is no doubt that prostitution in Bulgaria exists and that it is probably increasing as the economic circumstances of women continue to deteriorate, it does not yet seem that it is a factor enticing potential tourists to the country.

Of course, this situation could change in the future. The increasing presence of American military forces in the region may be having an effect on the demand for sexual services. American soldiers stationed in Bosnia and Kosovo during the late 1990s and early 2000s were taking their leaves in Bulgaria. Furthermore, there were rumors in 2003 that American military bases in Germany could be moved to Bulgaria after Germany's opposition to the second Gulf War. American soldiers stationed on Bulgarian territory could increase the demand for sex workers even further. At the same time, growing poverty among ordinary Bulgarian men and women, and continued high rates of unemployment could draw more Bulgarians into sex work as alternative economic opportunities disappear. This is a phenomenon in Bulgaria that should be very closely watched over the coming years. I reiterate, however, that my exclusion of an extended discussion on sex tourism is because it was not relevant to the Bulgarian context at the time of my research.

28   United Nations Development Program, *Bulgaria 2000: Human Development Report—The Municipal Mosaic* (Sofia: UNDP, 2000).

29   NSI, *Employment and Unemployment 1/2000*.

30   NSI, *Statistical Yearbook 1999*.

31   Ibid.

3. THE RED RIVIERA

1   There are only a handful of scholars who have studied tourism in the socialist context. The two best sources are Derek Hall, ed., *Tourism and Economic Development in Eastern Europe and the Soviet Union* (London: Belhaven, 1991); and the special issue of *Annals of Tourism Research*, vol. 17, no. 1 (1990).

2   Hall, *Tourism and Economic Development*.

3   Ibid.

4   F. W. Carter, "Bulgaria," in *Tourism and Economic Development*.

5   Peter Doitchev, *Zhivot: Otdaden na Turizma* (Life: Devoted to Tourism) (Sofia: Literaturen Forum, 1999).

6   Nadija Kutskova, marketing director, interview by author, Pamporovo, Bulgaria, 1 November 1999.

7   Boyan Stoev, former Orbita employee and president of Magic Tours, interview by author, Sofia, Bulgaria, 28 January 2000. As of January 2002, Orbita was still owned by the Bulgarian state.

8   Michael Pearlman, "Conflicts and Constraints in Bulgaria's Tourism Sector," *Annals of Tourism Research* 17, no. 1 (1990): 103–22.

9   There is also a Greek Macedonia, which lies within the political borders of Greece, and a Vardarska Macedonia that was once Yugoslavian Macedonia and is now FYROM, the Former Yugoslav Republic of Macedonia.

10   Peter Doitchev, "proto-Balkantourist" employee and author, interview by author, Sofia, Bulgaria, 19 July 2000.

11   Doitchev, *Zhivot: Otdaden na Turizma.*

12   Ibid.

13   World Tourism Organization, *Yearbook of Tourism Statistics* (Madrid: WTO, 1990).

14   Krassen Roussev, director of the Dutch-Bulgarian International School of Tourism, interview by author, Albena, Bulgaria, 23 May 2000.

15   This is one of the favorite stories of those over the age of fifty still employed in tourism. I heard the same story at least ten times from different sources.

16   Martin Groenendijk, professor and tourism consultant at the New Bulgarian University, interview by author, Sofia, Bulgaria, 30 November 1999.

17   Central Statistical Institute, *Tourism* (Sofia: Central Statistical Institute, 1990); and NSI, *Statistical Yearbook 1999.*

18   Lampe, *Bulgarian Economy.*

19   These are the Grand Hotel Varna, the New Otani, and two Novotel Hotels in Sofia and Plovdiv.

20   Carter, "Bulgaria."

21   Maria Vodenska, "International Tourism in Bulgaria: Problems and Perspectives," *Journal of Economic and Social Geography* 83, no. 5 (1992).

22   Krassimir Kanev, former Balkantourist employee and president of Alder Tours, interview by author, Sofia, Bulgaria, 20 January 2000.

23   The privatized airline ultimately went into receivership and was bought back by the Bulgarian state after the private investor had sold off its most lucrative assets.

24   Velitchko Velitchkov, former deputy minister of transportation and former head of Balkan Airlines, interview by author, Sofia, Bulgaria, 25 January 2000.

25   Kanev, interview.

26   Mariana Assenova, deputy minister of tourism, interview by author, Sofia, Bulgaria, 5 December 1999.

27   Todor Zhivkov, *Otchet na Tsentralniia Komitet na Bulgarskata Komunisticheska partiia za perioda mezhdu Desetiia i Edinadesetiia Kongres i predstoiashtite zadachi, 29 March 1976* (Report of the Central Committee of the Bulgarian Communist Party for the Period between the Tenth and Eleventh Congresses and on the Forthcoming Tasks, 29 March 1976) (Sofia: Sofia-Press, 1976).

28   Nedyalka Sandalska, former Balkantourist legal counsel and current managing director of Balkantourist, the private successor of the state-run enterprise, interview by author, Sofia, Bulgaria, 16 August 2000. Ms. Sandalska was personally responsible for the demonopolization of Balkantourist in the early 1990s.

29   Sandalska, interview. Ms. Sandalska was also employed as a lawyer for the Committee on Tourism and often mediated disputes between the resorts and the central government.

30   Diliana Zarneva, former Balkantourist employee and marketing director of Hotel Samokov, interview by author, Borovetz, Bulgaria, 11 July 2000.

31   Zarenva, Doitchev, Katya Koleva, and Rumijana Varajova in addition to many informal conversations about tourism with older workers still employed in the sector. In general, many older, former Balkantourist employees felt that tourism was better organized and more beneficial to Bulgarians in general under communism than it is in the post-1989 period.

32   For instance, the brochure for the 1999/2000 Crystal Ski packages advises customers to pay for as many services as possible in the UK before departure to Bulgaria due to the high rates of inflation. This is despite the fact that the lev has been linked to the German mark since 1997, when Bulgaria instituted a currency board.

33   Vladimir Kostov, Bulgarian journalist and former DS informant, revealed that "the degree of integration is such that nothing of importance takes place in Bulgaria without the knowledge of the USSR. Each department of the Bulgarian DS had Soviet 'counselors' responsible to Moscow. Resolutions of the Central Committee of the Bulgarian Communist Party concerning 'organic integration' envisage the coordination with their Soviet counterparts of all governmental decisions and actions in Bulgaria." *The Bulgarian Umbrella* (New York: St. Martin's, 1988), 11.

34   The study of the theory of socialism versus the practice of "really existing socialism."

35   Kostov, *The Bulgarian Umbrella*.

36   Barbara Carr, *Spy in the Sun: The Story of Yuriy Loginov* (Cape Town: Howard Timinis, 1969).

37   Carr writes: "The KGB has the means of surrounding every visitor to Russia with a human and technical surveillance net which ensures that no movement or contact goes unnoticed and that at any moment it can subject its victim to provocation or place him in a compromising situation . . . The most common devices are the involvement of the targets in extra-marital or homosexual relationships . . ." *Spy in the Sun*, 224. Vladimir Kostov, describing the Hotel Bulgaria in Sofia, wrote that "DS officers met their contacts there, and prostitutes, on instructions more often than not from these same officers, picked up foreigners staying at the hotel." *The Bulgarian Umbrella*, 116.

38   Christopher Andrew and Vasili Mitrokhin, *The Sword and the Shield: The Mitrokhin Archive and the Secret History of the KGB* (New York: Basic Books, 1999), 251.

39   Ibid., 429

40   Doitchev, interview.

41   The actual Bulgarian phrase translates to "jar bank."

42 PHARE stands for Poland and Hungary: Action for the Restructuring of the Economy. In December 1989, the Council of Ministers of the European Union decided to assist Poland and Hungary with the dramatic changes taking place in their countries. Within two years, however, the program was extended, and it has covered fourteen partner countries: Albania, Bosnia and Herzegovina, Bulgaria, Croatia, the Czech Republic, Estonia, the Former Yugoslav Republic of Macedonia (FYROM), Hungary, Latvia, Lithuania, Poland, Romania, Slovakia, and Slovenia.

43 Derek Jones and Takao Kato, "The Nature and the Determinants of Labor Market Transition in Emerging Market Economies: Evidence from Bulgaria," *Industrial Relations* 36, no. 2 (1997): 229–54.

44 See Pierre Bourdieu, *Practical Reason: On the Theory of Action* (Stanford: Stanford University Press, 1998).

45 Ironically, the lecture on political capital was delivered just weeks before the Berlin Wall collapsed, and the political capital became useless.

46 Bourdieu, *Practical Reason.*

47 In some ways, Bourdieu privileges "the market" as a natural state that communism has distorted and within which economic and cultural capital will always be ascendant. Judith Butler has questioned Bourdieu's conception of the market and points to the mid-1940s work of Karl Polanyi on how the market is not a "natural" preexisting phenomenon but a human institution shaped out of the social fabric. See Judith Butler, "Performativity's Social Magic," in *Bourdieu: A Critical Reader*, edited by Richard Shusterman (Oxford: Blackwell, 1999); and Karl Polanyi, *The Great Transformation* (New York: Beacon, 2001).

Informed by this bias toward a natural market, Bourdieu saw the activities and protests of the dissident intellectuals in Eastern Europe as proof that cultural capital would always struggle to translate itself into some kind of class privilege despite the efforts of those trying to suppress it (i.e., those with political capital in the Soviet variant). See George Konrád and Ivan Szelenyi, *The Intellectuals on the Road to Class Power*, translated by Andrew Arato and Richard E. Allen (New York: Harcourt Brace Jovanovich, 1979).

48 "The proletariat is forced to take power before it has appropriated the fundamental elements of bourgeois culture; it is forced to overthrow bourgeois society by revolutionary violence for the very reason that society does not allow it access to culture. The working class strives to transform the state apparatus into a powerful pump for quenching the cultural thirst of the masses. This is a task of immeasurable historic importance . . . The essence of the new culture will be not an aristocratic one for a privileged minority, but a mass culture, a universal and popular one." Leon Trotsky, "What is Proletarian Culture, and Is It Possible?" 1923, ⟨www.marxists.org⟩.

49 World Bank, *World Development Report 1981* (Washington, D.C.: World Bank, 1982), 179.

50 Ibid. These numbers, however, are not very reliable because of different definitions of higher education in the capitalist and communist worlds, and the fact that many of the socialist countries were not regularly reporting data to the World Bank.

51 Emma Goldman, *My Disillusionment with Russia*, 1923, ⟨www.marxists.org⟩.

52 Ibid.

53 Katherine Verdery has also objected to the use of some of Bourdieu's terminology and theoretical frameworks in the postcolonialst context. See Katherine Verdery, *National Ideology Under Socialism: Identity and Cultural Politics in Ceausescu's Romania* (Berkeley: University of California Press, 1991).

54 Karl Marx, *Capital: A Critique of Political Economy*, translated by Ben Fowkes (London: Penguin, 1990).

55 Cultural capital is referred to as "human capital" in economics. See Gary S. Becker, *Human Capital: A Theoretical and Empirical Analysis with Special Reference to Education* (Chicago: University of Chicago Press, 1964).

56 Recognizing, of course, that the system was admittedly far from ideal, and that many populations, especially the Roma, were still excluded.

57 This is not to deny that political capital under socialism was in some ways related to cultural capital. Certainly, the children of the communist elite were given preferences when competing for places in the university. But their "success" after university was more related to their political capital than to their cultural capital.

58 See Ivan Szelenyi, *Socialist Entrepreneurs: Embourgeoisement in Rural Hungary* (Madison: University of Wisconsin Press, 1988).

59 See Paolo Freire, *Pedagogy of the Oppressed*, translated by Myra Bergman Ramos (New York: Herder and Herder, 1970); and *Education for a Critical Consciousness* (San Francisco: Harper San Francisco, 1973).

60 This idea also explains the phenomenon of "qualification escalation" or the "diploma disease" in capitalist countries. As more and more people have access to education, the necessary educational requirements for employment increase. Qualification escalation is the capitalist system's way of ensuring that cultural capital always remains scarce (despite all of the rhetoric about educational opportunity to the contrary). See Ronald Dore, *The Diploma Disease: Education, Qualification, and Development* (Berkeley: University of California Press, 1976).

61 Other scholars have also found that women were better poised to deal with economic transition because of their higher levels of cultural capital. For instance, see: United Nations Development Program, *Women in Poverty* (Sofia: UNDP, 1997); Eva Fodor, "Gender in Transition: Unemployment in Hungary, Poland and Slovakia," *East European Politics and Societies* 11, no. 3 (1997): 470–501;

Tanja Van Der Lippe and Eva Fodor, "Changes in Gender Inequality in Six Eastern European Countries," *Acta Sociologica* 41, no. 2 (1998): 131–50; Julia Szalai, "From Informal Labor to Paid Occupations: Marketization from Below in Hungarian Women's Work," in *Reproducing Gender: Politics, Publics, and Everyday Life after Socialism*, edited by Susan Gal and Gail Kligman (Princeton: Princeton University Press, 2000); Lisa Giddings, *Does the Shift to Markets Impose Greater Hardship on Women and Minorities? Three Essays on Gender and Ethnicity in Bulgarian Labor Markets* (Ph.D. diss., American University, 2000).

62 Susan Gal and Gail Kligman, *The Politics of Gender after Socialism* (Princeton: Princeton University Press, 2000).

63 For instance, the 1987 feature film *Wall Street* starring Michael Douglas as Gordon Gekko did much to "masculinize" the financial-services sector of the economy.

64 There was no significant difference between the number of young men and women studying in the off-season, 20 percent and 19.8 percent respectively.

65 Julia Szalai has also suggested that women in Hungary who are able to withdraw from the labor force are able to take up "occasional, one-time, cash-payment or otherwise irregular" work in other sectors of the economy. "From Informal Labor." Despite the irregularity of this temporary work in Hungary, Szalai found that these opportunities actually afforded women a higher standard of living than those employed in steady but low-paying jobs; multiple jobs worked as "a protection against the excesses of a market economy" (220–21).

66 This difference is statistically significant at the 5 percent level.

67 This difference is statistically significant at the 10 percent level.

4. TO THE WOLVES

1 E. Kalinova and I. Baeva, *Balgarskite Prehodi 1939–2002* (The Bulgarian Transitions 1939–2002) (Sofia: Paradigma, 2002).

2 Zoya Mladenova and James Angresano, "Privatization in Bulgaria," *East European Quarterly* 30, no. 4 (1996): 495–517.

3 For more background see: Petya Kabakchieva, "The New Political Actors and Their Strategies," in *Bulgaria at the Crossroads*, edited by Jacques Coenen-Huther (New York: Nova Science Publishers, 1996); and *The Civil Society against the State: The Bulgarian Case* (in Bulgarian) (Sofia: Lik, 2001).

4 Mladenova and Angresano, "Privatization in Bulgaria."

5 Marvin Jackson, "A Crucial Phase in Bulgarian Economic Reforms," 1989, paper 72, Berichte des Bundesinstituts fur ostwissenschaftliche und internationale Studien, Cologne, Germany.

6 A joint-stock company consists of shares that are bought and sold by individual shareholders. These shareholders have no liability beyond the value of their

shares for the failures of the company. A limited-liability company is a partnership where individual partners own the company together; they have more liability than shareholders in a joint-stock company but less liability than a traditional partnership. In both cases in Bulgaria, the state was the only shareholder and the only partner in the early phases of privatization.

7   Marvin Jackson, "The Rise and Decay of the Socialist Economy in Bulgaria," *Journal of Economic Perspectives* 5, no. 4 (1991): 203–9.

8   Stark, "Path Dependence."

9   Jon Elster, Claus Offe, and Ulrich K. Preuss, *Institutional Design in Post-Communist Societies: Rebuilding the Ship at Sea* (Cambridge: Cambridge University Press, 1998).

10 Jackson, "Rise and Decay."

11 Mladenova and Angresano, "Privatization in Bulgaria."

12 Tomas Jezek, "The Czechoslovak Experience with Privatization," special issue "Privatization: Political and Economic Challenges," *Journal of International Affairs* 50, no. 2 (1997): 477–89.

13 Jackson, "Rise and Decay."

14 Between November 1989 and April 1997, Bulgaria had nine different prime ministers.

15 Boyan Koulov, "Market Reforms and Environmental Protection in the Bulgarian Tourist Industry" in *Reconstructing the Balkans: A Geography of New Southeast Europe*, edited by Derek Hall and Darrick Danta (Chichester, England: Wiley, 1996).

16 As Daniel Kaufmann and Paul Siegelbaum have insightfully pointed out, "even in corruption, entrepreneurship pays." "Privatization and Corruption in Transition Economies (Privatization: Political and Economic Challenges)," *Journal of International Affairs* 50, no. 2 (1997): 419–59.

17 Institute for Market Economics, *Economic Outlook of Bulgaria: 1995–1997* (Sofia: Bulgarian Academy of Sciences, 1995).

18 Mladenova and Angresano, "Privatization in Bulgaria."

19 Krassen Stanchev, "Bulgaria," *Journal of Southeastern Europe and Black Sea Studies* 1, no. 1 (2001): 140–58.

20 Kaufmann and Siegelbaum, "Privatization and Corruption."

21 *State Gazette, Law on the Transformation and Privatization of State and Municipal Enterprises*, art. 25, para. 3–4, no. 89: 7 (October 1997).

22 Bulgarian Foreign Investment Agency, *Bulgaria Business Guide 2000—Legal, Tax, and Accounting Aspects: Challenges of Joining Global Markets* (Sofia: BFIA, 2000).

23 For an interesting discussion of MEBOS and how mass-privatization schemes worked in the Romanian case see Duncan Light and D. Dumbraveanu, "Romanian Tourism in the Post-Communist Period," *Annals of Tourism Research* 26, no. 4 (1999): 898–927.

24 For instance, the Ministry of Industry, the Ministry of Trade and Tourism, the Ministry of Agriculture, etc.

25 For studies of corruption in Bulgaria, see: Ase Grodeland, Tatyana Koshechkina, and William Miller, "Foolish to Give and Yet More Foolish Not to Take: In-depth Interviews with Post-Communist Citizens on Their Everyday Use of Bribes and Contacts," *Europe-Asia Studies* 50, no. 4 (1998): 651–78; Transparency International, "Year 2000 Corruption Perceptions Index," ⟨www.transparency.de/documents/cpi/2000/cpi2000.html⟩; KPMG-Bulgaria, *Foreign Investors in Bulgaria* (Sofia: KPMG, 1998); Coalition 2000, "Corruption Assessment Report 1999," (Sofia: Coalition 2000), ⟨www.anticorruption.bg/eng/coalition/car1999.htm⟩; and Coalition 2000, "Corruption Assessment Report 2000," (Sofia: Coalition 2000, 2001), ⟨www.anticorruption.bg/eng/coalition/car2000.htm⟩.

26 Creed, *Domesticating Revolution*; and Meurs, *Evolution of Agrarian Institutions*.

27 Bulgaria is divided into 278 municipalities. These municipalities are legal entities and have the right of ownership and independent municipal budgets. The municipal council is the local government authority and is directly elected by the people.

28 Mladenova and Angresano, "Privatization in Bulgaria."

29 V. Nekova, privatization expert at the Ministry of Economy, interview by author, Sofia, Bulgaria, 25 July 2000.

30 Koulov, "Market Reforms."

31 Ibid.

32 Marin Bachvarov, "End of the Model? Tourism in Post-communist Bulgaria," *Tourism Management* 18, no. 1 (1997): 43–50.

33 Stanchev, "Bulgaria."

34 Deni Consult, *A Survey of the Tourist Industry in Bulgaria* (Sofia: Deni Consult, 1997).

35 Koulov, "Market Reforms."

36 Roussev, interview.

37 Sandalska, interview.

38 Ibid.

39 Koulov, "Market Reforms."

40 Ibid.

41 Donna Steiger, former M.B.A. corps consultant to the Committee on Tourism in 1991–1992, interview by author, Sofia, Bulgaria, 17 August 2000.

42 European Union, "Draft Concept for Statute, Classification and Management of Large Tourist Resorts in View of Accelerated Privatization and in the Post-Privatization Period (Discussion Paper)," Sofia, April 1988.

43 Carter, "Bulgaria."

44 Gergana Mantarkova, deputy managing partner at KPMG-Bulgaria, interview by author, Sofia, Bulgaria, 24 November 1999.

45 These included Golden Sands, Sunny Beach, St. Constantine and Elena, Riviera, Sunny Day, Dyuni, Elenite, Rusalka, Pamporovo, Borosport, and Rila-Borovetz. See European Union, "Large Tourist Resorts."

46 Jovo Nikolov, "Crime and Corruption after Communism: Organized Crime in Bulgaria," *Eastern European Constitutional Review* 6, no. 4 (1997), ⟨www.law.nyu.edu/eecr/vol6num4/feature/organizedcrime.html⟩.

47 Where the percentage of shares distributed freely to the population is inversely related to the possibility of future state expropriation. Kaufmann and Siegelbaum, "Privatization and Corruption in Transition Economies."

48 Kristen Ghodsee, "Tri Prikaski za Albena" (Three Tales of Albena), *Turistechicki Pazar* (Tourism Market), no. 7 (July 2000): 6–7.

49 Kazimierz Z. Poznanski, "Recounting Transition," *East European Politics and Societies* 13, no. 2 (1999): 328–45.

50 UNDP, *Annual Early Warning Report 2000*.

51 Bulgaria has historically been famous for its Olympic prowess in weightlifting and wrestling, winning many gold medals during the communist period. After "the changes," state support for athletes declined drastically, and after years of pampering, they had to find other ways to support themselves. In fact, the Bulgarian word for *wrestler*, *boretz*, is still used synonymously with the word for *thug* or *mobster*.

52 Roumen Daskalov, *The Things that Surround Us: Observations and Reflections on Social Change* (in Bulgarian) (Sofia: Lik, 1998).

53 One interesting exception is a novel where an American woman has an affair with a Bulgarian mobster and does a thorough description of the criminal underworld. Ann Ward, *The Making of June* (New York: Putnam, 2002).

54 Nikolov, "Crime and Corruption."

55 Venelin Ganev, "Bulgaria's Symphony of Hope," *Journal of Democracy* 6, no. 4 (1997): 125–39.

56 Nikolov writes, "The most intense turf wars took place over Bulgaria's attractive seaside resorts. Frequent dismissals of hotel managers, perennial uncertainty about the validity of legal titles, fuzzy property rights ambiguously assigned, and the unpredictable cancellation of privatization deals created favorable conditions for the spread of corruption and the cozy coexistence among criminals, former policemen, and members of the *nomeklatura*. The dynamics of criminal activity surrounding the seaside resorts is emblematic of emerging patterns of organized crime in Bulgaria." "Crime and Corruption," 3–4.

57 Emile Giatzidis, *An Introduction to Postcommunist Bulgaria: Political, Economic and Social Transformation* (Manchester: Manchester University Press, 2002).

58 BFIA, *Bulgaria Business Guide 2000—Legal, Tax and Accounting Aspects*. This figure, however, is most likely an overestimation of the actual amount. According to BFIA records, Cyprus is the third-largest foreign investor in Bulgaria. Cyprus,

however, is a well-known tax shelter, and many Bulgarian investments are routed through Cypriot companies in order to avoid taxation. Much of this money may also be Bulgarian money in the process of being laundered.

59 Government of Poland, "Foreign Direct Investment," ⟨www.poland.gov.pl/ ?document=468⟩.

60 An employee of KPMG-Bulgaria who was in charge of approaching foreign investors for their pool of hotels said that the investors would not even bother to ask about the individual assets. Once they heard where she was calling from they immediately said no.

61 There are many historical animosities the Bulgarians hold against the Turks, all related to the Ottoman domination of Bulgaria for the better part of 500 years.

62 It could be suggested that the UDF was interested in the promotion of tourism because they personally owned so many assets in the sector.

63 BFIA, *Bulgaria Business Guide 2000—Legal, Tax and Accounting Aspects*, 30.

64 For an interesting discussion of the problems with Bulgaria's legislative framework, see Thomas O'Brien and Christian Filipov, "Current Regulatory Framework Governing Business in Bulgaria," in *World Bank Technical Papers* (Washington, D.C.: World Bank, July 2001).

65 BFIA, *Bulgaria Business Guide 2000*, 16, 18.

66 Ibid.

67 National Statistical Institute, *Statistical Yearbook 2002* (Sofia: NSI, 2003), 373.

68 Ibid.

69 With the state and the market being the first two.

70 Minnesota Advocates for Human Rights, "Sex Discrimination and Sexual Harassment in the Workplace in Bulgaria," 1999, ⟨www.mnadvocates.org/Eastern_ Europe.html⟩.

71 Ibid.

72 Minnesota Advocates for Human Rights, "Domestic Violence in Bulgaria," 1996, ⟨www.mnadvocates.org/Eastern_Europe.html⟩.

5. FEMINISM-BY-DESIGN

1 There is an extensive body of literature on NGOs and civil society. For information on the role of NGOs and international aid in general see: James Petras, "Imperialism and NGOs in Latin America," *Monthly Review* 47, no. 7 (1997): 10–16; and "NGOs: In the Service of Imperialism," *Journal of Contemporary Asia* 29, no. 4 (1999): 429–41; James Petras and Henry Veltmeyer, *Globalization Unmasked* (Halifax, Nova Scotia: Fernwood, 2001); Julie Fisher, *Nongovernments: NGOs and the Political Development of the Third World* (West Hartford, Conn.: Kumarian, 1997); and "Third World NGOs: A Missing Piece to the Population Puzzle," *Environment* 36, no. 4 (1994): 6–17; Michael Edwards and David Hulme, *Beyond the*

Magic Bullet: NGO Performance and Accountability in the Post–Cold War World (West Hartford, Conn.: Kumarian, 1996); and *NGOs, States and Donors: Too Close for Comfort?* (New York: St. Martin's, 1997); Gerard Clarke, "Non-governmental Organizations (NGOS) and Politics in the Developing World," *Political Studies* 46, no. 1 (1998): 36–53; Marina Ottoway and Thomas Carothers, eds., *Funding Virtue: Civil Society Aid and Democracy Promotion* (Washington, D.C.: Carnegie Endowment for International Peace, 2000).

On the specific topic of Western aid to Eastern Europe see Janine Wedel's excellent book, *Collision and Collusion: The Strange Case of Aid to Eastern Europe* (New York: Palgrave, 2001). For information on NGOS in Eastern Europe, see Sarah Mendelson and John Glenn, *The Power and Limits of NGOS: A Critical Look at Building Democracy in Eastern Europe and Eurasia* (New York: Columbia University Press, 2002); and *Democracy Assistance and NGO Strategies in Post-Communist Societies*, Carnegie Endowment Working Papers, Democracy and Rule of Law Project, no. 8 (Washington, D.C.: Carnegie Endowment for International Peace, 2000); Kevin Quigley, "Lofty Goals, Modest Results: Assisting Civil Society in Eastern Europe," in *Funding Virtue*, edited by Ottaway and Carothers.

On women's NGOS in Eastern Europe and the former Soviet Union, see: Laura Grunburg, "Women's NGOS in Romania," in *Reproducing Gender*, edited by Gal and Kligman; Rebecca Kay, *Russian Women and Their Organizations: Gender, Discrimination, and Grassroots Women's Organizations, 1991–1996* (New York: St. Martin's, 2000); Valerie Sperling, *Organizing Women in Contemporary Russia: Engendering Transition* (Cambridge: Cambridge University Press, 1999); Gal and Kligman, *Politics of Gender*; Julie Hemment, "Global Civil Society and the Local Costs of Belonging: Defining Violence Against Women in Russia," *Signs: Journal of Women in Culture and Society* 29, no. 3 (2004): 815–40; Elissa Helms, "Women as Agents of Ethnic Reconciliation? Women's NGOS and International Intervention in Postwar Bosnia–Herzegovina," *Women's Studies International Forum* 26, no. 1 (2003): 15–34; Armine Ishkanian, "Working at the Global-Local Intersection: The Challenges Facing Women in Armenia's NGO Sector," in *Post-Soviet Women Encountering Transition: Nation Building, Economic Survival, and Civic Activism*, edited by Kathleen Kuehnast and Carol Nechemias (Washington, D.C.: Woodrow Wilson Center Press, 2004).

2 For discussions on NGOS in Bulgaria see: Keith Snavely and Uday Desai, "The Emergence and Development of Nonprofit Organizations in Bulgaria," *Nonprofit and Voluntary Sector Quarterly* 27, no. 1 (1998): 32–48; Krassimira Daskalova, "Women's Problems, Women's Discourses in Bulgaria," in *Reproducing Gender*, edited by Gal and Kligman; United Nations Development Program, *National Human Development Report 2001: Citizen Participation in Governance, from Individuals to Citizens* (Sofia: UNDP, 2001); Snavely, "Welfare State"; Gerald Creed and

Janine Wedel, "Second Thoughts from the Second World: Interpreting Aid in Post-Communist Eastern Europe," *Human Organization* 56, no. 3 (1997): 253–64; Cellarius and Straddon, "Environmental Nongovernmental Organizations," 188. Finally, for a more thorough discussion of women's NGOs in Bulgaria see: Kristen Ghodsee, "Feminism-by-Design: Emerging Capitalisms, Cultural Feminism and Women's Nongovernmental Organizations in Post-Socialist Eastern Europe," *Signs: Journal of Women in Culture and Society* 29, no. 3 (2004): 727–53.

3   Wedel, *Collision and Collusion*.

4   For examples, see chapter 1, note 1.

5   For examples from Hungary, see Szalai, "From Informal Labor"; and Fodor, "Gender in Transition."

6   Ghodsee, "Feminism-by-Design."

7   Manuel Castells, *The End of the Millennium*, vol. 3 of *The Information Age: Economy, Society and Culture* (Malden, Mass.: Blackwell, 1998).

8   Regina Indjewa and Stanimir Hadjimitova, "Mapping NGOs dealing with Gender Issues," report of the Women's Alliance for Development, 2002, ⟨www.women-bg.org/index_en.html⟩.

9   Cultural feminism proposes that there are critical biological and psychological differences between men and women that are irreversible, and make the literal equality of the sexes impossible. In this view, men and women are not the same, and have different needs that must be met separately in order for women and men to achieve social equity. Cultural feminism as an ideology has been "mainstreamed" into societies around the world through its gradual integration into the bilateral and multilateral aid agencies and the thousands of local and international women's organizations they fund. Cultural feminism is a convenient package of ideas for the promotion of a free-market agenda; it allows donors to recognize that women may be differentially affected by macroeconomic changes, and to address their "special" needs within the established status quo without challenging the logic of neoliberalism. Because men and women are so fundamentally different, cultural feminism argues, all women have more in common with each other than they do with men. This idea of a global sisterhood, however, erases important differences in power and access to resources among women of varying races, ethnicities, and nationalities. Previous critiques of cultural feminism have gone unheeded in the reconstruction projects of the former "Second World."

10   Theodore H. Moran, *Foreign Direct Investment and Development: The New Policy Agenda for Developing Countries and Economies in Transition* (Washington, D.C.: Institute for International Economics, 1998).

11   Microcredit schemes extend small loans to groups of poor women. These women either use the money to meet immediate basic needs or invest in some small

income-generating project that allows them to pay the money back after having made a profit.

12 In 2001, over 60 percent of BSP members were women. United Nations Development Program, *Human Development Report 2002* (New York: UNDP, 2002).

13 United Nations Development Program, *National Human Development Report 2000* (Sofia: UNDP, 2001).

14 Indjewa and Hadjimitova, "Mapping NGOs," 12. Emphasis added.

15 Kevin Quigley, "Lofty Goals, Modest Results: Assisting Civil Society in Eastern Europe," in *Funding Virtue: Civil Society Aid and Democracy Promotion*, edited by Marina Ottaway and Thomas Carothers (Washington, D.C.: Carnegie Endowment for International Peace, 2000); Jenny Pearce, "NGOs and Social Change: Agents or Facilitators?" *Development Practice* 3, no. 3 (1993): 222–27; Clarke, "Non-governmental Organizations."

16 Petras and Veltmeyer, *Globalization Unmasked*.

17 For comprehensive statistics on women in Bulgaria, see UNDP, *Human Development Report 2000*.

18 UNDP, *National Human Development Report 2000*, 41.

19 Indjewa and Hadjimitova, "Mapping NGOs."

20 For an interesting look at the role of intellectuals under communism see: George Konrád and Ivan Szelenyi, *The Intellectuals on the Road to Class Power*, translated by Andrew Arato and Richard E. Allen (New York: Harcourt Brace Jovanovich, 1979); and Szelenyi, *Socialist Entrepreneurs*.

21 After 2003, most of the gender "experts" had already moved on to Central Asia, Afghanistan, or Iraq.

Glossary

Balkantourist: Under communism, the state-owned enterprise that had a monopoly on tourism. After 1998, Balkantourist became a private tourism company.

Banitza: A breakfast pastry made of philo dough, eggs, and feta cheese

Boza: A sweet, thick drink made of fermented malt and usually had for breakfast

Chalga: Music that is a fusion between Roma music and traditional Bulgarian folk

COMECON: The economic organization that existed from 1949 to 1991, linking the USSR with Bulgaria, Czechoslovakia, Hungary, Poland, Romania, East Germany, Mongolia, Cuba, and Vietnam, with Yugoslavia as an associated member. Albania also belonged between 1949 and 1961. The COMECON was formally disbanded in June 1991.

Cyrene: Bulgarian white cheese similar to the Greek feta cheese

DS: State Security, the Bulgarian equivalent of the KGB

Gevrek (gevretsi): A Bulgarian bread that is a cross between a pretzel and a bagel and sold on the streets for breakfast

Lev (leva): The Bulgarian currency, for example: one lev, two leva, three leva, etc.

Meze: Any appetizer eaten with rakiya

Mutra: A Bulgarian mobster

Mutressa: The girlfriend of a mutra

Mutri: The plural of mutra, mobsters

Nomenklatura: Members of the former communist elite

Pochivni stantzii: Holiday houses owned by enterprises for their employees

Rakiya: Bulgarian brandy, usually distilled from grapes

Stotinki: The Bulgarian cent. There are one hundred stotinki in one lev.

Vitosha: The mountain that overlooks Sofia, and the main shopping street in Sofia

Vitoshka: A diminutive of Vitosha, which refers only to the street

Selected Bibliography

Alavi, Hamza, and Teodor Shanin, *Introduction to the Sociology of "Developing Societies."* London: Macmillan, 1982.

Alsanbeigui, Nahid, Steve Pressman, and Gale Summerfield. *Women in the Age of Economic Transformation: Gender Impacts of Reforms in Post-Socialist and Developing Countries.* New York: Routledge, 1994.

Anderson, Susan, and Bruce Tabb, eds. *Water, Leisure and Culture: European Historical Perspectives (Leisure, Consumption, and Culture).* Oxford: Berg, 2002.

Andrew, Christopher, and Vasili Mitrokhin. *The Sword and the Shield: The Mitrokhin Archive and the Secret History of the KGB.* New York: Basic Books, 1999.

Anzaldúa, Gloria, and Cherríe Morag. *This Bridge Called My Back: Writings by Radical Women of Color.* New York: Kitchen Table, 1983.

Bachvarov, Marin. "End of the Model? Tourism in Post-communist Bulgaria." *Tourism Management* 18, no. 1 (1997): 43–50.

Bebel, August. *Woman under Socialism.* New York: Labor News, 1904.

Becker, Gary S. *Human Capital: A Theoretical and Empirical Analysis with Special Reference to Education.* Chicago: University of Chicago Press, 1964.

Bourdieu, Pierre. *Distinction: A Social Critique of the Judgment of Taste.* Translated by Richard Nice. Cambridge: Harvard University Press, 1984.

——. *Practical Reason: On the Theory of Action.* Stanford: Stanford University Press, 1998.

Brown, J. F. *Bulgaria Under Communist Rule.* New York: Praeger, 1970.

Buckley, Mary. *Post-Soviet Women: From the Baltic to Central Asia.* Cambridge: Cambridge University Press, 1997.

Bulbeck, Chilla. *Re-orienting Western Feminisms: Women's Diversity in a Postcolonial World.* Cambridge: Cambridge University Press, 1998.

Bulgaria. Ministry of Economy. "2000: Silen start za mezhdunarodniya ni turizum." *Turisticheski Pazar* 4, no. 5 (2000): 6.

——. "Turizmut s polozhitelno saldo." *Turisticheski Pazar* 2, no. 3 (2000): 3.

Bulgarian Foreign Investment Agency. *Bulgaria Business Guide 2000—Legal, Tax and Accounting Aspects: Challenges of Joining Global Markets.* Sofia: BFIA, 2000.

Burawoy, Michael. *Ethnography Unbound: Power and Resistance in the Modern Metropolis*. Berkeley: University of California Press, 1991.

Carr, Barbara. *Spy in the Sun: The Story of Yuriy Loginov*. Cape Town: Howard Timinis, 1969.

Castells, Manuel. *The End of the Millennium*. Vol. 3 of *The Information Age: Economy, Society and Culture*. Malden, Mass.: Blackwell, 1998.

Cellarius, Barbara. " 'You Can Buy Almost Anything with Potatoes': An Examination of Barter During Economic Crisis in Bulgaria." *Ethnology* 39, no. 1 (2000): 73–93.

———. *In the Land of Orpheus: Rural Livelihoods and Nature Conservation in Postsocialist Bulgaria*. Madison: University of Wisconsin Press, 2004.

Cellarius, Barbara A., and Caedmon Straddon. "Environmental Nongovernmental Organizations, Civil Society, and Democratization in Bulgaria." *East European Politics and Societies* 16, no. 1 (2002): 182–222.

"Citizen's groups: The Non-governmental Order—Will NGOs Democratise, or Merely Disrupt, Global Governance?" *Economist*, 11 December 1999, 20.

Clayton, Andrew, ed. *Governance, Democracy and Conditionality: What Role for NGOs?* Oxford: INTRAC, 1994.

Clifford, James, and George Marcus. *Writing Culture: The Poetics and Politics of Ethnography*. Berkeley: University of California Press, 1985.

Coenen-Huther, Jacques, ed. *Bulgaria at the Crossroads*. New York: Nova Science, 1996.

Cohen, Colleen. "Marketing Paradise, Making Nation." *Annals of Tourism Research* 22, no. 2 (1995): 404–21.

Commission of the European Communities. *Report for the Commission to the Council, the European Parliament, the Economic and Social Committee and the Committee of the Regions: Equal Opportunities for Women and Men in the European Union*. Brussels, 8 March 2000.

Corrin, Chris. *Superwoman and the Double Burden: Women's Experience of Change in Central and Eastern Europe and the Former Soviet Union*. Toronto: Second Story, 1992.

Crampton, R. J. *A Short History of Modern Bulgaria*. Cambridge: Cambridge University Press, 1987.

———. *A Concise History of Bulgaria*. Cambridge: Cambridge University Press, 1997.

Creed, Gerald. *Domesticating Revolution: From Socialist Reform to Ambivalent Transition in a Bulgarian Village*. University Park: Pennsylvania State University Press, 1998.

Creed, Gerald, and Janine Wedel. "Second Thoughts from the Second World: Interpreting Aid in Post-Communist Eastern Europe." *Human Organization*, 56, no. 3 (1997): 253–64.

Cukier, Judie, Joanne Norris, and Geoffrey Wall. "The Involvement of Women in the

Tourism Industry of Bali, Indonesia." *Journal of Development Studies* 33, no. 2 (1996): 248–71.

Cukier-Snow, Judith, and Geoffrey Wall. "Tourism Employment: Perspectives from Bali." *Tourism Management* 14 (1993): 195–201.

———. "Tourism Employment in Bali, Indonesia." *Tourism Recreation Research* 19, no. 1 (1994): 32–40.

Daskalov, Roumen. *The Things that Surround Us: Observations and Reflections on Social Change* (in Bulgarian). Sofia: Lik, 1998.

Davin, Delia. "China: the New Inheritance Law and the Peasant Household." *Journal of Communist Studies* 3 (December 1987): 52–63.

Deni Consult. *A Survey of the Tourist Industry in Bulgaria.* Sofia: Deni Consult, 1997.

Dobrin, Bogoslav. *Bulgarian Economic Development Since World War II.* New York: Praeger, 1973.

Doitchev, Peter. *Zhivot, Otdaden na Turizma* (Life: Devoted to Tourism). Sofia: Literaturen Forum, 1999.

Drakulic, Slavenka. *How We Survived Communism and Even Laughed.* New York: HarperCollins, 1993.

Edwards, Michael, and David Hulme. *Beyond the Magic Bullet: NGO Performance and Accountability in the Post–Cold War World.* West Hartford, Conn.: Kumarian, 1996.

———. *NGOs, States and Donors: Too Close for Comfort?* New York: St. Martin's, 1997.

Einhorn, Barbara. *Cinderella Goes to Market: Citizenship, Gender, and Women's Movements in East Central Europe.* London: Verso, 1993.

Enloe, Cynthia. *Bananas, Beaches and Bases: Making Feminist Sense of International Politics.* London: Pandora, 1989.

European Commission. *Employment and Labour Market in Central European Countries.* Germany: European Commission, 2002.

European Union. *Human Resource Development Strategy for the Tourism Industry.* Report of the EU PHARE Program "Manpower Development and Training" Project. Madrid: Consultiberica, 1997.

———. Tourism Development Program—Bulgaria: Institutional Strengthening/Enterprise Development. *Draft Concept for Statute, Classification and Management of Large Tourist Resorts in View of Accelerated Privatization and in the Post-Privatization Period.* Discussion paper. Sofia, April 1998.

Eyal, Gil, Ivan Szelenyi, and Ellen Townsley. *Making Capitalism Without Capitalists: The New Ruling Elites in Eastern Europe.* London: Verso, 1998.

Ferguson, James. *The Anti-politics Machine: "Development," Depoliticization, and Bureaucratic Power in Lesotho.* Cambridge: Cambridge University Press, 1990.

Fisher, Julie. "Third World NGOs: A Missing Piece to the Population Puzzle." *Environment* 36, no. 7 (1994): 6–17.

——. *Nongovernments: NGOs and the Political Development of the Third World*. West Hartford, Conn.: Kumarian, 1997.

Fisher, William. "Doing Good? The Politics and Antipolitics of NGO practices." *Annual Review of Anthropology* 26 (1997): 439–64.

Fodor, Eva. "Gender in Transition: Unemployment in Hungary, Poland and Slovakia." *East European Politics and Societies* 11, no. 3 (1997): 470–501.

Foreign Investment Advisory Service. *Bulgaria: Administrative Barriers to Foreign Investment*. Washington, D.C.: World Bank, 1999.

Foucault, Michel. *Power/Knowledge: Selected Interviews and Other Writings 1972–1977*. New York: Pantheon, 1980.

Freeman, Carla. *High Tech and High Heels*. Durham, N.C.: Duke University Press, 2000.

Fukuyama, Francis. "Second Thoughts: The Last Man in a Bottle (Socialism and the End of Human Economy)." *National Interest*, no. 56 (summer 1999): 16.

Funk, Nanette, and Magda Mueller, eds. *Gender Politics and Post-Communism: Reflections from Eastern Europe and the Former Soviet Union*. New York: Routledge, 1993.

Gal, Susan, and Gail Kligman. *The Politics of Gender after Socialism*. Princeton: Princeton University Press, 2000.

——, eds. *Reproducing Gender: Politics, Publics, and Everyday Life After Socialism*. Princeton: Princeton University Press, 2000.

Ganev, Venelin. "Bulgaria's Symphony of Hope." *Journal of Democracy* 6, no. 4 (1997): 125–39.

Ghodsee, Kristen. "*Tri Prikaski za Albena*" (Three Tales of Albena.) *Turisticheski Pazar* (Tourism Market), no. 7 (July 2000): 6–7.

——. "State Support in the Market: Women and Tourism Employment in Post-Socialist Bulgaria." *International Journal of Politics, Cultural and Society* 16, no. 3 (2003): 465–83.

——. "Feminism-by-Design: Emerging Capitalisms, Cultural Feminism and Women's Nongovernmental Organizations in Post-Socialist Eastern Europe." *Signs: Journal of Women in Culture and Society* 29, no. 3 (2004): 727–53.

Giatzidis, Emile. *An Introduction to Postcommunist Bulgaria: Political, Economic and Social Transformation*. Manchester: Manchester University Press, 2002.

Giddings, Lisa. *Does the Shift to Markets Impose Greater Hardship on Women and Minorities? Three Essays on Gender and Ethnicity in Bulgarian Labor Markets*. Ph.D. diss., American University, 2000.

"Globalisation and Its Critics: a Survey of Globalisation." *Economist*, 29 September 2001, 28.

Grodeland, Ase, Tatyana Koshechkina, and William Miller. "Foolish to Give and Yet More Foolish Not to Take: In-depth Interviews with Post-Communist Citizens on

Their Everyday Use of Bribes and Contacts." *Europe-Asia Studies* 50, no. 4 (1998): 651–78.

Hall, Derek. "Tourism Development and Sustainability Issues in Central and Southeastern Europe." *Tourism Management* 19, no. 5 (1998): 423–32.

Hall, Derek, ed. *Tourism and Economic Development in Eastern Europe and the Soviet Union*. London: Belhaven, 1991.

Hall, Derek, and Darrick Danta, eds. *Reconstructing the Balkans: A Geography of New Southeast Europe*. Chichester, England: Wiley, 1996.

Harrison, David. "Bulgarian Tourism: A State of Uncertainty." *Annals of Tourism Research* 20, no. 3 (1993): 519–34.

——, ed. *Tourism and the Less Developed Countries*. London: Belhaven, 1992.

Hassan, Fareed M. A., and R. Kyle Peters Jr. "The Structure of Incomes and Social Protection during the Transition: The Case of Bulgaria." *Europe-Asia Studies*, 48, no. 4 (1996): 629–46.

Helms, Elissa. "Women as Agents of Ethnic Reconciliation? Women's NGOs and International Intervention in Postwar Bosnia–Herzegovina." *Women's Studies International Forum* 26, no. 1 (2003): 15–34.

Hemment, Julie. "Global Civil Society and the Local Costs of Belonging: Defining Violence Against Women in Russia." *Signs: Journal of Women in Culture and Society* 29, no. 3 (2004): 815–40.

Holmes, Leslie. *Post-Communism: An Introduction*. Durham, N.C.: Duke University Press, 1997.

hooks, bell. *Ain't I a Woman: Black Women and Feminism*. Boston: South End, 1981.

Huntington, Samuel. *The Clash of Civilizations and the Remaking of World Order*. New York: Simon and Schuster, 1996.

Institute for Market Economics. *Economic Outlook of Bulgaria: 1995–1997*. Sofia: Bulgarian Academy of Sciences, 1995.

International Monetary Fund. "IMF Approves Stand-By Credit and a Drawing Under the CCFF for Bulgaria." Press release no. 97/15, 11 April 1997.

——. "IMF Concludes Article IV Consultation with Bulgaria." Press information notice no. 97/15, 29 July 1997.

——. *Annual Report 1997*. Washington, D.C.: IMF, 1997.

International Organization for Migration. "IOM Launches Information Campaigns to Raise Awareness about Trafficking in Women in Bulgaria and Hungary." Press release no. 842, 12 November 1999.

Jackson, Marvin. "A Crucial Phase in Bulgarian Economic Reforms," 1989. Paper 72. Berichte des Bundesinstituts fur ostwissenschaftliche und internationale Studien, Cologne, Germany.

——. "The Rise and Decay of the Socialist Economy in Bulgaria." *Journal of Economic Perspectives* 5, no. 4 (1991): 203–9.

Jalusic, Vlasta. *Freedom Versus Equality?* IWM Working Paper, no 1. Vienna: Institute for Human Sciences, 1998.

Jalusic, Vlasta, and Milica Antic. *Prospects for Gender Equality Policies in Central and Eastern Europe.* SOCO Project Paper, no. 70. Vienna: Institute for Human Sciences, 2000.

Jezek, Tomas. "The Czechoslovak Experience with Privatization (Privatization: Political and Economic Challenges)," *Journal of International Affairs* 50, no. 2 (1997): 477–89.

Jones, Derek, and Takao Kato. "The Nature and the Determinants of Labor Market Transition in Emerging Market Economies: Evidence from Bulgaria." *Industrial Relations* 36, no. 2 (1997): 229–54.

Kabakchieva, Petya. *The Civil Society against the State: The Bulgarian Case.* Sofia: Lik, 2001.

Kalinova, E., and I. Baeva. *Balgarskite Prehodi 1939–2002* (The Bulgarian Transitions 1939–2002). Sofia: Paradigma, 2002.

Kaufmann, David, and Paul Siegelbaum. "Privatization and Corruption in Transition Economies (Privatization: Political and Economic Challenges)," *Journal of International Affairs* 50, no. 2 (1997): 419–59.

Kempadoo, Kamala. *Sun, Sex and Gold: Tourism and Sex Work in the Caribbean.* New York: Rowman and Littlefield, 1999.

Kennedy, Paul. *The Rise and Fall of the Great Powers: Economic Change and Military Conflict from 1500 to 2000.* New York: Random House, 1987.

Kinnaird, Vivian, and Derek Hall, eds. *Tourism: A Gender Analysis.* Chichester, England: Wiley, 1994.

Knott, David. "NGOs Foresee Better Business Ethics." *Oil and Gas Journal*, 31 August 1998, 27.

Kollontai, Alexandra. *Selected Writings of Alexandra Kollontai.* Translated with an introduction and commentaries by Alix Holt. Westport, Conn.: L. Hill, 1997.

Kossev, D., H. Hristov, and D. Angelov. *A Short History of Bulgaria.* Sofia: Foreign Language Press, 1963.

Kostov, Vladimir. *The Bulgarian Umbrella.* New York: St. Martin's, 1988.

Lalkov, Milcho. *A History of Bulgaria: An Outline.* Sofia: St. Kliment Ohridski University Press, 1998.

Lampe, John. *The Bulgarian Economy in the Twentieth Century.* London: Croom Helm, 1986.

Leebaert, Derek. *The Fifty-Year Wound: The True Price of America's Cold War Victory.* Boston: Little, Brown, 2002.

Levy, Diane, and Patricia Lerch. "Tourism as a Factor in Development: Implications for Gender and Work in Barbados." *Gender and Society* 5, no. 1 (1991): 67–85.

Lewis, David. *Sexpionage: The Exploitation of Sex by Soviet Intelligence.* New York: Harcourt Brace Jovanovich, 1976.

Light, Duncan, and D. Dumbraveanu. "Romanian Tourism in the Post-Communist Period." *Annals of Tourism Research* 26, no. 4 (1999): 898–927.

Lorde, Audre. *I Am Your Sister: Black Women Organizing Across Sexualities*. New York: Kitchen Table, 1985.

Marx, Karl. *The Portable Karl Marx*. Edited by Eugene Kamenka. New York: Penguin, 1983.

Mendelson, Sarah, and John Glenn. "Democracy Assistance and NGO Strategies in Post-Communist Societies" Carnegie Endowment Working Papers, Democracy and Rule of Law Project, no. 8., 2000. Washington.

Meurs, Mieke. *Many Shades of Red*. Lanham, Md.: Rowman and Littlefield, 1998.

Millar, James. "The Post Cold-War Settlement and the End of the Transition: Implications for Slavic and East European Studies." *NewsNet* 41, no. 1 (2001): 1–4.

Minassian, Garabed. "The Road to Economic Disaster in Bulgaria." *Europe-Asia Studies*, 50, no. 2 (1998): 331–49.

Mladenova, Zoya, and James Angresano. "Privatization in Bulgaria." *East European Quarterly* 30, no. 4 (1996): 495–517.

Moghadam, Valentine, ed. *Democratic Reform and the Position of Women in Transitional Economies*. Oxford: Clarendon, 1993.

——. *Patriarchy and Economic Development: Women's Positions at the End of the Twentieth Century*. Oxford: Clarendon, 1996.

Mohanty, Chandra Talpade, Ann Russo, and Lourdes Torres. *Third World Women and the Politics of Feminism*. Bloomington: Indiana University Press, 1991.

Monroe, Will S. *Bulgaria and Her People*. Boston: Colonial Press, 1914.

Moran, Theodore H. *Foreign Direct Investment and Development: The New Policy Agenda for Developing Countries and Economies in Transition*. Washington, D.C.: Institute for International Economics, 1998.

Narayan, Uma. *Dislocating Cultures: Identities, Traditions, and Third-World Feminism*. New York: Routledge, 1997.

Nash, Dennison. *Anthropology of Tourism*. London: Pergamon, 1996.

National Statistical Institute. *Integrated Statistics on Women, Women in Bulgaria and the World*. Sofia: NSI, 1991.

——. *Statistical Yearbook*. Sofia: NSI, 1998.

——. *Statistical Yearbook*. Sofia: NSI, 1999.

——. *Employment and Unemployment 1/2000*. Sofia: NSI, 2000.

——. *Tourism 2000*. Sofia: NSI, 2000.

——. *Statistical Yearbook 2000*. Sofia: NSI, 2001.

——. *Women and Men in the Republic of Bulgaria*. Sofia: NSI, 2002.

——. *Employment and Unemployment 1/2003*. Sofia: NSI, 2003.

——. *Tourism 2002*. Sofia: NSI, 2003.

Nee, Victor. "A Theory of Market Transition: From Redistribution to Markets in State Socialism." *American Sociological Review* 56, no. 5 (1989): 663–81.

Neuburger, Mary. "Bulgaro-Turkish Encounters and the Re-Imagining of the Bulgarian Nation (1878–1995)." *East European Quarterly* 31, no. 1 (1997): 1–20.

Nikolov, Jovo. "Crime and Corruption after Communism: Organized Crime in Bulgaria." *Eastern European Constitutional Review* 6, no. 4 (1997).

Oren, Nissan. *Bulgarian Communism: The Road to Power 1934–1944*. New York: Columbia University Press, 1971.

Pearce, Jenny. "NGOs and Social Change: Agents or Facilitators?" *Development Practice* 3, no. 3 (1993): 222–27.

Pearlman, Michael. "Conflicts and Constraints in Bulgaria's Tourism Sector." *Annals of Tourism Research* 17, no. 1 (1990): 103–22.

Petras, James. "Imperialism and NGOs in Latin America." *Monthly Review* 47, no. 7 (1997): 10–16.

———. "NGOS: In the Service of Imperialism." *Journal of Contemporary Asia* 29, no. 4 (1999): 429–41.

Petras, James, and Henry Veltmeyer. *Globalization Unmasked*. Halifax, Nova Scotia: Fernwood, 2001.

Phillips, Robin, and Cheryl Thomas. *Domestic Violence in Bulgaria*. Minneapolis: Minnesota Advocates for Human Rights, 1996.

Polanyi, Karl. *The Great Transformation*. Introduction by Joseph Stiglitz. New York: Beacon, 2001.

Prohaska, Maria, et al. *Social Consequences of the Implementation of a Currency Board in Bulgaria*. SOCO Project Paper, no. 66. Vienna: Institute for Human Sciences, 1999.

Rakadjiyska, Svetla. "Tourism Training and Education in Bulgaria." *Annals of Tourism Research* 17, no. 1 (1990): 150–53.

Roberts, Lesley, and Fiona Simpson. "Institutional Support for the Tourist Industry in Post-Socialist Europe: A Comparison of Bulgaria and Romania." *Tourism Recreation Research* 24, no. 2 (1999): 51–58.

Rona-Tas, Akos. "The First Shall Be Last? Entrepreneurship and Communist Cadres in the Transition from Socialism." *American Journal of Sociology* 100, no. 1 (1994): 40–70.

———. "Path Dependence and Capital Theory: Sociology of the Post-Communist Economic Transformation." *East European Politics and Societies* 12, no. 1 (1998): 107–32.

Rueschemeyer, Marilyn, ed. *Women in the Politics of Postcommunist Eastern Europe*. Armonk, N.Y.: M. E. Sharpe, 1994.

Runciman, Steven. *A History of the First Bulgarian Empire*. London: G. Bells, 1930.

Shaw, Gareth, and Allan Williams. *Critical Issues in Tourism*. Oxford: Blackwell, 1994.

Shusterman, Richard, ed. *Bourdieu: A Critical Reader*. Oxford: Blackwell, 1999.

Sinclair, Thea. *Gender, Work and Tourism*. London: Routledge, 1997.

Smith, Valentine. *Hosts and Guests: The Anthropology of Tourism*. Philadelphia: University of Pennsylvania Press, 1989.

Snavely, Keith. "The Welfare State and the Emerging Non-profit Sector of Bulgaria." *Europe-Asia Studies* 48, no. 4 (1996): 647–63.

Snavely, Keith, and Uday Desai. "The Emergence and Development of Nonprofit Organizations in Bulgaria." *Nonprofit and Voluntary Sector Quarterly*, 27, no. 1 (1998): 32–48.

Stacey, Judith. "Can There Be a Feminist Ethnography?" *Women's Studies International Forum* 11, no. 1 (1988): 21–27.

Stanchev, Krassen. "Bulgaria." *Journal of Southeastern Europe and Black Sea Studies*, 1, no. 1 (2001): 140–58.

Standing, Guy, and Victor Tokman, eds. *Towards Structural Adjustment*. Geneva: ILO, 1991.

Stark, David. "Path Dependence and Privatization Strategies in East Central Europe." *East European Politics and Societies* 6, no. 1 (1992): 17–54.

——. "Recombinant Property in East European Capitalism." *American Journal of Sociology* 101, no. 4 (1996): 993–1027.

Stoillova, Rumiana, et al. *Bulgarian Women in the Period of Transition: Inequalities, Risks, and Social Costs*. SOCO Project Paper, no. 78. Vienna: Institute for Human Sciences, 2000.

Swain, Margaret. "Women Producers of Ethnic Arts." *Annals of Tourism Research* 20, no. 1 (1993): 32–51.

——, ed. Special issue "Gender in Tourism." *Annals of Tourism Research* 22, no. 2 (1995).

Szelenyi, Ivan. *Socialist Entrepreneurs: Embourgeoisement in Rural Hungary*. Madison: University of Wisconsin Press, 1988.

Szivas, Edith, and Michael Riley. "Tourism Employment During Economic Transition." *Annals of Tourism Research* 26, no. 4 (1999): 747–71.

Tinker, Irene. *Persistent Inequalities*. New York: Oxford University Press, 1990.

Todorova, Maria. "Historiography of the Countries of Eastern Europe: Bulgaria." *American Historical Review*, 97, no. 4 (1992): 1105–18.

——. "Historical Tradition and Transformation in Bulgaria: Women's Issues or Feminist Issues?" *Journal of Women's History* 5, no. 3 (1994): 129–44.

——. "Situating the Family of Ottoman Bulgaria within the European Pattern." *History of the Family*, 1, no. 4 (1996): 443–60.

——. *Imagining the Balkans*. New York: Oxford University Press, 1997.

True, Jacqui. *Gender, Globalization, and Postcolonialism: The Czech Republic After Communism*. New York: Columbia University Press, 2003.

Tucker, Robert, ed. *The Marx-Engels Reader*. 2d ed. New York: Norton, 1978.

United Nations. *The Impact of Economic and Political Reform on the Status of Women* in Eastern Europe. Proceedings of a United Nations Regional Seminar. 8–12 April 1991, Vienna. New York: UN, 1992.

United Nations Development Program. *Human Development Report Bulgaria—1996.* New York: UNDP, 1996.

——. *Women in Poverty.* Sofia: UNDP, 1997.

——. *Human Development Report 1998.* New York: UNDP, 1999.

——. *National Human Development Report Bulgaria 1999.* Vol. 2, *Bulgarian People's Aspirations.* Sofia: UNDP, 1999.

——. *Human Development Report 1999.* New York: UNDP, 2000.

——. *Human Development Report 2000.* New York: UNDP, 2001.

——. *National Human Development Report 2001: Citizen Participation in Governance, from Individuals to Citizens.* Sofia: UNDP, 2001.

——. *Early Warning Report: Bulgaria.* Sofia: UNDP, April 2003.

Verdery, Katherine. *National Ideology Under Socialism: Identity and Cultural Politics in Ceausescu's Romania.* Berkeley: University of California Press, 1991.

——. *What Was Socialism, and What Comes Next?* Princeton: Princeton University Press, 1996.

Verloo, Mieke. "Another Velvet Revolution? Gender and Mainstreaming and the Politics of Implementation 2001." IWM Working Paper, no. 5, Vienna.

Vienna Institute for Comparative Economic Studies. *COMECON Data 1980.* Westport, Conn.: Greenwood, 1981.

——. *COMECON Data 1987.* Westport, Conn.: Greenwood, 1988.

——. *COMECON Data 1988.* Westport, Conn.: Greenwood, 1989.

——. *COMECON Data 1989.* Westport, Conn.: Greenwood, 1990.

——. *COMECON Data 1990.* Westport, Conn.: Greenwood, 1991.

——. "Depression and Inflation: Threats to Political and Social Stability." Working Paper, no. 80. Vienna: Vienna Institute for Comparative Economic Studies, 1992.

Vladimirov, Zhelyu, et al. *Bulgaria After 1997: The Current Situation and Development Tendencies.* SOCO Project Paper, no. 88. Vienna: Institute for Human Sciences, 2000.

Vodenska, Maria. "International Tourism in Bulgaria: Problems and Perspectives." *Journal of Economic and Social Geography* 83, no. 5 (1992).

Wallerstein, Immanuel. "What Are We Bounding, and Whom, When We Bound Social Research? (Defining the Boundaries of Social Inquiry)." *Social Research* 62, no. 4 (1995): 839–57.

Wallis, Tina, and Candida March. *Changing Perceptions: Writings on Gender and Development.* Oxford: Oxfam, 1991.

Wedel, Janine. *Collision and Collusion: The Strange Case of Aid to Eastern Europe.* New York: Palgrave, 2001.

Wight, Jonathan, and M. Louise Fox. "Economic Reform and Crisis in Bulgaria, 1989–1992." *Balkanistica* 11 (1998): 127–46.

Wolf, Diane. *Feminist Dilemmas in Fieldwork.* New York: Westview, 1996.

World Bank. *World Development Report 1980.* Washington, D.C.: World Bank, 1980.

——. *World Development Report 1981.* Washington, D.C.: World Bank, 1981.

——. *World Development Report 1988.* Washington, D.C.: World Bank, 1988.

——. *World Development Report 1989.* Washington, D.C.: World Bank, 1989.

——. *World Development Report 1991: The Challenge of Development.* Washington, D.C.: World Bank, 1991.

——. *World Development Report 1992: Development and the Environment.* Washington, D.C.: World Bank, 1992.

——. *World Development Report 1996: From Plan to Market.* Washington, D.C.: World Bank, 1996.

——. *World Bank Annual Report 1997.* Washington, D.C.: World Bank, 1997.

——. *World Development Report 1999/2000: Entering the 21st Century.* Washington, D.C.: World Bank, 1999.

——. *Bulgaria Country Economic Memorandum: The Dual Challenge of Transition and Accession.* Washington, D.C.: World Bank, 2000.

——. *Making the Transition Work for Women in Europe and Central Asia.* Washington, D.C.: World Bank, 2000.

——. *Engendering Development: Through Gender Equality in Rights, Resources, and Voice.* New York: Oxford University Press, 2001.

——. *World Development Report 2002: Building Institutions for Markets.* Washington, D.C.: World Bank, 2002.

——. *World Development Report 2003: Sustainable Development in a Dynamic World.* Washington, D.C.: World Bank, 2003.

World Tourism Organization. *Bulgaria.* International Tourism Report, no. 108. London: Economic Intelligence Unit, 1986.

——. *Yearbook of Tourism Statistics.* Madrid: WTO, 1990.

World Travel and Tourism Council. "Bulgaria–Travel and Tourism a World of Opportunity: The 2003 Travel & Tourism Economic Research." London: WTTC, 2003.

Yorov, Todor. "Record Low Trading Volume on the Stock Exchange." *Sofia Echo* 4, no. 25 (2000).

Zetkin, Clara. *Clara Zetkin: Selected Writings.* Edited by P. Foner and A. Davis. 1907. Reprint, New York: International Publishers, 1984.

Zetkin, Clara. *Reminiscences of Lenin; Dealing with Lenin's Views on the Position of Women and Other Questions.* London: Modern Books, 1929.

Zhivkov, Todor. *Otchet na Tsentralniia Komitet na Bulgarskata Komunisticheska partiia za perioda mezhdu Desetiia i Edinadesetiia Kongres i predstoiashtite zadachi, 29 March 1976.* (Report of the Central Committee of the Bulgarian Communist Party for the Period between the Tenth and Eleventh Congresses and on the Forthcoming Tasks, 29 March 1976.) Sofia: Sofia-Press, 1976.

Žižek, Slavoj. *NATO as the Left Hand of God?* Ljubljana, Slovenia: Bastard Press, 2001.

Index

Kristen Ghodsee is an assistant professor of gender and women's studies at Bowdoin College.

Library of Congress Catagloging-in-Publication Data

Ghodsee, Kristen Rogheh

The Red Riviera : gender, tourism, and postsocialism

on the Black Sea / Kristen Ghodsee.

p. cm.—(Next wave)

Includes bibliographical references and index.

ISBN 0-8223-3650-2 (cloth : alk. paper)

ISBN 0-8223-3662-6 (pbk. : alk. paper)

1. Women—Employment—Bulgaria.

2. Tourism—Bulgaria. 3. Post-communism—Bulgaria.

I. Title. II. Series.

HD6181.5.G46 2005 331.4'09499—dc22

2005010070